FROM NEAR
AND FAR

T0385452

FRANCE OVERSEAS:
Studies in Empire and Decolonization

SERIES EDITORS:
A. J. B. Johnston, James D. Le Sueur, and Tyler Stovall

FROM NEAR AND FAR

A Transnational History of France

Tyler Stovall

University of Nebraska Press   Lincoln

© 2022 by the Board of Regents of
the University of Nebraska

All rights reserved

The University of Nebraska Press is part of a land-
grant institution with campuses and programs on the
past, present, and future homelands of the Pawnee,
Ponca, Otoe-Missouria, Omaha, Dakota, Lakota, Kaw,
Cheyenne, and Arapaho Peoples, as well as those of the
relocated Ho-Chunk, Sac and Fox, and Iowa Peoples.

Library of Congress Cataloging-in-Publication Data
Names: Stovall, Tyler, 1954–2021, author.
Title: From near and far: a transnational
history of France / Tyler Stovall.
Description: Lincoln : University of
Nebraska Press, 2023 | Series: France overseas:
studies in empire and decolonization |
Includes bibliographical references and index.
Identifiers: LCCN 2022010875
ISBN 9781496232809 (hardback)
ISBN 9781496231505 (paperback)
ISBN 9781496233912 (epub)
ISBN 9781496233929 (pdf)
Subjects: LCSH: France—History—1789 |
France—Foreign relations. | France—
Civilization. | Transnational history—France. |
BISAC: HISTORY / Europe / France
Classification: LCC DC33 .S76 2023 |
DDC 944.06—dc23/eng/20220830
LC record available at
https://lccn.loc.gov/2022010875

Set in Garamond Premier by Mikala R. Kolander.
Designed by N. Putens.

To the memory of

Barbara Fuller Stovall

April 1933–July 2021

My mother, a beloved visionary
and a fighter for social justice:

You brought me across the river

CONTENTS

ILLUSTRATIONS

PREFACE AND ACKNOWLEDGMENTS

All books are the products of a specific time and place, but let me state at the outset that this project came to fruition in two rather singular circumstances. First, while writing this book I changed jobs, moving from UC-Santa Cruz to Fordham University. This rather monumental shift between two very different institutions located on opposite sides of the country certainly posed numerous challenges, making me adjust from one system to another, disrupting old relationships and creating new ones. At the same time, it introduced me to new possibilities and ways of looking at things, including my research, underscoring my conviction that life is a process of continuous learning, that the dynamism and shock of the new makes us all truly alive.

Second, I wrote much of this book during the great COVID-19 pandemic, literally composing it at my computer with a mask over my face. Coronavirus has created many difficulties for scholars: it has reduced the number of conferences and other venues where one can discuss and get feedback on one's work, not to mention making daily life more difficult by reducing childcare and other support networks. At the same time, the impact of COVID-19 speaks to some of the central concerns of this book in interesting ways. A key theme of *From Near and Far* is the relationship between the local and the global, something that coronavirus has reshaped since March 2020. In many ways the pandemic has made life much more local, often reducing our existences to our own homes. At the same time, it has powerfully reinforced the importance of global online networks, so that in general coronavirus has challenged us to rethink our ideas of space and what they mean to our lives. These issues have been on all our minds of late, so I imagine that they played an important role in the final form of my book, and how those who read it in this context will react to it.

It is my great pleasure to begin this book by thanking all those who played a role in bringing it from idea or fond hope to reality. First of all, let me express my gratitude to the people of the University of Nebraska Press who made this book possible. Nebraska's France Overseas series has played a leading role in not only preserving the study of French history in America but also integrating it into colonial, postcolonial, and global studies, thus rendering a tremendous service to our profession. I am very grateful to Matthew Bokovoy, senior acquisitions editor, for his vision, encouragement, and high standards. Permit me also to thank Heather Stauffer, associate acquisitions editor, for the rigorous attention to detail without which this book could not have come into being.

Many colleagues at Santa Cruz gave generously of their time and support to help me conceptualize and write this book. I am pleased and honored to thank Irena Polić and Nathaniel Deutsch of the Humanities Institute, who have kept the torch of humanistic inquiry burning at Santa Cruz and inspired so many of us. I am also grateful to friends and colleagues Jonathan Beecher, Alan Christy, Judy Plummer, Gail Hershatter, Bruce Thompson, and Alice Yang, for their support and collegiality over the years.

I arrived at Fordham in July 2020 as the new dean of the Graduate School of Arts and Sciences, and found myself immersed in a campus forced to adjust to the realities of COVID-19. This meant developing relationships with colleagues mostly by Zoom, so that I had no idea how tall many of my new friends are. In spite of these rather bizarre circumstances I am very grateful to have been welcomed into the Fordham community and to have my new colleagues acknowledge and recognize my work on this book and other scholarly projects. In particular I want to thank fellow deans Eva Badowska, Maura Mast, and Laura Auricchio for their support. I am also grateful to Rafael Zapata, chief diversity officer at Fordham University, for his warmth and advice about joining this new community.

In spite of the limits imposed by the pandemic, colleagues in the field of French history in general made important contributions to *From Near and Far*. Over the years former students have become one of my most important support networks, and I am very grateful to them for their wisdom and encouragement. Mike Vann, as always, inspired me with his own scholarship and insights. I would also like to thank Robin Mitchell, Minayo Nasiali, and Chris Church for their support. More broadly I wish to acknowledge colleagues like Jennifer Boittin, Emmanuelle Sibeud, John Merriman, Sylvain Pattieu, Richard Fogarty, Christy Pichichero, Alice Conklin, Ruth Ginio, Tip Ragan, Alyssa Sepinwall, Naomi Andrews, Nimisha Barton, and many others for creating a warm and supportive scholarly community. I'm proud to be a French historian, and it's thanks to all of you.

Let me end by recognizing and thanking my family for all their love and support. My wife, Denise Herd, has always been in my corner and has not only taken many concrete steps to help me write this book but has always, always encouraged me and made me believe my work matters. My son, Justin Stovall, grew through adolescence to adulthood during the years it took to write this book, and while he no longer wants to be a fireman or a French historian I am nonetheless very proud of the paths his life has taken so far. My thanks and my love to you both, now and forever.

In July 2021 my mother, Barbara Stovall, passed from this earth, after a long and rich life of eighty-eight years. She was a dynamic force of nature, a social worker, a political activist, and a crusader for civil rights. She was also an intellectual and a believer in historical scholarship: her most damning critique of someone was to say they didn't know their history. I will be forever grateful for her influence on my life, firmly believing that without her example I would never have become a historian. My own work thus reflects and continues her legacy, and in that spirit I dedicate this book to her memory.

FROM NEAR
AND FAR

Introduction

France in the World, the World in France

This book has a somewhat curious history; initially I did not plan for it to be a book at all. While writing my textbook on modern French history, *Transnational France*, I decided to craft and include a series of vignettes—specific tales about people, places, and events that illustrated the transnational and universal character of modern French history. I planned to choose a wide variety of case studies corresponding to specific historical eras, ones that showed how the broader themes of the book figured into a series of ordinary, extraordinary lives and events. With this schema in mind I drafted twelve microhistories, one for each chapter.[1]

Yet things often do not turn out as planned, and so it proved in this case. By the time I finally finished *Transnational France* I had exhausted all the room my publisher would allow for the book, leaving the case studies orphaned, as it were. This occurrence certainly speaks to poor planning on my part, but it also raises the broader question of the place of individual people and events in grand historical narratives. In writing history it is all too easy for overarching narratives to edge out and ultimately overwhelm particular tales of the past. What is the relationship between history and (auto)biography, and how do the two forms intersect with and shape each other? How do specific historical incidents and events interact with broader patterns of human history? To take one example, in rejecting the narrative of history as the story of great men, have social and cultural historians adequately accounted for the ways in which history is shaped by individuals or, perhaps more importantly, the ways in which individuals are shaped by their own histories? How does one integrate the writings of professional historians and the tales told by one's grandparents into a common vision of the past?[2]

This book resulted from my attempt not just to salvage the work I had already done but to find a place for it in my own recapitulation of French history. Like the previous study from which it arose, it takes a transnational approach to the history of France and considers the many different ways in which people and places beyond the conventionally accepted borders of the nation shaped its life. It underscores the fact that the nature of these borders has always been contested, and that their indeterminacy, and the ambivalent nature of what it has meant in the past to be French, has been both a national and a global issue.

In many ways transnationalism overlaps with another vision of global interactions, internationalism, but the two are not the same. While historians and other scholars frequently differ on the meanings of these terms, many have argued that internationalism refers to the relationships *between* nations, whereas transnationalism characterizes processes *beyond* nations— transcending boundaries rather than merely crossing them. As Eliezer Ben-Rafael and Yitzhak Sternberg argue in their book, *Transnationalism: Diasporas and the Advent of a New Dis(order)*: "The notion of transnationalism . . . differs from what is usually meant by 'international' and which designates activities setting in contact official bodies—states, universities, associations or parties—belonging to different states. While by 'transnational' one also understands relations that run across states and societies, this term focuses on people and groups and do [*sic*] not necessarily refer to official bodies."[3] This distinction makes a good deal of sense, yet it is by no means absolute. The modern-era nation-states, and in particular the cultures they engender, retain a considerable presence, so that one cannot completely disentangle global processes from them. To take the classic example of the twenty-first century, the internet is a fundamentally global phenomenon, yet differences in national cultures and economies have played and continue to play a seminal role in shaping it. Consequently, this study, like *Transnational France*, sees transnationalism not as a rejection of the national for the global, but rather the interaction between the two, the life of the nation-state and its citizens being shaped by forces beyond its frontiers.[4]

At the same time, however, this book focuses much more intensively on specific individuals and events, exploring how in concrete fashion they illustrate and exemplify the transnational character of French history. It adds another dimension, the local-microhistorical, to the relationship between national and global histories. Historians and other scholars have long explored the relationship between local and national. During the 1970s and 1980s the Italian school of microhistory, led by scholars such as Carlo Ginzburg and Giovanni Levi, emphasized local history, as did the group of West German historians who developed at roughly the same time an approach they called *alltagsgeschichte* (history of everyday life).[5] A generation ago Steven K. Vincent and Alison Klairmont Lingo published *The Human Tradition in Modern France*, a book dedicated to reaffirming the importance of personal and local stories in modern historiographies that often are dominated by the analysis of impersonal social structures and trends.[6] For another example, a classic study by Peter Sahlins, *Boundaries*, not only portrays the history of a small valley in the Pyrenees split between France and Spain, but shows how ideas of the nation were constructed locally and how in effect the modern nation grew up on its margins.[7]

How does a transnational approach add to and reshape our understanding of interactions between national and local, between individual experience and broader history? Isn't there a risk that studying history at the global level might further marginalize individuals and localities? One important influence on my thinking about these matters has been the theory of *glocalization*, of the relationship between local and global. The term and concept originated in the business world, developed by Japanese entrepreneurs in the 1980s to refer to the adaptation of global products and services to local conditions. During the early 1990s Scottish sociologist Roland Robertson adopted the term for use in the social sciences, using it to intervene in scholarly debates about globalization. In his seminal article "Glocalization: Time-Space and Homogeneity-Heterogeneity," Robertson argues:

> The need to introduce the concept of glocalization firmly into social theory arises from the following considerations. Much of the talk about globalization has tended to assume that it is a process which overrides

locality . . . This interpretation neglects two things. First, it neglects the extent to which what is called local is in large degree constructed on a trans- or super-local basis. In other words, much of the promotion of locality is in fact done from above or outside . . . Second, while there has been increasing interest in spatial considerations and expanding attention to the intimate links between temporal and spatial dimensions of human life, these considerations have made relatively little impact as yet on the discussion of globalization and related matters. In particular, there has been little attempt to connect the discussion of time-and-space to the thorny issue of universalism-and-particularism.[8]

Glocalization theory, by addressing the mutual interactions of local and global life and the ways in which each creates and shapes the other, provides a useful perspective from which to address transnational history. It shows how life can be both local and global at the same time, and how the nation-state draws upon the interaction of both in creating a distinct national culture.

France is in many ways an ideal case study for exploring the interactions between local and global history in the modern era. As the pioneering work of Eugene Weber demonstrates, the struggle to create a unified nation-state out of many disparate local traditions and cultures occupies a central role in French history, a struggle that never came to a definitive conclusion. Even in the national capital, life often proceeded according to the rhythms of the *esprit de clocher* (spirit of the clock tower), with individual Parisian neighborhoods resembling small provincial villages. Charles de Gaulle once famously asked how one could govern a country with more than 250 different kinds of cheese, underscoring the fact that such differences are both the glory and despair of the French nation. By the early twentieth century the French educational system aspired to be so centralized that at any given moment of the school day all students in the same grade throughout the country were turning the exact same page of the exact same book. However, how they interpreted what they found in those books varied widely, as did the impact of these varying interpretations on the school system in general.

In the modern era France has carved out some of the greatest empires ever seen in world history, empires held together (if not necessarily united) not just by force of arms or even laws, but also by political culture. At the height of his reign Napoleon controlled virtually the entire European continent, a feat not rivaled until the era of Adolf Hitler's Third Reich more than a century later, and he did so in the name of the French Revolution. The French Third Republic overthrew an imperial regime only to go on to create its own even vaster vision of empire, one similarly inspired by the values and political culture of 1789. Rather than relegating it to the periphery, this book considers the colonial empire to be a central part of modern French history, and the interactions between citizens and natives a prime example of the making of transnational France.

From Near and Far thus explores how the experiences of specific individuals, events, and organizations have contributed to the transnational culture of modern France. I tend to focus on a few specific types of glocal transnationalism, of people, places, and events that bring together the local and the global. The reader will find several accounts of individual migrants, of those who came to France and those who left it to go elsewhere. The category migrants includes people who traveled between the French metropole and its colonies, a gray zone that embraces journeys both internal and external to France.

The book also examines major world historical events and their impact in France, bringing together local French life and global histories. How did the French experience phenomena like the world wars of the early twentieth century, for example, and what does their experience reveal about worldwide events? Some sections deal with the history of international organizations, both those originating in France and those shaping French life from abroad.

A key theme of the book concerns universalism, both French and global. A belief in universal values and ideals has been a major characteristic of French life since the Revolution, and any study of modern France must address the ways in which the nation's citizens saw themselves as exponents of principles relevant to all humankind. But universalism has not just existed in France, and this book will also tell the tale of the interactions between French and other universal ideologies. Whether it be American universalism, Marxist and socialist universalism, or the universalism of the Jewish diaspora, totalizing belief systems from abroad influenced and were influenced by the universalist principles of the French Revolution. Universalism represents an important example of the interaction between local and global, and its central role in modern French history makes France a vital case study in transnational glocalization.[9]

From Near and Far thus looks at modern France from two perspectives, the small-scale and individual, and the large-scale of global scope, and considers the impact and the interaction of both in the history of the French nation. It argues for the centrality of the nation-state to modern history, but at the same time contends that one cannot fully grasp this history without looking both within and beyond its borders. Above all, it attempts to show how what it means to be French has made major contributions to what it means to be human in our modern world.

Chapter Outlines

This book is divided into four main parts, proceeding in roughly chronological order. Each part begins with a short introduction, setting forth major themes of the period in both French and world history. The introduction is then followed by three chapters dealing with specific events, individuals, or movements. Part 1 covers the history of France from the Revolution through the Second Empire, roughly 1789 to 1870. The first chapter explores the history of Gallipolis, founded by a group of émigrés who left France during the Revolution to settle in the Ohio frontier during the 1790s. It shows how their ideals of a Rousseauian paradise in the wilderness of the New World collided with the realities of land speculation and conflicts with the native peoples, and the ways in which they nonetheless struggled to create an outpost of French civilization in the Americas. Chapter 2 considers the life of the young Karl Marx in Paris during the 1840s. Marx came to France as part of a large German immigrant community in the French capital, and this chapter explores his political life there and its influence on the subsequent development of Marxist ideology, in particular his first meeting with life-long collaborator Friedrich Engels. Chapter 3 returns to the New World with a history of the French invasion of Mexico during the 1860s. It shows how this imperial adventure overseas collapsed in the face of opposition from the Mexican people as well as the United States, and foreshadowed the end of empire in France itself a few years later.

Part 2 focuses on France during the late nineteenth century, from the Second Empire to the Third Republic. Chapter 4 explores one of the great symbols of modern French life, the fashion industry. It examines in particular the rise of *haute couture* and the life of its founder, English fashion designer Charles Worth, and explores how an industry founded by an Englishman and sustained by an international clientele could be so emblematically French. The fifth chapter looks at the history of the Alliance Israélite Universelle, an organization founded by French Jews in 1860 to promote the ideals of the Enlightenment to Jews throughout the world. Inspired by the French Revolution's liberation of the nation's Jews, it combined French and Jewish universalism in its efforts to educate and elevate the Jews of the Ottoman empire in particular with the culture of modern France. Chapter 6 explores the history of the great Impressionist painter Paul Gauguin, a Frenchman of Franco-Peruvian ancestry who married a Danish woman and spent much of his life abroad. It focuses on the last stages of his life, in Tahiti, and the ways in which his art articulated and combined both Polynesian influences and a colonial French gaze.

Part 3 brings us to the early twentieth century and the era of the great world wars. Chapter 7 considers the impact of the American soldiers who came to France as allies during World War I. It examines how the French saw these strangers from a different shore, as well as the effect their sojourns in France had upon the young American warriors. Chapter 8 looks at the Parisian stay of the young Vietnamese radical Nguyen Ai Quoc, later to become famous to history as Ho Chi Minh. Like Karl Marx almost a century earlier, Quoc lived briefly in France, becoming engaged with both French and Vietnamese activists before leaving as a mature revolutionary. The ninth chapter looks at the Manouchian group, a network of foreigners involved in the French Resistance to German occupation during World War II. It explores their tragic history as a way of considering both the important role played by foreigners in the Resistance, and why it has often been difficult for the French to acknowledge the importance of that role in what has often been seen as a struggle for national renewal.

The final section of the book covers life in France since the Second World War. Chapter 10 looks at the great American expatriate performer Josephine Baker, having transcended her early years in Paris to become a French citizen and heroine of the Resistance. It considers her creation of a "Rainbow Family," adopting children from all over the world to live together in a beautiful castle in the Dordogne, discussing it in the context of France's postwar baby boom and history of decolonization. The issue of decolonization also looms significantly in the next chapter, which examines the history of Club Méditerranée. Created by Jewish entrepreneurs, Club Med fostered a new vision of French culture at once global and national, emphasizing a new empire of French culture and leisure in a world where the old patterns of imperial domination were no longer viable. The last chapter in the book brings the history of France up to the present day, looking at what I call the "postcolonial soundtrack," the world of French hip-hop. It explores how this powerful art form brings together many different influences on contemporary French life as well as projecting French cultural influence on a global scale.

From Near and Far thus presents a variety of histories of modern France. Some deal with individuals or small groups, others focus on larger events and movements. Several combine the two, working in multiple registers. All, however, speak to important themes in both French and global history, and help to illustrate how the history and culture of France as a nation is intimately bound up with peoples, places, and events beyond its borders. I write this book neither with the intention to downplay the importance of French history in global comparison, nor conversely to promote and boast of France as the center of the world. Rather, I want to emphasize how impressed I am with the richness of French culture and history, in the belief that one major explanation for this richness is precisely the openness the nation has shown in the past to foreign influences.

I write these words fully conscious of, and intent upon, their political implications. We live in a world today where many voices and political actors see immigration and the presence of foreigners as an evil, as a danger to national integrity and even existence. In sharp contrast, I argue that the history of a great nation like France—in many ways a leading representative of the modern nation-state—has been shaped in many important ways by foreign and global influences, and that without those France would simply not be recognizable as the nation and the culture we know today. The same is true of most other nations, certainly including my own. To explore transnational history is, therefore, an investigation into the ways in which we all have multiple identities, as citizens of our own nations and as members of a global human community.

At the same time transnational history, like most other forms of history, looks at the human experience through the act of storytelling. This emphasis on individual and local history, in a national and global context, enables the historian to embrace the power of narrative while also analyzing the structures of historical change at a variety of spatial and temporal levels. It helps us to engage in the challenging but necessary task of exploring the configurations of the world that shaped the movement of history as we also try to understand how the people whose lives we explore saw their own world and time. Hopefully this intersection of structure and narrative will facilitate our comprehension of that foreign country we call the past. So settle back and get comfortable, dear reader, for I have a few tales to tell.

Part 1

The World of the French Revolution

By the late eighteenth century France was clearly one of the dominant nations of Europe. Its great "Sun King," Louis XIV, had both extended its national boundaries and made it the leading military power on the Continent. The intellectual school known as the Enlightenment, led by great thinkers such as Diderot, Voltaire, and Rousseau, had made France the center of Western civilization and culture. The nation's capital, Paris, was the largest city in Europe with 600,000 inhabitants. France had a prosperous peasantry living in an abundant and fertile countryside, and a growing middle class brought wealth to its towns and cities. The old Yiddish saying "Happy as God in France" seemed to describe French life accurately.

This happy land would, however, soon enter into a period of extraordinary political turmoil that would fundamentally transform France, with echoes far beyond its borders. The French Revolution that began in 1789 would abolish both feudalism and the monarchy, create the first republic in French history, and transform the subjects of the king into the citizens of the nation. It would initiate wars with the rest of Europe that would ultimately lead to Napoleon's conquest of most of the Continent, and would give rise to ideas about human liberty and sovereignty that many considered both the heritage of the French nation and the universal property of humankind. Even more than the American War of Independence, it lay at the center of the Age of Revolution that would transform the Atlantic world. Moreover, even after Napoleon's defeat and the restoration of the monarchy in 1814, after a quarter century of revolutionary turmoil, France would not achieve stability. The nation would experience several more regime changes and revolutions before the Third Republic could finally create a stable national political consensus.

The essays in this first section will consider the transnational history of revolutionary France, from the fall of the Bastille in 1789 to the Second Empire in the mid-nineteenth century. They show how the French Revolution was, in the idea of the German philosopher Georg Hegel, a world historical event, and the impact the turbulence of late eighteenth and early nineteenth century had on peoples and places far beyond its borders. The French Revolution and its aftermath played a key role in the shaping of the modern world, and in doing so helped make France a universal nation.

The French Revolution and the Napoleonic Empire

In 1789 France was a monarchy, ruled according to the tenets of divine right absolutism by King Louis XVI. As we have seen, it was a prosperous and powerful land, yet one also experiencing a variety of intellectual, political, and economic crises. Many Enlightenment thinkers strongly opposed royal rule, demanding instead individual and political liberty. Absolute monarchy was expensive, and the wars and grandeur of Louis XIV, followed by those of his successors, had burdened the kingdom financially. French support for the American War of Independence had dealt a powerful blow to France's great rival, Britain, but its costs pushed France into a financial crisis. The only solution was to raise taxes, but this need pushed up against the structure of old regime society. As in the Middle Ages, France was divided into three estates: the clergy and the church, the aristocracy, and the commoners (or everyone else). Even though the first two estates possessed great wealth, feudal tradition exempted them from paying taxes. The clergy and aristocracy strongly resisted the monarchy's increasingly assertive attempts to tax them, in the end precipitating a full-fledged political crisis. They forced Louis XVI to call into session the Estates General, the traditional legislative body of feudal society, one so moribund it hadn't met since 1614.

Elections for the Estates General took place from late 1788 to early 1789, and the electoral process mobilized political and popular opinion across France to an unprecedented degree. When the Estates General did meet in May 1789, in the royal capital of Versailles outside Paris, it immediately confronted a demand by representatives of the Third Estate to change the voting system. Traditionally each estate had had the same number of votes, but despite representing 97 percent of the population, the Third Estate had only one-third of the vote. Its representatives initially pushed for doubling their representation, and then for the full replacement of the Estates General by a new National Assembly. Louis XVI conceded to their demands, ordering the other two estates to join the National Assembly, but at the same time began assembling troops to reinforce his authority.

Popular reaction to the events in Versailles during the summer of 1789 transformed the political crisis into a revolution. A harsh winter and bread shortages, combined with fears that the king intended to crush the new National Assembly, prompted popular action throughout the country. In Paris thousands of ordinary men and women began arming themselves to seize grain and resist despotism, and the popular mobilization culminated on July 14 with the seizure of the Bastille, a royal fortress in the eastern part of the city. In the countryside rumors of royalist bandits led peasants to rise up and attack the castles of the nobility throughout the country. The so-called Great Fear, along with the mobilization of the Paris crowd, forced Louis XVI to accept the National Assembly and the dissolution of the traditional order. To underscore this, in October a group of armed Parisian women marched to Versailles and forced the king and his family to move to Paris, where they would remain under the watchful eyes of the revolutionary crowd.

Over the next two years the now empowered National Assembly transformed France from a feudal monarchy into a modern nation. It formally abolished feudalism, serfdom, and the aristocracy, made French men and women citizens of the nation rather than subjects of the king or queen, and decreed that national sovereignty resided with the people rather than the monarch, who now became a constitutional ruler. It implemented civil liberties and freedom of religion, granting full citizenship to members of religious minorities; France became the first nation in Europe to make Jews equal citizens. Power was vested in the National Assembly, to be elected by all men of property. Above all, it emphasized the Enlightenment idea that reason and freedom were the universal values of mankind. As *The Declaration of the Rights of Man and Citizen*, adopted in August 1789, declared, "Men are born and remain free and equal in rights."

This was the liberal phase of the French Revolution, one that achieved many of the goals of the Enlightenment and French liberals. But the movement did not stop there. It continued in part thanks to growing resistance, both at home and abroad, against the revolution. Starting in 1789 many French aristocrats fled their homeland for other parts of Europe and America, warning whoever would listen that the anarchy unleashed in France would soon infect the rest of the world. Monarchs and aristocrats throughout Europe watched the events in Paris with increasing apprehension. At the same time, the National Assembly's decision to nationalize the Catholic Church split the French clergy, pushing many into opposition to the new regime, especially after the pope condemned the revolution in general. Louis XVI's abortive attempt in June 1791 to flee France in disguise, only to be apprehended at the border and brought back to Paris as a prisoner, convinced many French people that the revolution was in danger, a belief strengthened by the increasing hostility of European royalty.

At the same time, voices in France challenged the restrictive nature of the liberal revolution, demanding that its universalism truly apply to all peoples. In September 1791 the Parisian playwright Olympe de Gouges published *The Declaration of the Rights of Woman and the Female Citizen*, demanding that women be given civil rights and legal equality with men. A month earlier a massive slave revolt broke out in the Caribbean colony of Saint-Domingue, as Black slaves asserted their rights under the universal principles of the Revolution to be treated as free men and women. For many members of the Third Estate, especially the activists in Paris, the revolution had to go beyond granting liberal civil rights, and in addition ensure social and economic justice.

In 1792, revolutionary France declared war on Austria, whose king was the brother of the much-hated French queen Marie Antoinette. For the next twenty years the French would wage war against much of the rest of Europe, and the dynamics of war abroad tended to polarize politics at home. In August members of the Paris crowd, known as *sans-culottes* (those without fashionable knee-breeches) invaded the National Assembly, convinced that traitors at home were responsible for military losses abroad. They forced the deputies to abolish the National Assembly in favor of a National Convention, one elected by universal manhood suffrage. At the same time supporters of the revolution flooded into the national armies, stopping the Prussian and Austrian advance on Paris at the battle of Valmy in September. The new National Convention abolished the monarchy, making France a republic for the first time in its history.

This shift to the left was a prime example of politics as a glocal phenomenon, vividly illustrating the interplay between war among European states and local activism in Paris. Like many revolutions, the French Revolution quickly assumed the form of a civil war. In this case, however, because one side of the conflict (the aristocracy) had significant connections throughout Europe, this became an international affair. Much of the opposition to the Revolution fled abroad, establishing its main center in the German city of Coblenz on the Rhine River. War between revolutionary France and aristocratic Europe thus evolved naturally out of the conflict between different French factions. The Paris uprising of August 10, 1792, underscored the belief of the *sans-culottes* that their struggle was part of a glocal crisis, both local and global at the same time.

This began the radical phase of the French Revolution. New elections brought to political dominance the Jacobin party, originally formed during the elections of 1789. The Jacobins split into two factions, the moderate Girondins led by Jacques-Pierre Brissot, and the more radical Montagnards led by Maximilian Robespierre. The Montagnards prevailed in the Convention by allying themselves with the radical Parisian crowd, first accepting their demand to condemn the king for treason. The Convention duly placed Louis XVI on trial, and on January 21, 1793, "citizen Louis Capet" was executed by that new instrument of revolutionary justice, the guillotine.

The execution of the king and the abolition of the monarchy precipitated the greatest crisis yet for the Revolution. It galvanized the rest of Europe in opposition against France, which soon faced a broad coalition of states pledged to overthrowing the revolutionary government. The Convention leaders also confronted a major domestic counterrevolution, an armed insurgency spurred in particular by the Revolution's attacks on the church. In May 1793 the *sans-culottes* again invaded the national government, forcing the expulsion of the Girondins who now joined the counterrevolution. Surrounded by numerous and determined enemies at home and abroad, it seemed the days of the Revolution were numbered. The movement led by the people of Paris would survive as a global phenomenon, or it would not survive at all.

The Montagnards who now ran the Convention responded not with compromise but rather by further increasing the radicalism of the movement. They reorganized the government to create an effective dictatorship, forming the Committee of Public Safety led by Robespierre and a small group of Montagnards. To face the military threat the government instituted conscription on an unprecedented scale, creating a massive army of 1.5 million men by late 1794. The Committee also fixed the price of essential foods, especially bread, to ensure the loyalty of the *sans-culottes*. Most notoriously, it instituted a wide-ranging program of political repression known as the Terror, a search for traitors to the Revolution that resulted in the convictions and executions of several thousand French women and men. The Montagnard dictatorship also decreed the formal de-Christianization of France, turning the cathedral of Notre Dame into a temple of reason, and in February 1794 formally abolished slavery, the first European colonial power to do so.

These measures, especially the new draft that created an army much larger than those of France's European opponents, ensured the survival of the Revolution. By the spring of 1794 French armies were able to take the offensive in the east, occupying Belgium and the Rhineland, and at the same time crushed the counterrevolution at home. However, greater military security did not lead to liberalization at home. On the contrary, the Committee ramped up the Terror, increasingly targeting all political opponents. In March 1794 it executed the radical journalist Jacques Hébert, who had accused Robespierre of being too moderate. A few weeks later the Terror took the lives of Georges Danton and other prominent Jacobins. These executions not only divided the Jacobins but also alienated many of the *sans-culottes*, who had looked to Hébert as their champion. This provided an opening for the Committee's opponents; on July 27, 1794, they arrested Robespierre and other Committee members, in their turn sending them to the guillotine.

The death of Robespierre and the downfall of the Committee of Public Safety marked the end of the Terror and the radical phase of the French Revolution. A massive counterreaction set in, far more extreme than the plotters against Robespierre had expected, as political prisoners were freed from prison and the Jacobin club was legally banned. Conservatives unleashed a so-called White Terror, hunting down revolutionary militants, beating and sometimes killing them. The government also ended price controls on food, not only triggering a new round of inflation but also sparking a new *sans-culottes* uprising in Paris, one that the army violently suppressed. With the breaking of the political and military power of the Paris crowd the political pendulum shifted back to the right. The Convention wrote a new constitution, abolishing universal manhood suffrage and concentrating executive power in a five-person committee called the Directory.

From 1795 to 1799 the Directory ruled France, striving to preserve the gains of the liberal revolution from both Jacobin radicalism and a return to monarchical rule. For a time it prevailed, managing to control inflation and restore prosperity to France. It also successfully continued prosecuting the war against the nation's European enemies, so that French armies occupied the Netherlands and pursued their offensive into Italy and Germany. The Directory did not succeed, however, in marginalizing its political opponents, facing armed uprisings from both royalists and radicals. This did not matter so much as long as times were good, but in 1798 the nation experienced a new economic downturn while French armies also lost several battles against a new coalition of British, Russian, and Austrian forces. By 1799 it seemed the Directory's days were numbered, and it only remained to be seen what would replace it.

The answer was surprising. The lengthy wars of the French Revolution and the new emphasis on an egalitarian army had allowed many young talented officers to rise through the ranks to positions of power. The most notable of these, Napoleon Bonaparte, came from the minor Corsican aristocracy. He had distinguished himself as an artillery officer in several campaigns against both foreign and domestic enemies, crushing the Austrians with a series of impressive victories in Italy in 1796 then leading a dramatic expedition to Egypt in 1798. Hailed as a military hero, the thirty-year-old Napoleon returned to Paris in October 1799, where the Directory appointed him military commander of Paris. In November he used this position to surround the Convention with troops, forcing it to transfer power to a new government of three Consuls, himself being one. Over the next few years Napoleon used his military power to shove the other consuls to the side, appointing himself consul for life in 1802, and then emperor in 1804, the first emperor of France since Charlemagne a thousand years earlier. His coronation marked the end of the First Republic and its replacement by the First Empire.

Napoleon ruled France for well over a decade, until 1814, and during those years he made major changes in French life, both building upon and transforming the legacy of the Revolution. He further increased the centralization of the French state, strengthening the departments that the Revolution had created out of the old royal provinces. He also introduced a new civil code, the Napoleonic Code, that emphasized the Revolutionary ideal of the equality of all men before the law. In addition, the First Empire confirmed the end of feudalism, and the supremacy of Paris in national politics. At the same time Napoleon turned back some of the innovations of the revolutionary era. He reestablished the aristocracy and made the nation's peace with the church. He also restricted civil liberties and increased government censorship, as well as stripping the legislature of any significant power. In addition, he reversed the First Republic's abolition of slavery, restoring it throughout the French Caribbean. Napoleon ruled France as a modernizing despot, but a despot nonetheless.

The heart of Napoleonic rule, however, was warfare against France's enemies, and his brilliant military campaigns more than anything else created his popularity and his legend. He forced the European allies to accept peace largely on his terms at the Peace of Amiens in 1802, then when war broke out again he crushed the alliance of Britain, Prussia, and Russia, occupying first Berlin then Vienna. By 1810 Napoleon controlled most of central Europe plus the Iberian and Italian peninsulas, giving him and France the largest empire the continent had seen since the days of the Romans. In the modern era only Adolf Hitler's Nazi Germany would come close to repeating Napoleon's success as the master of Europe. His one major defeat came in the Caribbean, where his failure to reassert French control over the rebel slaves of Saint-Domingue led to the permanent loss of that colony and the emergence of Haiti. Napoleon's empire marked the culmination of a central characteristic of the Revolution that began in 1792, its interplay between political conflicts at home and military expansion abroad, highlighting the transnational roots of the modern French nation.

In ruling the conquered lands, Napoleon imposed many of the achievements of the French Revolution, including the abolition of feudalism and serfdom, the liberation of the Jews, and the imposition of the Napoleonic code. He also redrew the administrative map of the continent, creating a new Polish state, abolishing the Holy Roman Empire, and redrawing the maps of Germany and Italy. Many people in occupied Europe, especially at the beginning of French rule, welcomed the new era as bringing the modernity and liberalism of revolutionary France to their own lands. They applauded the abolition of feudalism and the liberation of the Jews, for example. Even as far away as India, French expatriates set up a Jacobin club in the kingdom of Mysore to organize against British influence. However, as French rule gradually became more oppressive (and expensive), some began to see it as conquest rather than liberation, and guerrilla wars against the French arose in Spain, Germany, and other parts of the empire.

In the end, Napoleon's empire fell victim not to internal dissent and revolt but to military defeat. By 1810 France controlled all of Europe except Britain and Russia. Unable to defeat the British navy, Napoleon therefore resolved to subjugate the Russians, invading that vast empire in 1812. French armies scored several victories and occupied Moscow, but failed to destroy Russian armies that waged a scorched-earth strategy that forced the French into a ruinous retreat during the brutal Russian winter. The Russian campaign so fatally weakened Napoleon's forces that by the end of 1813 France lost several major battles against Britain and her allies. In April 1814 the allies forced Napoleon to abdicate the throne and exiled him on the Italian island of Elba. In a bizarre postscript to the imperial story,

Napoleon escaped from Elba in March 1815, making his way back to France and regaining control of the nation. Once again, he led French armies to battle against the powers of Europe, but suffered a crushing defeat at the Battle of Waterloo. This time he was exiled to the island of St Helena off the African coast, and after years of military glory the First Empire faded into history and legend.

The Early Nineteenth Century: Restoration, Revolution, and Empire

On May 3, 1814, after more than twenty years in exile, Louis XVIII, the brother of the martyred Louis XVI, returned to Paris in the train of the conquering European allies to take up his duties as the new king of France. By that spring the French nation had been convulsed by war and revolution for a quarter of a century, and many hoped for a return to some semblance of stability, if not necessarily the good old days. It was not to be. For the next several decades France would experience a succession of regimes, including two monarchies, a republic, and a new empire, as well as two different revolutions. At the same time, the rise of the new industrial economy would transform French economic and social life. The French Revolution had raised but not conclusively resolved fundamental questions of governance, national identity, and social justice, and these conflicts would continue to preoccupy French women and men during the new century.

France under the Restoration was a society deeply divided about the legacy of the Revolution and empire. The aristocrats who flooded back into the country after years of foreign exile wanted nothing less than a return to the Old Regime and royal absolutism. Louis XVIII himself had a more moderate perspective, and was willing to embrace the idea of constitutional monarchy. This became difficult when the Ultra party, representing the extreme right, won control of the new legislature, the Chamber of Deputies, in the fall of 1815. During most of Louis XVIII's reign they dominated French political life, and their position was reinforced when the king died in 1824 and was succeeded by his very conservative brother, Charles X. The liberal opposition remained a force to be reckoned with, however, its appeal bolstered by an economic downturn beginning in 1827. That year and again in 1830 the liberal opposition won control of the Chamber. These victories underscored increasing discontent in the nation as a whole with royalist policies, discontent Charles X tried to allay with foreign adventurism. In June 1830, after a series of diplomatic incidents, French forces invaded Algiers, seizing that nation in a major expansion of France's colonial empire.

This overseas success did nothing to pacify the opposition at home, however, and Charles X's refusal to compromise with his opponents produced an explosion. Not for the last time in the history of modern France would military campaigns in the colonial world and political upheaval in Paris coincide. On July 27 mass protests began in Paris and demonstrators began barricading key streets and intersections. The next day the movement turned into a full-scale revolution, with insurgents occupying key points in the capital; many soldiers sent to suppress the revolutionaries joined them instead. By July 29 the rebels had seized control of most of the capital and called for the abdication of the king. Charles X, deserted by most of his supporters, formally resigned a few days later and fled to exile in Britain. The uprising, later known as the Three Glorious Days, had triumphed, and the restoration of the monarchy had ended with a new revolution in Paris, a revolution that like the great predecessor of 1789 was both local and transnational.

The Revolution of 1830 did not bring an end to the French monarchy, however. The leaders of the opposition did not want a republic, but instead a truly constitutional monarch. They found one in the Duke of Orleans, who now took power as King Louis Philippe, the ruler of what became known as the July Monarchy. Louis Philippe rejected absolutism and considered himself a citizen king, one who accepted the legacy of the liberal phase of the French Revolution and was willing to work with the legislature. In particular, he reached out beyond the narrow ranks of the aristocracy to those families who had risen to prominence under the Revolution and Empire, and to the new bourgeois society that developed in the early nineteenth century.

This new society arose out of the transformation of the national economy. During the July Monarchy France entered the industrial age, with social and political life adjusting to the new shape of the economy. Following the lead of the Industrial Revolution in Britain, French industries such as textiles, mining, and iron and steel grew dramatically. The spread of railroads around the country not only helped knit its various regions closer together but also symbolized the entrepreneurial spirit of the age. The burgeoning industrial sector produced vast amounts of new wealth, symbolized by the growth of the banks and the rise of a prosperous commercial and industrial bourgeoisie. At the same time, millions of unskilled laborers streamed into the nation's cities, above all Paris, finding hard work and harsh living conditions. The new industrial society represented not only great wealth, but equally a sharp contrast between the lives of rich and poor.

The nouveaux riches of the July Monarchy looked to the regime to protect their interests, and Louis Philippe's government was happy to oblige. Those who favored the heritage of the Revolution and the Jacobin republic did not share their enthusiasm, however, and often advocated the overthrow of the monarchy and the establishment of a republic. The July Monarchy also witnessed the rise of new radical ideologies. The plight of the working poor inspired the birth of socialist ideologies, often taking the form of utopian visions of postcapitalist communal societies. Young dissident intellectuals and artists christened themselves Bohemians, making opposition to bourgeois society a matter of lifestyle as much as politics. The royal regime, for all its vaunted liberalism, showed little tolerance of these oppositions, frequently resorting to military force to preserve the established order.

As with the Restoration, an economic depression produced a political crisis for the July Monarchy. The mid-1840s saw major crop failures and industrial collapse all across Europe, symbolized especially by the great famine in Ireland. In France the crisis precipitated a call for political reform. In particular, the opposition demanded electoral reform, since under the restrictive franchise most Frenchmen, including most members of the middle class, could not vote. In February 1848 Louis Philippe responded to the campaign for reform by trying to ban a popular meeting in Paris. The people of the capital reacted with fury, taking to the streets and building barricades. When the soldiers in Paris rallied to the revolution, Louis Philippe, like Charles X eighteen years earlier, decided his cause was lost and fled to England.

The victorious revolutionaries decided that, unlike in 1830, there would be no new king. Instead, they appointed a provisional government to rule the country until elections could be arranged. The government proclaimed the Second Republic, to be based on universal manhood suffrage. It also proclaimed the final abolition of slavery in the French Empire, prompting slave uprisings in Martinique as news of the decision filtered across the Atlantic. France was once again a republic, yet like the First Republic the Second was divided between liberals and radicals, between those who emphasized civil liberties and law and those who looked to build a more egalitarian or socialist society. In June 1848 the two sides clashed when Parisian workers staged an insurrection, only to be defeated by the forces of the newly-elected National Assembly. This was 1848's version of the defeat of Robespierre in 1794, and henceforth the new republican regime would move decisively to the center.

This became abundantly clear with the December 1848 elections for the president of the republic. The most unusual candidate, and the surprise winner in a landslide, was Louis-Napoleon Bonaparte, the nephew of the great emperor who had spent most of his life in exile. Louis-Napoleon appealed successfully to both the left and the right, as well as to all those enamored of the Napoleonic legend. As president he moved decisively to repress the left, going so far as to ban the great Revolutionary anthem, *The Marseillaise*. Elected to a single four-year term, he was legally obligated to step down in 1852. Instead, in December 1851 he staged a coup d'état, dissolving the National Assembly and placing much of the country under martial law. A year later he won popular approval through a plebiscite for abolishing the Second Republic and, like his famous uncle had done a half-century earlier, replacing it with an imperial regime. He then took power as emperor Napoleon III.

Many French people at the time, and many historians and other commentators ever since, have castigated the Second Empire as an inferior sequel to the First, a tired re-run lacking genius or glory. "First time as tragedy, second time as farce," ran Karl Marx's famously nasty putdown of Napoleon III. Yet the regime, the last empire in French history, lasted for nearly twenty years and left an important imprint on the life of modern France. Even though it essentially abolished elections and reduced the power of the legislature, the Second Empire retained universal manhood suffrage, making it a permanent part of French political life. The fact that the emperor could and did appeal to both the political right and left was certainly opportunistic at times, but also contributed to formulating a national political culture that eventually brought stability to the nation. In terms of foreign and colonial policy Napoleon III blended the old and the new: while he continued to intervene in the affairs of other European states, unlike his famous uncle his vision of empire was increasingly an overseas one. The Third Republic that succeeded him would build on this tradition, crafting the greatest colonial empire in modern French history.

Historians have traditionally divided the Second Empire into an authoritarian phase during the 1850s and a liberal one during the 1860s. The 1850s were boom years in France, representing a reprise of the economic prosperity the nation had known under the July Monarchy. This brought the regime significant popular support, especially from the newly rich bourgeoisie and the peasantry. The Second Empire also expanded the French presence overseas, notably in Indochina, New Caledonia, and West Africa. It continued to suppress discontent at home, however, to keep the legislature largely powerless, and to ban working class organizations.

In the 1860s Napoleon III decided to liberalize his regime, legalizing unions, for example, reducing state censorship of the press and increasing the authority of the legislature. Unfortunately for him, these changes helped empower the opponents of his regime without significantly winning them over to his side. In response to elections at the end of 1869 that saw the opposition win nearly half the vote, the emperor proposed a new constitution to create a more liberal empire. He submitted it to a popular referendum that passed by more than 80 percent of the vote, seeming to validate the new direction of his rule. Things looked promising for the Second Empire until a diplomatic crisis with Prussia in the summer of 1870 led France to declare war against its increasingly powerful neighbor. The Franco-Prussian war was a complete disaster for the French: not only were their armies handily defeated in the field, but at the battle of Sedan on September 1 the Prussians took Napoleon III himself prisoner. The news reached Paris two days later, prompting a popular insurrection on the following day, September 4, that overthrew the regime and proclaimed a new Third Republic. No one lifted a hand to defend the empire, and like deposed French rulers before him, Napoleon III fled to England to spend the rest of his days in exile.

The eighty years between the outbreak of the French Revolution and the fall of the Second Empire transformed France from a kingdom into a nation, saw the development of an industrial economy, prompted the migration of millions from the countryside to the cities, and brought about the decline of the old Caribbean colonies and the birth of a vast new empire in Asia, Africa, and the Pacific. During these years France not only entered the modern world but to a significant extent created it. In many ways revolution in the modern world has been transnational, integrating local, national, and global concerns, and the Revolution of 1789 and its successors played a key role in establishing this pattern. The political turbulence of these years reflected debates about citizenship, national identity, class, and society that the Revolution had brought to the forefront of public debate. It would be up to the new Third Republic to resolve them, and in doing so it position France as a great nation and a major player on the world stage.

1

Strangers in a Strange Land
The Saga of the French Five Hundred

While the French Revolution was certainly an event of global importance, few people would normally look for traces of its history in the small towns of the American Midwest. Yet the aftershocks of that cataclysmic event reached even into that area, thousands of miles from Paris. The history of Gallipolis ("City of the Gauls") Ohio, on the banks of the Ohio River, testifies to the impact of the Revolution far from its birthplace. Here a group of French émigrés founded a new settlement in the 1790s, hoping to escape the turmoil of their native land and at the same time create a utopian community rooted in Enlightenment philosophy. The story of this community brings together the history of the French Revolution with that of the American frontier, showing how both were shaped by global patterns and events.

The history of Gallipolis begins with the mania for things American that swept France in the era of the American Revolution. French veterans of Lafayette's armies returned to Paris full of admiration for the new republic, and the presence of Benjamin Franklin further nourished this fascination. At the same time, the primitivist ideal developed by Enlightenment thinkers like Rousseau suggested that freedom and morality were to be found in the "state of Nature," far removed from urban civilization. These influences led many Parisians to contrast the decadent, despotic societies of the Old World with the possibility of building virgin Edens in the New. Thousands of miles away, one could easily conceptualize America as a utopian, imaginary land whose virtues closely reflected the vices of one's own society.

Such ideas might have remained just that, ideas, but for the confluence of two forces: the Revolution itself, and land speculation on the Ohio frontier. America's successful struggle for independence from Britain opened the doors to settlement of what was then called the Northwest Territory, the area between the Appalachian Mountains and the Mississippi River, north of the Ohio River. Speculators founded companies to purchase land in this vast area and sell it to settlers. In 1787 a group of businessmen from New England formed the Ohio Company and signed a contract with the U.S. government to purchase more than a million acres of land along the Ohio River. At the same time Manasseh Cutler and Winthrop Sargent, the Ohio Company's agents, signed a second contract giving themselves the right to purchase land along the Scioto River, a tributary of the Ohio, and transferred this option to Colonel William Duer. Using this option, Duer then created the Scioto Company.

In 1788 the Scioto Company began operations in Europe, hiring as its principal agent Joel Barlow, a young man from Connecticut with legal training and literary ambitions. Barlow arrived in Paris at the end of June and set about trying to sell plots of land in Ohio to the French. At first his efforts were less than successful, and by the spring of 1789 Barlow could point to few sales and was ready to admit defeat. However, a chance meeting with an English businessman in Paris, William Playfair, changed his mind, and by August the two started collaborating as representatives of the Scioto Company in France, opening an office in an affluent neighborhood of Paris. Playfair and Barlow began publicizing the possibilities of buying land in the Scioto valley, writing several papers about the venture, notably the *Prospectus for the Establishment on the Scioto and Ohio Rivers in America*. The *Prospectus* tantalized interested Parisians with visions of a fertile, virgin land where they could become independent and prosperous farmers, living in peace and security:

> The terrain of this area is one of the most fertile in the world. To the mildness of the climate and the excellence of the soil one must also add the virtues of the local government; in fact this may be one of the area's primary advantages, making this area superior to all others. Europe,

Asia, and Africa were peopled during times of ignorance, whose traces one can never entirely erase; it is only in America that one can enjoy all the happiness to be expected from freedom and a wonderful climate and terrain.[1]

Timing is everything. The Scioto Company proclaimed the attractions of life in Ohio to a country convulsed by political change. The summer of 1789 saw the seizure of the Bastille by the revolutionary Paris mob, followed in short order by the creation of a National Assembly and the abolition of the feudal order. The dramatic political events led some aristocrats and others to emigrate, a phenomenon that would only increase as the revolution became more radical. The beginnings of the French Revolution in 1789 thus created a huge amount of interest in the company. Together, idealistic fascination with America and fears of the political situation in Paris made the fortunes of the Scioto Company. One no longer need just dream of the New World, one could actually go there!

A veritable wave of Sciotomania engulfed the elite circles of the French capital. Parisians flocked into the company's offices to buy what they thought were the deeds to plots of land. As one aristocrat, Count Volney, commented, "Nothing was talked of, in every social circle, but the paradise that was opened for Frenchmen in the western wilderness: the free and happy life to be led on the blissful banks of the Scioto."[2] Visions of a Rousseauian pastoral paradise in America contrasted sharply with gathering political turmoil in Paris that had already prompted members of the aristocracy to flee their homeland. As one young Parisian commented, "I dream only of Scioto . . . Paris has no more charm. France is nothing next to Scioto."[3]

By the beginning of 1790 the company had sold more than one hundred thousand acres of land in the Ohio wilderness to eager French settlers. Who answered the Scioto's siren song? Most came from Paris, although some people from the French provinces responded to the call, and one man came from as far away as Hamburg, Germany. Most were young men, bourgeois but not wealthy and searching for new horizons to explore. As one wrote, "Young, native of Paris, independent, I have some small savings that could perhaps allow me to acquire an establishment in my homeland, if in the midst of the general upheaval one can still nurture such hopes. But a secret unrest which makes me want to travel . . . has turned my eyes toward the New World."[4] Some priests, facing the increasing confrontation between the new revolutionary government and the church, also opted to flee France for the Scioto. Many artisans, like the brothers François and Jean Germain Vallot, jewelers, bought property from the Scioto Company. The economic crisis and the flight of many aristocrats dealt a body blow to the luxury trades in France, forcing skilled craftsmen to consider other alternatives. Although the emigration to the Scioto mostly attracted men, some women, both married and single, also chose to go. Blondel de Beauregard, a widow with young children, seized in desperation upon the opportunity for a better life across the sea. Ironically, given the desire of the new settlers to create a rural Arcadia, only a few had any experience working the land.

Although Sciotomania and the desire to move to the Ohio territory captured the imagination of many different types of people in France, attention tended to focus on the aristocrats who saw in the venture an alternative to increasingly desperate conditions in their homeland. Young men from titled families, often younger sons with few prospects of inheriting the family estate, found Scioto an attractive prospect, while their elders regarded it as a prudent investment in a time of political anarchy. The Count d'Eprémesnil and the Marquis de Lezay-Marnésia, two leaders of the Parisian aristocracy, alone bought thirty-two thousand acres between them. In January 1790 they convened a group of like-minded wealthy investors, taking the name "The Society of Twenty-Four," that crafted plans not only to buy land in Ohio but also to create a utopian aristocratic community there. As Lezay-Marnésia's son later observed, "Despairing of the fate of the monarchy, he decided to search in America for a refuge against the savage anarchy breaking out everywhere, and to found there a French colony."[5]

These would-be settlers did not of course begin the tradition of French settlement in the New World, which dated back well over two centuries. Starting with Jacques Cartier's travels in the Saint Lawrence River valley during the early sixteenth century, France had established a considerable presence in North America. In 1608 the French founded Quebec City, which became the capital of the colony of New France. At the end of the century France created the colony of Louisiana at the mouth of the Mississippi River, and in 1718 founded the city of New Orleans. Thousands of French subjects settled in both colonies, working primarily as farmers but also as traders, clerks, and servants.[6]

In particular, the French developed a thriving trade in furs with the Indigenous population. The *coureurs de bois* or *voyageurs* (fur trappers), French entrepreneurs who both bought beaver pelts from the Indigenous inhabitants and eventually learned how to trap them on their own, prospered by selling luxurious furs to European aristocrats. They also, much more than other Europeans in North America, lived alongside and integrated into Indigenous communities, notably the Algonquian peoples who dominated the region. Many engaged in sexual relations, *marriages à la façon du pays* (common-law marriages between French men and Indigenous women), fathering mixed-race offspring and becoming part of the Indigenous population. In general, the *coureurs de bois* came to symbolize what by the eighteenth century had become French Canada.[7]

The French left a lasting cultural presence on the areas of the New World they colonized, one that endures to this day, but ultimately their rule would not survive into the modern era. New France gradually found itself outstripped by the more heavily populated and dynamic British colonies in North America. The outbreak of the Seven Years War in Europe during the 1750s and 1760s triggered fighting between the two colonial areas in America, known as the French and Indian War. Although the French maintained their alliance with the Algonquian nation, the British won over the powerful Iroquois peoples, rivals of the Algonquians. This alliance helped London win the war, dramatically conquering the great French fortress at Quebec in 1759 and annexing New France to the British Empire. In 1803 Napoleon would sell New Orleans and the entire Louisiana Territory to the United States, reducing North American France to a few rocky outposts. The colony in Gallipolis would thus take root in a continent whose French presence had largely been relegated to history.

In February 1790 hundreds of French men and women took ship in Le Havre for the promised land of Ohio. They were forced to wait in the city for more than a month before the Scioto Company was able to procure five small ships to transport them overseas. The voyage was arduous and monotonous, lasting two to three months. One ship sank in the middle of the Atlantic; fortunately for the passengers, a passing English ship rescued them, although they lost all their luggage. The first ship arrived in Alexandria, Virginia, on May 1, full of hopeful settlers eager to begin their new lives.

At this point, however, they learned of the scandal around the Scioto Company that had erupted in Paris soon after their departure. Even during the height of Sciotomania not all Parisians had warmed to the expedition. Supporters of the revolution often condemned it as merely another type of emigration, an aristocratic attack on the French people. At the same time rumors had begun to circulate that the company was a fraud, leading angry Parisians to besiege the company's offices, and it turned out the rumors were true. The Scioto Company never actually owned any land, just an option from the Ohio Company, and as a result the French settlers' deeds were worthless. Parisian journalists piled on in their denunciations of the Scioto Company as swindlers who had defrauded innocent French men and women. One caricature of a company advertisement proclaimed "Sale of desert land in Scioto by Anglo-Americans. Citizen Mignard draws attention to those English companies that sell imaginary lands in the United States."[8] The company collapsed and William Duer was imprisoned for debt.

All this proved small consolation to the French settlers, stranded in Virginia, having in many cases lost everything on this venture. When the first ship arrived, the passengers had been surprised that no representatives of the Scioto Company were there to greet them, so they began wandering around the port city looking for them. They soon encountered friendly locals, who marveled at their elegant Parisian wigs and clothes, but who also informed them about the realities of the Scioto Company and their situation. As ship after ship arrived, full of hopeful émigrés who soon learned the bitter news, the French debated what course to take. The people of Alexandria supported the stranded pioneers as best they could, while they negotiated with American officials. Eventually agents of the Ohio Company, which did in fact own the land, allowed the stranded French settlers to move onto its property. It hired woodsmen to clear out a townsite and build log cabins. They also arranged to transport them to their new home, moving them in rough-hewn wagons to the Ohio River and then on riverboats downriver to their destination.

Of the roughly one thousand French men and women who set sail for Ohio in 1790, only about five hundred eventually came to Gallipolis. Few aristocrats and members of the Society of Twenty-Four made it to the Scioto valley. Count d'Eprémesnil never left France at all, sending agents to America in his stead. Lezay-Marnésia did cross the Atlantic and ventured as far as Marietta, but disillusioned by the scandal of the Scioto Company soon left for Pittsburgh. Those who completed the journey to the Scioto found that their idea of an aristocratic utopian community in the wilderness held little appeal for most of their fellow émigrés, enticed instead by the prospect of becoming independent landholders. Ultimately the vision of the Society of Twenty-Four did not survive the journey from France, coming to naught in the New World.

On October 17, 1790, the first group of French settlers finally arrived at the place they had risked so much to see, a small collection of rustic houses next to the river. Upon their arrival one of the French settlers wrote about his hopes for their new home:

> We hope soon to arrive at our new territory, where we shall find things in their original state, such as God made them and not perverted by the ungrateful hand of man. To some these surrounding woods might appear frightful deserts; to me they are the paradise of nature; no hosts of greedy priests; no seas of blood to wade through; all is quiet, and the savages themselves shall soon be taught the art of cultivating the earth, refinement of manners, and the duties of genuine devotion. Under this free and enlightened dominion the unfortunate and oppressed of our nation shall ever find an asylum, our language and customs will here be preserved in their original purity for ages to come, and France shall find herself renovated in the Western World, without being disgraced by the frippery of kings or seeing the best blood wasted in gratifying the ambition of knaves and sycophants.[9]

They named the new settlement Gallipolis, a little piece of France in the Ohio wilderness. Legend has it that on their first night in their new home, the settlers put on their best clothes and held a formal ball, dancing the minuet and the gavotte.

As the settlers soon learned, life on the frontier had little in common with the primitivist fantasies nourished in France. Arriving in the autumn instead of the spring meant they could not plant crops and bring in a harvest until the following year. A collection of middle-class Parisians, cabinet makers, jewelers, and other artisans lacked the basic skills needed for survival in the wilderness. Woodsmen from the Ohio company helped the little colony through the first winter, but after that the French were on their own. Locals soon began to joke about the incompetence of the newcomers, how they knew next to nothing about the basic tasks of planting crops and clearing the land of the massive sycamores of the forest. In addition, Gallipolis was built on swampy soil, so that some settlers succumbed to fever. Many others wearied of the hardships of frontier life and left for the more established cities of the East Coast.

The settlers also came into conflict with local Indigenous populations. During the eighteenth century a variety of different Indigenous communities settled in the Ohio country, in particular the Algonquian Indians but also the Senecas, Cherokees, Miamis, and Shawnees. Indigenous men pioneered the lucrative fur trade of the area, while Indigenous women developed a rich and sophisticated agrarian economy, growing corn and fruit trees and raising domestic animals. After their conquest of New France, the British had sought to win over the Indigenous peoples by limiting, then prohibiting white colonial settlement in the Ohio River Valley. This helped provoke the American Revolution and led the United States to resume the settlers' attempt to invade the region and seize the Native peoples' lands. This triggered what became known as the Ohio Indian Wars during the 1780s, as local communities resisted the American invasion and the destruction of their way of life. Gallipolis was thus founded in the middle of a war zone.[10]

At first many Indigenous peoples regarded the French as allies against the Americans because of the legacy of the French and Indian War. Lezay-Marnésia initially viewed them as noble savages and tried to win their favor, with little success. Not surprisingly, the thousands of Indigenous peoples who lived in the area considered the Scioto their land, not that of the Scioto or Ohio companies. As the French came to rely upon protection from American soldiers the Indians' attitude changed, creating another danger for the new colony. In May 1791 American forces launched a major military attack on the Indigenous peoples in the area, only to be routed and annihilated by their intended victims. French militiamen from Gallipolis had fought with the American forces, so in consequence their Indigenous neighbors turned hostile. Thus for its first few years Gallipolis was under the constant threat of Indian attack. This danger prompted many more to leave, and within a few years Gallipolis shrunk to one-third of its founding population. In this case, the rejection of the French Revolution led the pioneers of Gallipolis to embrace settler colonialism and Indian removal, a far cry from the Rousseauian vision (in which Native Americans had often played an important role) of America that had inspired so many.

And yet the French colony survived, at least for a time. Those who remained mastered the skills they needed to live in Gallipolis, while at the same time reestablishing their former trades. The French settlers never succeeded in building the kind of large farms that increasingly dotted the American frontier, but they learned to grow grapes and fruit and established numerous vineyards; soon Gallipolis was making its own wine and brandy. The French also created productive vegetable gardens that after the first two winters enabled them to supply their own needs and to trade for commodities with other communities along the Ohio River, as far afield as New Orleans. In particular, the numerous artisans of the community gave Gallipolis a reputation for fine craftsmanship. One visitor described this aspect of the city:

> The most interesting shops . . . were those of goldsmiths and watchmakers. They showed us work on watch, compasses and sun-dial[s] finer than any I had ever beheld. Next in interest was the sculptor and stonecutter. The latter had two finished mantels, most artistically carved . . . The worker in glass seemed to be a born artist. He made us a thermometer, a barometer, a glass tobacco pipe, a small bottle (which could contain about a thimble-full), and a most diminutive stopper.[11]

Several French inhabitants became noteworthy for their picturesque character. Jean Gervais was born in Paris in 1764, where he grew up in a middle-class family and studied law. After arriving in America in 1790, he was one of the French settlers who chose to return to France after learning about the realities of the Scioto venture. Unlike most, however, he chose to go back to Ohio as the Revolution became more radical and threatening in France. He arrived in Gallipolis in 1792 and began organizing the French inhabitants to plead their case and demand redress from the U.S. Congress. He became noteworthy for his elegant manner, frequently strolling around town twirling a silver-headed cane. Gervais was an accomplished dancer, artist, poet, musician, and raconteur, a man who brought a whiff of Parisian sophistication to the Ohio wilderness.

Dr. Antoine Saugrain was perhaps the most famous of the French settlers in Gallipolis. From an illustrious Parisian family (his brother-in-law was Joseph Guillotin, inventor of the guillotine), Saugrain trained as a physician and had traveled widely in Europe and America before settling down in Gallipolis. He was in fact one of the very few French settlers to have visited Ohio before moving there, a fact that led William Playfair to recruit him for the new colony. Described as the merriest man in Gallipolis, the diminutive Dr. Saugrain attended tirelessly to the medical needs of the small colony. In addition to working as a doctor, he ran a small inn and created a scientific laboratory where he made thermometers and barometers. Dr. Saugrain moved to St. Louis in 1799, becoming the first physician in that city. There he supplied medical equipment for the Lewis and Clark expedition.

By 1795 the American forces of General "Mad" Anthony Wayne had largely "pacified" the Indigenous peoples, and things seemed to be looking up for the French colony. In March Congress awarded twenty-four thousand acres of land along the Scioto River to the settlers, an award known as the French grant. However, the community still faced the problem that the land they had originally bought, most of the land in Gallipolis, actually belonged to the Ohio Company. In negotiations with the company the settlers asked to be granted their lands outright. The company refused, instead offering to sell the lots to the settlers. Some accepted, submitting to the indignity of having to buy their own lands twice. But many others refused, seeing the company's decision as the ultimate humiliation and the death knell of the colony.

After 1795 the French population of Gallipolis declined inexorably. Some returned to France, but many more left for other American communities, either nearby villages and towns like Marietta, Ohio, or cities such as Pittsburgh, Philadelphia, and New York. When Count Volney visited Gallipolis from Paris in 1796 he described it as a sad, poor community peopled by sickly, anxious inhabitants. In January 1798 none other than Louis Philippe, the twenty-five-year-old future King Louis XVIII of France, passed through Gallipolis on his way to New Orleans. The thrilled French inhabitants welcomed him warmly and planned a formal ball for him the next evening, only to be disappointed when the eminent visitor left early, taking advantage of a thaw that melted the ice on the Ohio River.

By the beginning of the nineteenth century the number of settlers had dwindled to a few families, but Gallipolis survived: Yankees from New England began moving in, as did immigrants from Wales. The original settlers moved elsewhere in the United States, helping to found other French colonies such as Paris, Kentucky, and Demopolis, Alabama. But within a few decades little remained of the French presence in Gallipolis beyond the name itself. With its origins in the turmoil of the French Revolution, the city had now become integrated into the history of America. At the same time, however, its history spoke to the global vision of the French Revolution, and the ways that vision manifested itself in a small corner of the world thousands of miles away from Paris and Versailles. It provides a localized illustration, on a transnational scale, of the creation of modern France.

The history of the French Five Hundred is in many ways a sad tale. In some respects, like the Revolution itself, it moved from idealism to disenchantment, from the hopes for a new world to a realization of the difficulties involved in building one. And yet, also like the Revolution itself, this history underscores the power of dreams to shape the affairs of men. As we shall see in other parts of this book, fantasies of life overseas as a solution to problems at home would resurface during the history of modern France, inspiring migrations and settlements around the world. Such beliefs would also bring many foreigners to France. The fact that some dreams end bitterly has never stopped men and women from dreaming, and hopefully never will. The settlers of Gallipolis contributed to the history of America, and it is worth noting that relatively few returned to France. Yet they also belong to French history, their saga illustrating one reaction to their country's great revolution and one example of how fundamentally that event transformed the lives of its people.

2

World Revolutionary in a Universal Nation
Karl Marx in Paris

In 1845 the Prussian government received a secret report from the Paris police on the activities of German expatriates in the French capital, one whose dramatic tone underscored the image of Paris as a revolutionary center and a corrupter of youth:

> It is a really lamentable situation . . . to see here how a few intriguers are misleading the impoverished German workers, not simply the laborers but also young tradesmen, clerks, etc., and attempting to attract them to communism. Every Sunday the German communists assemble outside the Barrière du Trone in a hall belonging to a wine merchant on the Chausée; coming from the gate it is the second or third house on the right in the Avenue de Vincennes. Sometimes 30, sometimes 100 or 200 German communists collect here; they have rented the hall. Speeches are made openly advocating regicide, abolition of property, down with the rich, etc.; there is no longer any talk of religion; in short it is the crudest, most abominable nonsense . . . I write you this in all haste to prevent such people as Marx, Hess, Herwegh, A. Weil and Börnstein continuing to lead young people to disaster.[1]

For both French and German officials the activities of a few radical expatriates were annoying but nothing new; anyone familiar with popular activism in Paris had seen this before. None had any sense of the impact that the young agitator Karl Marx would have, not just on the disaffected workers of his time but on the shaping of the modern world in general.

Marx arrived in Paris in 1843 at the age of twenty-five, spending most of the next two years in the French capital. His life there showcases two important characteristics of the city during the July Monarchy: its large working-class immigrant population and its role as a center of progressive intellectuals from throughout Europe. As the above quotation suggests, Marx actively participated in both milieux, preaching socialist ideas among working class Germans and others and participating actively in the society of the city's cosmopolitan intelligentsia. At the same time Marx wrote prolifically, beginning to develop that corpus of theoretical and political literature we know today as Marxism. It was in Paris that he met his life-long friend and collaborator, Friedrich Engels. Karl Marx came to Paris drawn by the legacy of the French Revolution and the city's reputation as a tolerant host for expatriates and dissidents. During his life there he developed his own forceful ideas about capitalism and political change, setting out on the path that would ultimately make him the greatest revolutionary prophet of the modern world.

When we think of Germans in Paris, the Nazi occupation of the 1940s usually comes to mind. Yet one hundred years earlier a far larger German population settled in the French capital, under vastly different circumstances. Germany in the years after Napoleon was a largely rural and poor country, a far cry from the prosperous powerhouse it would eventually become. A series of economic crises struck the nation in the early nineteenth century, starting in the 1820s and culminating with the famine years of the 1840s. In response, during the first half of the nineteenth century hundreds of thousands of Germans left their native land in search of new lives elsewhere; among European nations only Ireland sent more of her children abroad. The majority went to the United States, but the German emigration was truly a global phenomenon, affecting lands as far distant as Australia and Puerto Rico. The political turbulence of 1848 and the defeat of the era's revolutionary hopes also spurred emigration, sending a wave of Red '48ers across the Atlantic.[2]

Not all German émigrés chose to cross the sea. Whereas those who went to America were mostly peasants leaving their homeland for good, German artisans and workers more often moved elsewhere in Europe, often following the traditional routes of young journeymen seeking to perfect their craft by traveling to different workplaces. Many traveled to England, attracted by the opportunities of major industrial centers like London and Manchester. Yet France, particularly Paris, also attracted large numbers. Even though many of these immigrants stayed in the French capital for only a short time, as they left others replaced them so that by the 1840s a substantial German community had taken root in the city. By 1844 more than forty thousand Germans lived in Paris, and some members of the community claimed a population as high as one hundred thousand.[3] Consequently, not only did natives of Germany constitute the largest foreign immigrant group in the French capital, but they also accounted for a sizeable fraction of the Parisian working class during the 1840s. When one thinks of the revolutionary crowd that mounted the barricades in February and June 1848, one must consider the fact that many of them probably spoke German.

Their destination was unique among cities not just in France but in all of Europe. Mid-nineteenth-century Paris was the largest city on the European continent, the capital and center of its largest and arguably greatest nation. Throughout the eighteenth century France was the cultural and intellectual center of Europe, and under the Napoleonic empire it dominated the continent militarily and politically as well. Even after the defeat of Napoleon and the abolition of the Empire, the nation remained a force to be reckoned with on the European stage, and Paris its beating heart.

The early nineteenth century was a period of tremendous growth for the French capital. By 1846 Paris had more than one million inhabitants, almost double its population at the beginning of the century. The new industrial economy that developed during the July Monarchy prompted much of this unprecedented urban growth. While France came relatively late to what historians call the Industrial Revolution compared to Britain, by the 1840s the nation experienced its first major industrial boom. The transformation of traditional industries such as textiles and mining and the creation of new ones such as railroads brought new prosperity but also misery to the French people. The extremes of wealth and poverty were nowhere greater than in Paris, where the newly affluent *haute bourgeoisie* often lived near the impoverished masses of the population.

Most of the city's growth came not from the birth of more children but rather from immigration, primarily from the countryside of northern France. Although French peasants enjoyed relative prosperity during these years, their high birthrate prompted many to seek new opportunities in the nation's capital. What most new Parisians found, however, was not wealth and success but hard work, cramped quarters, filth, and disease. Thousands of immigrants crowded into slums like the Ile de la Cité or the Faubourg Saint-Antoine, where an entire family would live in one small room without heating or plumbing. In a city of seven- and eight-story buildings without elevators they usually lived on the top floors, in the famed Parisian garrets, and if they wanted water they had to carry it up the stairs themselves. The newcomers would search for employment in the city's workshops, or in bourgeois households as maids and servants, hoping to earn enough to pay for the coarse brown bread that was the poor Parisian's staff of life. This was the world of Victor Hugo's *Les miserables*, one of deprivation and at times despair.[4]

As Hugo showed in his great novel, it was also a world of revolution. The poor of Paris had demonstrated their dedication to social justice and insurrection during the French Revolution, and in the early nineteenth century the city's extremes of wealth and poverty remained striking. The French capital had a strong and proud working-class tradition: it was a center of luxury manufacture by skilled and often independent artisans. The abolition of the guilds—traditional workingmen's associations—by the French Revolution and the restrictions on unions had challenged their role in society, but artisans remained the leaders of working-class Paris. Increasingly, however, the new industrial economy and the massive influx of unskilled laborers into the city made it more difficult for them to own their own workshops or even tools. Instead, they faced the dangers of pro-letarianization, of losing their skills and autonomy, being reduced to the level of unskilled workers.

Some responded to this threat to their social and economic status with a new language of radical politics. The term "socialism" first appeared in France in the early nineteenth century, and both artisans and middle-class intellectuals began creating socialist clubs and newspapers. Thinkers and activists including Etienne Cabet, Charles Fourier, Louis Auguste Blanqui, and Henri de Saint-Simon drew up schemes for a new egalitarian society based upon communal ownership of property, and at times resorted to violent insurrection to realize their dreams. Increasingly, those on the left in France sought to go beyond traditional republicanism, arguing for social justice as well as political liberalism, often termed "la république sociale" (the social republic). For this reason Paris became one of the early centers of the rise of modern socialism.

Many of the German immigrants of the early nineteenth century were themselves skilled artisans, and like their French colleagues faced the pressures of proletarianization and loss of status. In addition, as immigrants they usually could not reestablish the professions they had practiced in Germany, often having to resort to unskilled labor. In their case the combination of foreign status and the constraints of the new industrial economy intensified the experience of proletarianization. The development of socialism in France, and of socialist theory in general in the early nineteenth century, thus had an important transnational dimension.

The large German working-class population made Paris a natural destination for Karl Marx and other German socialist intellectuals during the 1840s. Émigrés created a number of socialist organizations during the July Monarchy, such as the Patriotic German Association, Young Germany, and the Communist League. Newspapers such as the *Franco-German Yearbook* and especially *Vorwärts (Forward)* also helped knit the community together around progressive ideas. In 1836 German progressive workers in Paris founded The League of the Just, a revolutionary organization that joined with French socialists led by Auguste Blanqui in a failed attempt to overthrow the government of Louis Philippe three years later. When thousands of weavers in the German province of Silesia staged a major insurrection in 1844, German exiles in Paris rallied to their defense and hailed the movement as a signal event in the dawn of German Communism. Men including Wilhelm Weitling, Moses Hess, Heinrich Börnstein, and Arnold Ruge not only worked with each other but also associated with French and other foreign leftist intellectuals in Paris, among them Louis Blanc, Pierre-Joseph Proudhon, and the Russian anarchist Mikhail Bakunin.

Beyond the large German colony, Paris offered a cosmopolitan society unmatched anywhere in Europe, perhaps the world. In the early nineteenth century conservative monarchies ruled most European countries, and they had little tolerance for republicans, liberals, or other dissenters. The July Monarchy, in contrast, not only espoused a more progressive ideology but also allowed political exiles from other countries to settle in France, creating a tradition of the nation as a center of expatriates and refugees. France beckoned them not only because of its liberalism, but equally because of its reputation as a center of culture and intellectual life. After 1830 foreign intellectuals and activists flooded into Paris. Hundreds of Poles, notably the great musician Frederic Chopin, settled in Paris after the defeat of revolution in that country. They founded émigré newspapers and even a Polish government in exile, headed by Prince Czartorysky. Exiles from Italy, Spain, and elsewhere in Europe also gathered in the French capital, plotting to liberate their homelands from reactionary rule. As the German expatriate Arnold Ruge argued, "One can judge the intelligence and independence of a man in Germany by his appreciation for France . . . Any German who understands France becomes an enlightened man, a free man."[5] For a young revolutionary, no place could be more exciting.

This was the world Karl Marx entered when he and his pregnant young wife Jenny moved to Paris in October 1843. Two years earlier Marx had finished his dissertation in philosophy at the University of Berlin. Already deeply involved in the radical politics of young German intellectuals, especially the group known as the Young Hegelians, Marx decided against an academic career, opting instead to go into the world of leftist journalism. At the age of twenty-four he became the editor of the *Rheinische Zeitung*, a prominent newspaper that sharply criticized the politics of the Prussian government and the Concert of Europe in general, and was frequently censored as a result. Marx's work on this paper brought him to the attention of Arnold Ruge, who had decided to launch a new journal, the *Franco-German Yearbook*. Ruge had established himself in Paris as a way of avoiding the Prussian censors and recruited Marx to join him there. He and his family lived communally with other German émigrés at 23 rue Vaneau, in the city's elite seventh arrondissement (district). After Marx and his wife tired of this extreme intimacy with other German exiles, they moved down the street to number 38.

Marx enjoyed his life in Paris and threw himself into both political activism and scholarship there. He worked actively on the *Franco-German Yearbook*, only one issue of which was ever published, as well as its successor, *Vorwärts*. Neither of these publications lasted very long, but they did provide Marx entrée into the activist circles of the French capital. Indeed, his revolutionary activism in Paris were extensive enough to convince the Prussian government to announce in the spring of 1844 that he would be arrested immediately if he ever set foot again in his home country. Solid financial support from family and friends back in Germany freed him from the necessity of earning a living, so he was able to devote his considerable energies to writing and activism. Initially, Marx came to Paris interested in studying the history of the French Revolution, especially its most radical phase, and read widely on the subject. At the same time, however, his studies and political efforts in Germany had awakened in him an interest in materialism, in particular the dialectical materialism championed by the most prominent Young Hegelian, Ludwig Feuerbach.

Marx's life in Paris turned him toward materialism by giving him a much greater familiarity with working class life. He went to meetings of both French and German artisans, getting to know members of the League of the Just. He both observed their poverty and listened to their hopes for a new, more just society. These personal experiences complemented his readings in German philosophy and French revolutionary history, giving him a new perspective on materialism and social change. As he noted after one such encounter:

> When communist *workmen* gather together, their immediate aim is instruction, propaganda, etc. But at the same time they acquire a new need—the need for society—and what appears as a means has become an end. This practical development can be most strikingly observed in the gatherings of French socialist workers. Smoking, eating, and drinking etc., are no longer means of creating links between people. Company, association, conversation, which in its turn has society as its goal, is

enough for them. The brotherhood of man is not a hollow phrase, it is a reality, and the nobility of man shines forth upon us from their work-worn faces.[6]

In Paris Marx came to see the working class as the key vector of revolutionary change and the creation of socialist society, a theme that would become fundamental to Marxist theory.

At the same time, Karl Marx lived a very active social life, one that had a major influence on his political thought. Not all of his friends were socialists: he and his family were very close to the great German Jewish poet Heinrich Heine (who was in fact a distant relative). At one point Heine helped a distraught Marx and his wife take care of their ailing infant daughter. Yet most of his friends in Paris, like the impecunious Russian aristocrat and anarchist Mikhail Bakunin, were fellow socialists and agitators. In the 1830s the French coined the term "bohemia," using the Gypsies of Eastern Europe as a model for young intellectuals and artists who rejected the bourgeois society of the July Monarchy. Paris became the world center of bohemia, a counterculture in which a young foreign intellectual like Karl Marx could find new friends and make his mark. Marx met his friends and comrades in a variety of venues in Paris, including German cafes like the Scherger and the Schiever, salons of the liberal Russian aristocracy, and meetings of Communist secret societies. For a brief time, he enjoyed the heady experience of spending one's youth in Paris, an experience that has continued to attract dreamers from his day until ours.

While the young Marx enjoyed bohemian entertainments and society, political discussions and polemics lay at the heart of his social life. He delighted in attacking other activists, notably the romantic socialists like Fourier and Saint-Simon, whose ideas he encountered in Paris. In February 1845 Marx published *The Holy Family*, which showcased his conversion to materialism and constituted a frontal attack on his fellow Young Hegelians. His most famous polemic targeted Pierre-Joseph Proudhon, whom he had met in the company of Bakunin and assorted German exiles. Proudhon was one of the leading socialists in Paris who saw the capitalist state and its defense of private property as the major cause of working-class poverty and oppression. Marx had met him socially and for a time admired his ideas, praising his rejection of private property in *The Holy Family*. Eventually he turned against the socialist leader, however, wickedly lampooning Proudhon's *The Philosophy of Poverty* with his own *The Poverty of Philosophy*. Marx attacked the Frenchman's rejection of revolutionary politics, arguing that class oppression was ultimately a political question.

In 1844 a series of articles appeared in the Paris *Vorwärts* that would change not only Karl Marx's life but the history of what would come to be known as Marxism. The articles dealt with the industrial revolution in Britain, written by the son of a German manufacturer who had worked in a factory in Manchester. The author, Friedrich Engels, visited Paris in September, where he met Marx on August 28 at the Café de la Régence, one of the city's great meeting spots. The two spent the next ten days engaging in intense discussions of Engels's work and their mutual interests. Like Marx, Engels had traveled abroad to explore working class life, in his case studying the city at the heart of the Industrial Revolution. The gritty realities of proletarian life in both Paris and Manchester led them to a common belief in historical and revolutionary materialism. The meeting in Paris began a life-long friendship and one of the greatest intellectual and revolutionary collaborations in world history.

Reading Engels reinforced Marx's interest in the study of political economy as the key to revolutionary history and activism. This new concern led him to produce the essays eventually known as the *Economic and Philosophical Manuscripts*, which he completed in Paris between April and August 1844. Also known as the *Paris Manuscripts*, the four essays combined a sharp critique of Hegelian philosophy with discussions of wage labor, profits, and rents. In these writings Marx first introduced his concept of alienation, one that would become central to Marxist philosophy. The *Economic and Philosophical Manuscripts* are a key text in Marx's transition from philosopher to political economist, an orientation that would bloom fully in his magnum opus, *Capital*. At the same time, they show how in Paris Marxian socialism remained a fluid ideology, open to both humanist and more quantitative interpretations.

Marx's activism soon brought the wrath of both Prussian and French officialdom down upon his head. At the end of January 1845 French police issued an order requiring him to leave the country within 24 hours. Marx immediately departed for Brussels, his wife Jenny following with their young daughter a few months later. Engels moved to Brussels as well in April and the two began their long literary collaboration in the city, culminating with the writing of the book that would make them famous, *The Communist Manifesto*. Marx stayed in Brussels until the February 1848 revolution erupted in France. In March the provisional government invited him to return to France, writing: "Good and loyal Marx: The soil of the French Republic is a field of refuge for all friends of liberty. Tyranny exiled you; now free France opens its doors to you."[7] Under an expulsion order from the Belgian government Marx returned to Paris only to leave a few weeks later for Köln in Germany, attracted by the burgeoning revolution in his homeland. He came back to Paris over a year later, in June 1849, where it soon became clear that the hopes of 1848 had turned to ashes in the capital of revolution. Once again facing expulsion by the French police, Marx left Paris in August for London, the city where he would spend the rest of his life. In 1849 his brief Parisian sojourn came to a definitive end.

What impact did Paris have on Karl Marx, and on the early history of Marxism in general? The French capital was the young philosopher's first experience of exile; aside from his year in Köln he would never return to his homeland to live again. It exposed him to Europe's leading constellation of revolutionaries and scholars, while at the same time immersing him in a large working-class German expatriate community. No other city could offer such a brilliant array of activist intellectuals, nor bring them together in such a vibrant social life. In comparison, Marx's considerably longer life in London was much more difficult and isolated. Paris also first introduced Marx to Engels and to the study of political economy, a subject that would become the bedrock of Marxism after the publication of *Capital*. While the outlines of Marxism as a definite philosophy matured in London, they were born in Paris.

Marx's brief but important sojourns in Paris thus underscored the position of the French capital as a world center of revolution. The combination of an active working class and expatriates from throughout Europe gave the city an incomparable political and intellectual culture. At the same time Paris was France's capital, and as Marx's different brushes with the law demonstrated, the nation's political culture had a definite impact on his life and thought there. Here local, national, and global politics interacted in a complex and creative manner. Paris left an enduring imprint on the thought of the great revolutionary in his intellectually formative years, and through him would give global significance to Parisian political life and thought. Ultimately Marxism would return to France as a more defined ideology at the end of the nineteenth century, in the form of Marxist political parties and unions. But although at times rejected as a foreign import, it always had an indisputably French lineage. In the 1840s the capital of insurrection gave birth to the greatest revolutionary ideology of the modern era, one that continues to count millions of followers worldwide to this day.

3

The Other Second Empire
France's Intervention in Mexico

When people think of France as a global power and cultural presence, Latin America rarely comes to mind. Whereas the nation is central to European affairs, and has exercised an imperial presence in Africa and Asia, south and central America have seemingly occupied only a small place in the French national experience. French influence in the Americas has paled compared with that of Spain, the United States, and even Britain. Nonetheless, the law and culture of the universal nation have played an important role in Latin America. Indeed, the term "Latin America" was first coined in Paris during the 1850s by French and Hispanic American scholars to emphasize the affinities between Catholic, Latin France and America in contrast to the "Anglo-Saxon" United States. To this day France retains a toehold on the South American continent in French Guiana, and in Argentina it is still said that an Argentine is an Italian who speaks Spanish, wishes he were English, and acts as if he were French.[1]

At no time in the history of modern France has Latin America been more important to the nation than during the Second Empire. Nothing more clearly underscores the global vision of Napoleon III than the French intervention in Mexico from 1862 to 1867. Many contemporaries and historians have viewed the French attempt to create a Mexican empire headed by the Austrian Hapsburg prince Maximilian as a bizarre attempt to transpose traditional European dynastic politics into a New World utterly unsuited to them. Napoleon III's Mexican policy was not necessarily an aberration, however, but offers important insights into the history of the Second

Empire in general. The tragic outcome of the French emperor's adventure in Mexico underscored for his critics at home and abroad the deficiencies of his regime as a whole. More broadly, the French intervention brought together European and overseas visions of empire as well as illustrating in exaggerated form the emperor's constant hesitation between conservative and liberal beliefs and policies.

France's Second Empire was perhaps the strangest political regime in that nation's modern history. The culmination of a turbulent early nineteenth century that brought multiple regimes and revolutions, it was established by Louis Napoleon, the nephew of the great Napoleon Bonaparte. Louis Napoleon had been elected president of the Second Republic in 1848 before overthrowing that regime and replacing it with the Second Empire in 1852, taking the crown as Napoleon III. A curious blend of authoritarianism and liberalism, the Second Empire had crushed the republican opposition but at the same time justified its rule with popular plebiscites based in universal manhood suffrage. During the 1860s Napoleon III began liberalizing his reign, relaxing censorship and legalizing unions. He embraced the idea of modernizing France from above, using authoritarian means to create a liberal democratic empire. His invasion of Mexico would prove to be one of the most prominent examples of this goal, and its failure illustrated the broader bankruptcy of the imperial project.[2]

Napoleon III's invasion of Mexico also occupies an interesting position in the history of French colonialism. It represented the last French imperial venture in the Americas, taking place at a time when the nation's colonial interests had already shifted to Asia, Africa, and the Pacific. It also illustrated the gradual transformation of the *mission civilisatrice*, the "civilizing mission" that would play such a major role in the overseas expansion of France. The concept of the civilizing mission owed a lot to Napoleon I's conquest of Europe and his imposition of liberal regimes by force on the subject nations. Napoleon III's intervention in Mexico both resembled his uncle's famous conquests, and at the same time foreshadowed subsequent French adventures overseas and its construction of a new empire. Both in domestic and foreign policy, therefore, the invasion of Mexico cast a key transnational perspective on the history of the Second Empire. In more than one way, the essence of Napoleon III's imperial regime revealed itself south of the Rio Grande.

The history of Mexico in the early nineteenth century was a complex affair. After winning independence from Spain in 1822, the new nation experienced a prolonged period of political instability dominated by conflicts between two main factions, the Liberals and the Conservatives. Whereas the Conservatives supported the church and the Liberals demanded more progressive political institutions, both largely ignored the needs of the Indian peasantry. Mexico first achieved independence as a constitutional empire, one quickly overthrown by a republican government in 1824, only to give way to the dictatorship of General Santa Anna after 1834. The next year Texas began its successful struggle for independence, followed a decade later by the even more disastrous and humiliating war with the United States, which cost Mexico control of California just as gold was discovered there, turning the area into a modern El Dorado. In 1858 Conservative general Felix Zuloaga overthrew the Liberal regime in a coup d'état. The Liberal opposition, headed by Benito Juárez, established a rival government in Vera Cruz, beginning a civil war between the two factions. In 1861 the Liberals triumphed and Juárez set up his government in Mexico City, becoming the country's first president of Indian origin.

France followed the travails of the new nation for a variety of reasons. After Mexico achieved independence a number of French people moved there—the country counted some five thousand French inhabitants by the early 1860s, with only Spain accounting for a larger community of foreign nationals. France also had substantial commercial interests in Mexico, larger than in any other of Spain's former American colonies. The confluence of French interests and the chaotic state of Mexican politics led to conflict before the 1860s. When a French pastry chef in Mexico City sued the Mexican government in 1838 for damages caused by looting soldiers, Paris backed his demands by blockading the nation's Gulf Coast and capturing the port city of Veracruz, only relenting when the government met the baker's demands and paid an indemnity to France. The so-called Pastry War underscored France's determination to protect its position in Mexico, foreshadowing Napoleon III's massive intervention there.

In addition, Mexico played an important role in the French view of the world and its own place therein. Napoleon III viewed Mexico as an opportunity for France to exercise its civilizing mission, to use the light of French culture to uplift a people struggling to free itself from barbarism. In particular, French influence over the new nation was part of a broader hegemonic project to create a transatlantic Latin civilization, one that could increase France's power and resist that of the "Anglo-Saxon" United States, already seen as a growing threat. Hegemony over Mexico therefore seemed a key element in France's position as a world civilization.

The crisis of the 1860s that led to France's invasion was prompted by the continuing anarchy in Mexico that threatened foreign nationals living there, and by the chronic indebtedness of the Mexican government. In July 1861 President Juárez suspended payments on foreign debts, prompting France, Britain, and Spain to demand that Mexico honor its debts and protect their citizens residing in the country. On October 31 the three nations signed a pact in London threatening military intervention if Mexico City did not pay up. Spain became the first to send troops, its fleet setting sail from its Cuban colony in early December. On December 8 Spanish forces landed in the Mexican Gulf port of Veracruz, quickly securing control of the city. A month later France and Britain followed suit. When the French demanded an immediate payment of twelve million dollars to call off the invasion, Spain and Britain withdrew, judging this too harsh and unrealistic. British and Spanish troops left Mexico in April, leaving the way open for France's unilateral intervention. The American Civil War also emboldened the French to take action. Embroiled in its struggle with the rebel Confederacy, Washington was in no position to impose the Monroe Doctrine or effectively challenge European intervention along its southern border. The time was thus ripe for the French to establish a new presence in the Americas.

Napoleon III soon made it very clear that France intended not just to collect money from the Mexican government, but more fundamentally to remake the country along progressive lines. He consistently argued he invaded Mexico in support of the Mexican people against a corrupt local government, and that he prioritized establishing a more efficient and just political order. For the emperor that meant renewing the imperial tradition in

Mexico. Napoleon III felt that Mexico, like France, first needed a firm hand at the tiller in order to steer state and society into the waters of modernity. As he noted in 1863, "What is needed in Mexico is a *liberal* dictatorship, that is to say, a strong power which shall proclaim the great principles of modern civilization."[3] This idea of empire mirrored the desires of the Mexican elite, many of whom looked with fondness upon the First Empire and considered republican rule a recipe for anarchy.

Since Mexico's Conservatives treasured their Spanish heritage, who better to serve as emperor of Mexico than a scion of the Hapsburg dynasty that had conquered the Americas as kings of Spain in the first place? In fact, a Mexican delegation had tried to persuade Archduke Karl of Austria to accept the throne of the First Empire, only to be refused. By the late 1850s Conservative Mexicans such as Don Gutiérrez de Estrada and José Hidalgo began trying to convince Napoleon III, using their connections to his Spanish-born empress Eugénie, to help them find a European prince to take over the leadership of their country. With the onset of the Mexican crisis the emperor decided to take their advice, and settled on Archduke Maximilian of Austria, brother of the emperor Franz-Joseph, as the most promising candidate. When Maximilian indicated his interest in the possibility, the stage was set for Napoleon III's invasion.

The first French forces landed in Veracruz in early January 1862, reinforced by new detachments over the next several months. They won considerable support from the Conservatives and members of the Mexican social and economic elites, who looked to the French to overthrow the Liberals and restore the monarchy of the First Empire. Eventually French troops numbered close to forty thousand, aided by twenty thousand Mexican soldiers.

The Mexican government responded by mobilizing to resist the invaders, both the European armies and the Conservative Mexican elites who welcomed them. When President Juárez learned of the French landings in Mexico he issued an appeal to the Mexican people calling for resistance:

> Mexicans! If they intend to humiliate Mexico, to dismember our territory, to intervene in our internal administration and politics, or even to extinguish our nationhood, I appeal to your patriotism to drive out those

pestilent and hostile forces which have been the cause of our differences of opinion, to contribute your efforts and your blood, and to unite around the government in defense of the greatest and most sacred cause which exists among men and among peoples: the defense of our country.[4]

The French, widely regarded as some of the best fighters in the world, met unexpectedly fierce resistance; President Juárez decreed harsh penalties against those who collaborated with the enemy in any form. On May 5, 1862, Mexican forces handily defeated the French at the battle of Puebla, forcing their adversaries into retreat in a victory that would be commemorated by one of Mexico's great national holidays, Cinco de Mayo.

This was only a temporary setback for the French, who soon went back on the offensive. More troops came from France in September and October, led by General Achille Bazaine. By the end of the year they had captured the port city of Tampico, and early in 1863 returned to conquer Veracruz. From there the French armies went on to mount a second attack against Puebla, which they took control of in May, a year after their initial defeat there. By the end of the month President Juárez fled the capital to establish a government in exile in the north of Mexico. Bazaine's army entered Mexico City on June 7, 1863, proclaiming the overthrow of the Liberal republic. By the end of the following summer the French had assumed effective control of most of the country, forcing Juárez to flee to the border with the United States.

Napoleon's armies in Mexico did not consist just of French soldiers. Not only did thousands of Mexicans ally join him, but France also enlisted fighters from different parts of the world. Several Belgian detachments took part in the invasion of Mexico. Paris also brought in some 450 African soldiers, courtesy of the Egyptian government who had kidnapped them from their homes in the Sudan. The French considered them particularly appropriate to the war, believing them more resistant to tropical disease and the strains of a hot climate. Their presence in Mexico prompted a protest from the United States, which pointed out it also had Black soldiers and threatened to use them to invade Egypt. The French Foreign Legion, first created in 1831 and already tested in the conquest of Algeria and in the

Crimean War, also took part. On April 30, 1863, a company of sixty-four Legionnaires fought a battle against some two thousand Mexican troops, refusing to surrender in spite of overwhelming odds; only three survived. To this day, Legionnaires commemorate the Battle of Camerone every year, considering it the greatest example of the Legion's heritage of military heroism. In general, France's war in Mexico underscored Napoleon III's belief in his country's identity as a universal nation.

Once the victory of his forces was assured, Napoleon III began working out the final plans for creating the new Mexican empire. Like the French sovereign, the would-be emperor of Mexico was a complex figure, heir to one of Europe's greatest dynasties yet at the same time a man of progress and strong liberal beliefs. Maximilian had indicated his willingness to take up the leadership of Mexico, but his interest was based on his belief that this was not only in the interest of the Mexican people but also desired by them. When a Conservative Mexican delegation offered him the imperial crown in October 1863 the archduke replied that he would only accept if it was the will of the people. Accordingly, Napoleon's forces hastily organized a national plebiscite in December, in which voters overwhelmingly approved the offer to Maximilian. The dubious character of the vote, taken under the shadow of French guns and with no clear population or voter statistics, was evident to many, notably the American government which refused to recognize it. Nonetheless, it convinced Maximilian, who formally accepted the crown as emperor of Mexico at his palace in Italy on April 10, 1864. He then set sail from Europe with his wife, the empress Carlota, for his new empire, arriving in Veracruz at the end of May. During his voyage across the Atlantic Maximilian addressed the following proclamation to the Mexican people:

> Mexicans: You have desired my presence. Your noble nation, by a voluntary majority, has chosen me to watch henceforth over your destinies. I gladly respond to this call. Painful as it has been for me to bid farewell forever to my own, my native country, I have done so, being convinced that the Almighty has pointed out to me, through you, the mission of devoting all my strength and heart to a people who, tired of war and

disastrous contests, sincerely wish for peace and prosperity; to a people who having gloriously obtained their independence, desire to reap the benefit of civilization and true progress.[5]

Napoleon III could now claim that the ideal of liberal empire thrived on both sides of the Atlantic.

Maximilian strongly desired to bring progress to the Mexican people as their emperor, and naively believed he would be accepted even though he came in the train of the French army. At the time it was not unusual for titled nobility from one European nation to become rulers of another, and one of his Hapsburg relatives reigned in Brazil as Emperor Dom Pedro II. Maximilian hoped that his combination of impeccable royal lineage and liberal political views could make him attractive to both factions in Mexico and enable him to reconcile the two. Thus, like Napoleon III in his liberal phase, he reigned as an emperor with a progressive agenda. Strikingly, in spite of his opposition to President Juárez, he upheld most of the latter's liberal reforms, including land reform and broadening the franchise to include parts of the Indian and mestizo populations. As he noted, "The more I study Mexico, the more I am convinced that the regeneration of the country must be based on the Indians, who make up the vast majority of the population. It is a duty for me to try to lift up this fascinating and easily governable race from the state of abjection under which large land-owners seek to maintain them, and to achieve this goal, I have had a draft decree prepared."[6]

Unfortunately for Maximilian and his regime, this position alienated much of his Conservative support without in the least winning over the Liberal opposition. Conservatives in particular hated his refusal to embrace fully the Catholic Church and his support of religious tolerance. For Liberals he remained to the end el Austriaco, the Austrian imposed upon them by French bayonets. Like another infamous Austrian aristocrat brought in by French royalty, Marie Antoinette, his foreign presence provoked derision and contempt. His mixture of compassion and condescension toward the Indians left them unmoved. Maximilian was smart enough to realize that the future of Mexico lay with the nation's Indian and mestizo majority, but he failed to understand that in the end a European monarch, especially one who sought to overthrow the nation's first Indian president, could never win their trust or loyalty.

By the end of 1865 Napoleon III had been forced to admit that the Mexican venture was a failure. Mounting criticism at home focused on its cost and lack of tangible results, as well as seeing it as a symbol of the same autocracy the republican left opposed in France itself. Napoleon III increasingly considered Maximilian inept both administratively and politically, incapable of building a lasting imperial regime. The emperor also worried about the growing military power of Prussia, especially after that nation handily defeated the Austro-Hungarian empire in 1866, and calculated that France would need to keep its armies closer to home to contend with this new threat.

Then there was the American factor to consider. The Civil War ended in April 1865, freeing Washington to devote greater attention to the Americas in general and the French presence in Mexico in particular. By the end of the year the Americans had stationed an army of fifty thousand soldiers, larger than the entire French force in Mexico, along the Rio Grande. While not explicitly threatening to intervene, Washington made it clear it would not tolerate Napoleon III's presence south of its border indefinitely. As Benito Juárez commented, "Maximilian has now not the slightest proba-bility of cementing his so-called throne. . . . The United States will never permit him to consolidate his power, and his sacrifices and victories will have counted for nothing."[7]

In fact, the French emperor had always planned to withdraw his forces once the situation in Mexico stabilized. As Maximilian failed to consolidate popular support and the Liberal opposition gained strength, he gradually concluded the whole experiment was a lost cause. Accordingly, in January 1866 he announced plans to withdraw French troops from Mexico, starting in May. This decision sealed Maximilian's fate. The Liberal guerrilla armies went on the offensive as soon as the French departed, handing defeat after defeat to the imperial forces. In February 1867 Napoleon's troops left Mex-ico City, and a few days later Maximilian abandoned the capital for the northern city of Querétaro. The republican armies laid siege to the city in early March, capturing it and the emperor himself in May. President Juárez sentenced Maximilian to death and, in spite of appeals for clemency from throughout the world, executed him on June 19, 1867. If the history of Mexico's Second Empire paralleled that of France in many respects, three years later the fall and personal capture of Napoleon III at Sedan during the Franco-Prussian war would eerily echo the battlefield demise of Maximilian's ill-starred regime.

France's tragic intervention in Mexico underscored Napoleon III's determination to make his country a force in world affairs at the same time as it became one of the greatest examples of his failure to do so. It neatly illustrated the shifting boundaries of French approaches to empire in Europe and overseas with its attempt to impose a European monarchy upon an underdeveloped Latin American nation. It also underscored the ultimate weakness of the liberal idea of empire as a governing principle, in both Mexico and ultimately France itself. In both nations republicanism would overthrow empire, yet at least in France empire would not entirely disappear, instead assuming new forms under the Third Republic. In spite of its failure in Mexico, the dream of civilizing other peoples through the force of French arms and culture would remain a powerful one. Maximilian's regime might perish, but as the French would learn, in the late nineteenth century there remained other worlds to conquer, ultimately reinforcing the idea of France as a universal nation.

Finally, it is worth noting an interesting postscript to this story of France's failed Mexican adventure. Many people around the world took inspiration from the heroic struggle of the Mexican republicans against the Hapsburgs and the French empire. For the liberals and progressives of Italy's *Risorgimento*, or movement for national unification, who similarly fought against both to achieve their own national liberation, the defeat of Maximilian was especially meaningful. One Italian socialist worker was so moved by it that he named his son after President Juárez. Young Benito Mussolini would grow up embracing his father's progressive ideas, but as an adult would leave a very different mark on the history of Europe and the world.

Part 2

The Rise of the Imperial Republic

The late nineteenth century, from the creation of the French Third Republic in 1870 to the outbreak of World War I in 1914, gave birth to the modern age. During these years industrial production not only came to dominate economies in Europe and America but also reshaped society, politics, and culture in vast regions of the earth. Societies traditionally populated by a small aristocracy ruling over masses of peasants gave way to more complex social formations in which the middle and working classes produced by the new industrial society increasingly voiced their own needs and demands. The world became interconnected as never before—decisions made by financial elites in London, Paris, or New York could have a dramatic impact half a world away. Powerful nationalist movements progressively challenged, and in some cases replaced, the traditional multinational empires with new nation-states, while republicanism, democracy, and socialism mobilized to demand a voice in government for all people. The rise of mass literacy and mass consumer markets created a world where the desires of millions shaped global economies and cultures. In short, the decades before the Great War produced the age of modernity, an era that celebrated the onrush of the new, where the only constant was change.

At first glance France would seem to contradict this global emphasis on upheaval and transformation. The Third Republic arose from a revolutionary seizure of power on September 4, 1870, in the best tradition of early nineteenth century revolutions. It went on, however, to become the most durable regime in French history, outlasting the reign of Louis XIV. Even

World War I, which shattered so many governments across Europe, could not destroy the Third Republic; only the German conquest of 1940 would bring it to an end. Yet a closer look at France in the late nineteenth century reveals a society and nation in constant turmoil, so much so that until the beginnings of the twentieth century one could not reasonably rest assured that the regime would survive. A society in the throes of major economic, political, and cultural change, France symbolized both prosperity but also the shock and anxiety of the new.

That the French chose and maintained a republican form of government made their nation exceptional in the late nineteenth century. Aristocratic monarchies and empires, ranging from the increasingly constitutional kingdom of Great Britain to the absolutism of imperial Russia, dominated Europe in these years. Among the great industrial powers of the era only the United States, which was never a monarchy or an aristocracy, joined the French in choosing a republican form of government. Many people around the world viewed republicanism as a revolutionary ideology, bent on overthrowing the established order not just in politics but in economics and culture as well. The Third Republic had after all come to power via the revolutionary overthrow of the Second Empire. Its great challenge, and ultimately great achievement, was to demonstrate that a republic could protect the established capitalist order by providing a stable yet democratic form of government.

France thus represented, perhaps to an extreme degree, the patterns of economic and political modernity that developed in the world of the late nineteenth century. The explosive growth of the global economy transformed life in Western Europe and North America, creating a mass society and culture of affluence unparalleled in world history. It sharpened class divisions between rich and poor, generating powerful socialist movements throughout the industrialized world while also creating a large middle class and even providing a certain amount of working-class affluence. At the same time, the increased unity of the world economy went along with increased political unity through imperial expansion and conquest. The unprecedented economic and political integration of human societies across the planet gave a crucial transnational dimension to countries like France engaged in developing their own national political cultures. To be French under the Third Republic, therefore, was to be at the same time a member of a powerful nation-state and part of a global community.

Modernity in Europe and America

What historians and economists have termed the second Industrial Revolution reshaped the global economy during the late nineteenth and early twentieth centuries, making it more of an integrated whole than ever before. Much of this arose from breakthroughs in industrial technology. The Bessemer process, conceived by British inventor Henry Bessemer in the 1850s, dramatically lowered the price of steel, enabling industrialists to replace iron with a much stronger and more flexible building material. Thomas Edison's work with electricity made electrical energy a tremendous new source of power, replacing industry's dependence on coal. The rise of modern chemistry also transformed industrial production. Together, these innovations facilitated the rise of heavy industry during the late nineteenth century in Europe and America.

To survive and prosper heavy industry needed labor to run its machines and markets to purchase its products. The new economy provided employment for a vast new working class, luring them from rural communities to the burgeoning cities and factory towns of the era. The growth of urban areas also provided markets for industrial products, used heavily in industries such as construction and transportation. In addition, they provided markets for a vast array of consumer goods. Unlike their rural cousins, city dwellers had to buy most of what they used, and a wide array of institutions, ranging from department stores to the advertising industry, arose to cater to their needs. In an era of mass literacy major newspapers relied on advertising revenues to fund their outreach to millions of readers. The rise of heavy industry thus went together with the development of mass society and culture, with their implications for ideology and politics.

If the late nineteenth century witnessed the rise of heavy industry and mass industrial society, it also facilitated a new emphasis on political liberalism and ultimately liberal democracy. While monarchies continued to dominate Europe for much of the nineteenth century, they increasingly gave room to democratic pressures from the middle and working classes. Britain gradually expanded the franchise to allow most men to vote by the end of the century, while imperial Germany established a legislature and regular elections. In the Americas the United States represented a successful republican, non-aristocratic form of government, especially after the North's victory in the Civil War abolished slavery. By 1900 powerful feminist movements demanded that all their societies grant adults, men and women, the right to vote. Ultimately mass society and mass culture brought about the mass franchise, a movement for democratization that would not ultimately triumph until the enfranchisement of French women after World War II.

Moreover, the push for political inclusion went together with national integration and the rise of a new national consciousness. Italy and Germany achieved political unification by 1870–71, and the American Civil War represented another successful example of national integration. The rise of mass culture, as we shall see in the case of France, encouraged people think of themselves as members of a national community.

Paradoxically, overseas empires became one of the great symbols of national glory after 1870. In one of the great ironies of modern history, the rise of liberal democracy went hand in hand with the triumph of imperialism; indeed, one of the most progressive nations, Britain, established the greatest empire of all. Similarly, the United States, after destroying the Confederacy and extending (at least in theory) citizenship to all Americans, went on to a series of imperial adventures—subjugating the Native peoples of the West, defeating Spain in the Spanish American war, and annexing colonies as far-flung as the Philippines, Puerto Rico, and Hawaii. By 1914 Europe controlled 84 percent of the planet's land mass; the British Empire alone accounted for one quarter of the world's land and population.[1] Empire provided raw materials for industry and mass markets for industrial products such as cotton cloth. It also served to bolster national prestige, so that by the end of the nineteenth century to be a great nation meant having overseas colonies. Building a national community, therefore, included the goal of extending control over masses of people who would be excluded from full membership in that community.

France in the late nineteenth century both shaped and reflected this broader global history. It pioneered national unity and culture while at the same time establishing one of the world's great empires. It led the move toward democracy in Europe, trimming republicanism of its more radical associations and combining liberalism and democracy into the strange hybrid of liberal democracy. For France the period from 1870 to 1914 began with one war and ended with another, and during the years in between interactions with other nations and cultures constantly shaped what it meant to be French. A period that in many ways represented the consummation of France's national culture thus also had an important transnational dimension.

France under the Third Republic, 1870–1914

From the outset the Third Republic seemed a bundle of contradictions. Resulting from a popular insurgency, it brought to power social and political conservatives. In fact, a solid monarchist majority dominated the first National Assembly elected by popular vote after the establishment of the new regime. Moreover, the Third Republic immediately had to suppress a radical revolution in the national capital, as Paris attempted first to overthrow then secede from the republic. Perhaps most bizarre of all, given the instability of French governments since the Revolution of 1789, the Third Republic would not only survive its revolutionary beginnings but go on to become the longest-lived regime in French history. The quintessential modern French regime, from 1870 to 1914 the Third Republic would remake the nation, establishing republican liberal democracy as the permanent center of national political culture.

A divided nation overthrew the Second Empire on September 4, 1870. Many, especially residents of the countryside, hoped the defeat would bring about a quick peace. In contrast, the working-class political left in Paris and other cities looked back to the tradition of the *levée en masse* (mass uprising) during the French Revolution, hoping that a new republican government would redouble its military efforts and wage a revolutionary war of national defense. Both sides reckoned without the intentions of the German invaders. When the new government of the Third Republic rejected Berlin's proposed armistice, the German armies continued their invasion of France, reaching Paris on September 18 and placing the city under siege. For four months the invaders cut the national capital off from the rest of France, forcing Parisians to subsist on cats, rats, and even the animals of the Paris Zoo. In spite of this the city's inhabitants reacted with outrage to the French government's admission of defeat in late January. Prussia and her German allies imposed heavy peace terms on France, including a large indemnity and the annexation of the nation's German-speaking provinces of Alsace and Lorraine. Prussia further humiliated the French nation by holding the formal unification of Germany in Versailles's famed Hall of Mirrors, and by staging a victory march of the German armies through Paris to celebrate France's formal capitulation.

Anger at their government's surrender, compounded by Parisian land-lords' decision to demand back rent not paid during the siege, created an explosion in the French capital. As during the Revolution, working class Parisians saw the foreign enemy working in league with the class enemy, and in response launched France's last great revolutionary uprising of the nineteenth century. On March 18 Parisian soldiers in the National Guard refused to turn over cannon to the national government and instead occupied Paris City Hall and proclaimed the overthrow of the regime. The National Assembly fled for Versailles while troops across the city rallied to the revolution. Taking the name of the Paris Commune, the traditional designation of the Paris municipality, the new regime called for the overthrow of the national government and a renewal of the struggle against Germany. Similar uprisings took place in other French cities — notably Marseilles and Lyons—but unlike 1830 and 1848 the revolution of 1871 failed outside of Paris, leaving the French capital alone against the power of the nation. This marked a major turning point in French history, in effect the end of political revolution as a motor of national sociopolitical change.

Over the next two months, while the Communards launched a series of impressive social measures in line with their goal of creating an ideal socialist society, the National Assembly gathered its forces in Versailles. On May 21, after weeks of shelling the city, the Versailles forces invaded Paris, gradually forcing the defenders of the Commune back in a series of bloody battles. Over the next several days, known to history as Bloody Week, national troops overwhelmed the Commune, summarily executing thousands while the Communards executed their own bourgeois hostages (including the Archbishop of Paris) and lit fires throughout the city, threatening to burn it to the ground rather than surrender. The infant Third Republic thus took as one of its first major actions the fiery suppression of the radical left in France, making it clear that, in the words of President Adolphe Thiers, "the republic will be conservative or it will not be at all."

By suppressing the Commune, the Third Republic defeated the threat of the revolutionary left, but it remained to be seen whether it could overcome that of the monarchist right. During the early 1870s the royalist majority in the National Assembly assumed that the republic would soon give way to a royal restoration, and worked hard to make that happen. Ultimately they failed, stymied both by the rivalry between the Bourbon and Orléans dynasties, and especially by the unrealistic expectations of the royal pretender to the throne, the Comte de Chambord, who made it clear he would rule by divine right or not at all.

In rejecting Chambord's demands, the nation made it clear that it permanently, and irrevocably, embraced the heritage of the French Revolution; the monarchy would never return. By the end of the 1870s the French had clearly (if grudgingly) accepted the new republic, electing a republican majority to the National Assembly. It had paid off the indemnity imposed by the victorious Germans as well as ending the state of martial law ordered for Paris after the Commune. In 1880 the government amnestied former members of the Paris Commune and allowed them to return to France.

The next thirty years brought the triumph of the Third Republic, and of liberal democracy in general. This triumph did not come easily, and until the end of the century it was not always certain that the regime would survive the growing pains of mass democracy. In May 1877 the royalist president Patrice de MacMahon tried to replace the republican prime minister with a royalist, only to bow before the determined and unified opposition of the republican majority in the National Assembly. A decade later the dashing general Georges Boulanger mobilized a mass movement against the republic, drawing upon nationalist resentment of Germany and appealing to French men and women on both the Left and the Right. Winning election after election, Boulanger seemed poised to become another Napoleon and seize power in a coup d'état until his movement collapsed after he fled the country to avoid accusations of treason.

At the end of the nineteenth century the Third Republic would survive its greatest crisis of all. In 1894 the French Army convicted a Jewish captain, Alfred Dreyfus, of treason and sent him to the grim prison colony of Devil's Island in French Guiana. Doubts soon surfaced about his conviction, however, and within a few years the Dreyfus affair had become the cause célèbre of political life in France, bitterly splitting families and communities all over the nation. It became a major clash between socially conservative forces like the church and the military, on the one hand, convinced of Dreyfus's guilt, and advocates of liberal republicanism, on the other, viewing him as an innocent victim of reactionary politics. The controversy also revealed dangerous undercurrents of antisemitism in French life, representing a rejection of the modernity embraced by the Third Republic. The affair convulsed France for a decade, only coming to an end when the French government pardoned Dreyfus in 1905.

The triumph of the left in the Dreyfus Affair, and more generally France's political evolution from monarchism to radical republicanism, illustrated and arose out of fundamental changes in French society and culture during the late nineteenth century. France became a leading industrial nation during these years, witnessing the first examples of large factories—such as the Le Creusot steel plant in the Loire Valley—in an economy that had always emphasized small-scale artisanal production. The Freycinet Plan of 1879 gave the nation its first modern railway network, tying the nation's economy together as never before. Economic growth changed the structure of French society, replacing an old nation of peasants and aristocrats with a new society increasingly dominated by the middle and working classes of small towns and cities. The rise of modern industry and commerce required a large new working class, increasingly centered in urban areas as young people left the countryside in search of a better life. It also required more white-collar managers, clerks, and bookkeepers, as did the growth of government itself. By the beginnings of the twentieth century, and for the first time in French history, only a minority of men and women earned their living from working the land. Rural life changed as well, as so many sons and daughters of the peasantry left for the bright lights of cities and towns. As a result, peasant life became more integrated into that of the nation as a whole, as the farmers' children brought new ideas and habits back home from their lives in cities and towns.

Above all, the nation's capital represented the success of the Third Republic and its transformation of France. Under the Second Empire Baron Haussmann made Paris a glamorous world capital, but the social and political contradictions of life in the city—suppressed under the reign of Napoleon III—had exploded during the Siege and Commune in 1871, laying waste to much of the French capital. However, like France as a whole, Paris recovered spectacularly from the devastation of the Franco-Prussian war; public authorities repaired damaged streets and buildings and completed projects begun in the Second Empire, including the Paris Opera. The city became more than ever a site of broad elegant boulevards and luxurious department stores. At the same time, the rise of impressionism and post-impressionism, centered in the new bohemian neighborhood of Montmartre, ensured the city's intellectual and cultural dominance. In the late nineteenth century, the French government hosted several world's fairs in Paris, underscoring the city's (and the nation's) global prominence. These fairs featured exhibitions of new technologies and of traditional cultures from throughout France and across the world. Rising dramatically above the Exposition Universelle of 1889, the new Eiffel Tower, at the time the tallest structure in the world, proudly proclaimed Paris' identity as a world city, the capital of a transnational nation.

In both Paris and the provinces, therefore, the Third Republic created a new vision of France. It prepared for and shaped this new society by investing tremendously in public education, especially but not only primary education. Creating the modern republic meant wresting control of the vital task of educating the next generation out of the hands of the Catholic Church. From 1879 to 1885 minister of education Jules Ferry enacted laws that made primary education compulsory and free throughout France, creating an army of primary school teachers, "the hussars of the Republic," to teach and champion the values of the French nation across the country. Generations of schoolchildren grew up learning the values of secular republicanism in classrooms invariably decorated with French flags and maps of France. The Third Republic also reestablished military conscription for men, another heritage of the French Revolution, and the Army became known as "the school of the nation." Military service took young men far away from their native towns and villages, in the process teaching them that their loyalty was to the French nation above all.

The Third Republic thus succeeded in creating not just a unified nation but a national culture, one grounded in the values of republicanism, science and rationality, and a belief in progress and the future. This increased national unity led the Third Republic to expand overseas, in effect combining republican and imperial rule. Given that most Europeans at the time considered empires and republics mortal enemies—not to mention that ever since the French Revolution republics in France had achieved power by overthrowing kings and emperors—this fusion was a singular, and rather bizarre, achievement. In one of the great ironies of French history in this period, and perhaps generally, the Third Republic both made republicanism the dominant force in the nation's political culture and at the same time forged the greatest empire France had ever seen. It tremendously expanded the Second Empire's imperial holdings, creating vast new colonies in Africa and Asia, so that by the end of the nineteenth century the French empire was second only to that of Britain in the world.

The Third Republic had inherited a significant overseas presence from earlier regimes: the restoration monarchy of Charles X had conquered Algiers, for example, and the Second Empire had expanded French holdings in Africa, Asia, and the Pacific, annexing Dakar, Saigon, and New Caledonia. The Third Republic's colonial policy built upon, but went far beyond these legacies. Jules Ferry, the architect of mass public education, also championed imperial expansion, earning the sobriquet *le Tonkinois* (the Tonkinese) for his efforts in southeast Asia. During the 1880s France conquered Vietnam, Cambodia, and Laos, creating French Indochina. France also took an active role in what became known as the "scramble for Africa" after the Berlin conference of 1884. French adventurers and soldiers ranged widely across west and central Africa in the late nineteenth century, "discovering" the legendary city of Timbuktu in 1893 and annexing it to France. They carved out a vast new empire, organized into French West Africa and French Equatorial Africa, ranging from Mauritania to the Congo. The French also took possession of Tahiti and Madagascar in the late nineteenth century, and by the eve of World War I had established protectorates over Morocco and Tunisia. By 1914 France had created one of the largest empires in world history; including metropolitan France, it covered over four million square miles and had one hundred million inhabitants.

The French sought to apply the ideas of republicanism to their huge new empire, with little success. In some colonies, notably the old Caribbean possessions of Martinique, Guadeloupe, and French Guiana, the natives held French citizenship, yet both the economic power of the white planters and the political control of the French colonial administration severely limited their ability to exercise power. Elsewhere, residents of the empire were mostly subjects and could only become voting citizens by demonstrating that they had "assimilated" into French culture, something achieved by few. The French doctrine of assimilation assumed that all men and women could become French, but the fact that colonial administrations invested relatively little in native education made the concept essentially a dead letter.

An empire without an emperor, a republic with both citizens and subjects, Third Republic France combined increasingly republican and democratic politics in Europe with a growing authoritarian, paternalistic empire in Asia and Africa. To a large extent, although not entirely, this distinction rested upon racial difference, making France a nation of white citizens and nonwhite colonial subjects. All were French, but not all were French equally. One cannot, therefore, separate the intensifying national integration of French political culture in the late nineteenth century from its increasingly transnational character. The contradictory character of republican imperialism lay at the heart of the politics and life of the Third Republic, and would constitute a powerful legacy for France in the twentieth century.

As we shall see in the following chapters, the rise of a modern French nation and culture during the late nineteenth century had an important transnational dimension. Paris became to an important extent one of the world's great centers of modernity, while the exceptional growth of France's empire brought French ideas of republican liberal democracy to a global audience, even though those ideals did not at all take the same form that they did in metropolitan France. Between 1870 and 1914 France became more than ever before a transnational nation, the rise of a national political culture working in tandem with the spread of French ideas and influences around the world.

4

Capital of Fashion
Paris and the Rise of Haute Couture

Few things more typify the image and global presence of Paris than the world of haute couture, high fashion. To people throughout the world today it often seems second nature to look to France in general, and Paris in particular, for the latest styles and trends. Most notably, the French capital has dominated the world of women's fashion for much of the modern era, and clothing designers still look to the Paris runways during the spring shows for inspiration. High-quality women's clothing has come to represent the ultimate example of both Parisian traditions of luxury manufacture more generally, and the city's image as a consumer paradise. The importance of haute couture was made clear at the 1900 Exposition, where the fashionably dressed, beautiful woman was regarded as the very symbol of Paris.[1]

The world of high fashion represents Paris, and indeed France, at its most transnational. The French capital has been an international fashion center since the court of Louis XIV made style a key marker of prestige and, ultimately, political power. In the nineteenth century the industrialization of European and American society, together with the increased globalization of modern culture, gave fashion a new prominence. Improvements in transportation made it easier for wealthy women to travel to Paris to buy fashionable clothing, and the advent of mass-mailed catalogs spread images of Parisian style throughout the world. If French haute couture influenced women's ideas of beauty throughout the world, it was also shaped by designers from abroad who came to make their way in the world's fashion capital.

High fashion represented not only the influence of Paris on the world, but also the impact of the world on the life of Paris.

Paris as a Fashion Mecca

The French capital has been so central to the world of clothing manufacture and style it is easy to forget that modern fashion did not begin there. Like many other major aspects of French history, fashion arose out of the interactions of local, national, and global developments. Historians of Europe have traced the history of fashion back to the Middle Ages, and the rise of new views of clothing as one aspect of the transition to the modern era. The Crusades brought Europeans into contact with the cultures of the Middle East, cultures with a much stronger tradition of elaborate costumes, a contact which played a role in the rise of courtly fashion in Europe. During the late Middle Ages, European aristocrats and the wealthy began to pay careful attention to their dress, for not only aesthetic but also political reasons. Especially in royal courts, clothing styles indicated prestige and power.

Aristocratic and royal courts did not by themselves produce the modern world of fashion, however. Renaissance Italy, with its vibrant urban life and culture, became the real birthplace of modern ideas of style. Tight-fitting, often sexually revealing, clothing became the order of the day in fourteenth century Italian cities, generally developed and worn by members of the middle classes. The rise of proto-capitalist economies facilitated the development of fashion as an industry as well as a culture, an early example of a phenomenon that would characterize the Parisian garment industry in the modern era as well. Finally, as they would centuries later in the French capital, in the city-states of Renaissance Italy art and fashion intersected, both products of cultures that championed the vibrant and the new.[2]

Modern fashion spread from Italy to France during the early modern era. Unlike in the Renaissance Italian cities, fashion in France first arose in royal courts. During the fourteenth century the dukes of Burgundy ruled a regime more powerful—and more fashionable—than that of the kings of France, stretching from Switzerland to the North Sea. Their court in Dijon became known for luxurious style, called by some "the cradle of fashion." In the early sixteenth century Francis I became king of France, bringing to the court in Paris a new emphasis on style, dressing himself and his followers in elaborate, colorful silks and satins. Under his reign the French provided a counterpoint to the fashion sense of Europe's dominant power, Spain. The Spanish court, influenced by the somber logic and crusading zeal of the Counter-Reformation and the conquest of the Americas, strongly emphasized heavy black clothing. This style also appealed to the Calvinist Dutch, who in spite of their political and military opposition to Madrid agreed with and reinforced its sartorial style.[3]

France became a true leader of European fashion in the seventeenth century, above all under of the monarchy of the Sun King, Louis XIV. His regime represented one of the greatest eras of modern French history; under his rule, France replaced Spain as the leading power in Europe, and the nation expanded to its present-day geographical boundaries. The royal court at Versailles dazzled visitors from throughout Europe with its splendor, and Paris became the largest city on the continent. Under Louis XIV France also increasingly challenged Italy as the cultural leader of Europe.

Yet for many the most striking aspect of Louis XIV's reign, and its most memorable, lay in its emphasis on aesthetic magnificence and style. The king himself supposedly said, "Fashion is the mirror of history," and his court's emphasis on bright colors, extraordinary costumes, and incredibly elaborate rituals of dress proclaimed the power of his reign.[4] The great king's wars against Spain went hand in hand with his successful campaign against Spanish fashion, emphasizing bright colors rather than the dour black of Madrid. Fashion also represented good business, a source of wealth for the national economy. Under Louis XIV the French state invested in the nation's textile industry, seeing it as ultimately capable of producing the same kind of wealth that the Spanish crown drew from its empires in the Americas.[5]

The beginnings of the eighteenth century brought the decline of the royal court at Versailles and a new prominence to the city of Paris, which soon emerged as the center of French fashion. The proximity of the French court provided lots of business for the city's clothing industries, and thousands of Parisian artisans labored to make stylish costumes and dresses for the aristocrats of Versailles. At the same time, Paris offered an escape from the court's strict rules of etiquette and power governing fashion, as well as a large upper middle-class market for aristocratic fashion. By the time Louis XIV died in 1715, fashion in France had become somewhat more democratic, no longer dictated by the court to the broader society but increasingly developed in the French capital. Paris grew famous for its style: as one commentator noted in 1712, "To be in Paris without seeing the fashions, you have to close your eyes ... Whenever a fashion begins to dawn, the capital is infatuated with it, and no one dares to show himself, unless he is done up in the new finery."[6]

During the eighteenth-century Paris reinforced and expanded its identity as the fashion center of Europe. Although the styles of the royal court still carried weight, increasingly the garment industry catered to the city's large bourgeois consumer market. Shops arose around the rue Saint-Honoré and the Palais Royal to cater to the tastes and needs of upper middle-class consumers. Moreover, Paris began to dictate fashion standards to people living far beyond the city's boundaries. Provincial elites increasingly looked to the capital for the latest styles, as opposed to following the traditions of the local aristocracy. Parisian dressmakers sent dolls clothed with their latest creations to clients throughout Europe and beyond. At the same time, Paris fashion drew upon influences from abroad, especially England. The English came to dominate men's fashion in particular, part of a broader shift from the flamboyant masculine costumes of seventeenth-century Versailles to the more understated black menswear that would prevail in the nineteenth century. During the eighteenth century Paris fashion became increasingly women's fashion, a gendered pattern that has persisted down to the present day.

The career of Rose Bertin exemplified the new prominence of Paris fashion, both its growing international scope and its continued ties to the royal court. Bertin was born in Picardy in northern France in 1747, and at the age of sixteen moved to Paris as an apprentice in the shop of a milliner, Mademoiselle Pagelle. Bertin thrived in the shop, eventually becoming Pagelle's partner, and became close to many of her aristocratic clients. In 1770 she opened her own shop in the rue Saint-Honoré, and soon developed a substantial clientele in Versailles. Two years later she met Queen Marie Antoinette, who fell in love with her dresses. Bertin became the official dressmaker to the queen, a position which placed her at the apex of Parisian style. Dubbed "the Minister of Fashion," she used her influence at Versailles to create dresses and hairstyles that made France, and Paris in particular, the center of fashion in Europe.

Rose Bertin fled Paris for London in February 1793 as revolutionary turmoil convulsed the life of the capital, depriving her of many of her aristocratic clients; Queen Marie Antoinette herself would fall victim to the guillotine that October. The French Revolution marked a new stage in the history of Paris fashion, illustrating the deeply political ramifications of the art of clothing. As in the English revolution a century earlier, different political sides dressed differently, using style as a marker of political identity. The lower-class revolutionaries who made up the Paris crowd and overthrew the monarchy became known by their plain long trousers, not the stylish short pants of the aristocracy. The *sans-culottes* also adopted other sartorial symbols of liberty, notably the red cap or *bonnet rouge*, modeled on the Phrygian cap worn by freed slaves in antiquity. Parisian designers also incorporated the tricolor flag into clothing.

The overthrow of Robespierre's radical dictatorship in 1794 brought momentous changes in fashion as well as politics. The White Terror and the return of the royalist refugees from the Revolution brought a new assertion of aristocratic style and excess. The gangs of stylishly dressed young men who beat up *sans-culottes* and revolutionaries after the fall of Robespierre took the name of *jeunesse dorée*, or gilded youth, their clothing symbolizing their aristocratic and political identities. More generally, supporters of the new conservative regime, or *Merveilleuses*, as they were often called, emphasized wearing luxurious, extravagant clothing. Rose Bertin returned from English exile in 1795, and in 1797 fashion magazines reappeared in the French capital. In postrevolutionary Paris fashion reasserted itself with a vengeance that was both aesthetic and political.

France restored royal government in 1814, and kings ruled the country during the Restoration and the July Monarchy until a new revolution erupted in 1848. Yet as the world of fashion made clear, ultimately the nation would not return to the aristocratic world that had vanished with the Revolution. The great royal court at Versailles was no more (when the palace reopened in 1837, it did so as a national museum), and during the early nineteenth century the balance between court and city as arbiters of style shifted decisively in favor of the latter. As the contemporary novels of Honoré de Balzac reveal, the *haute bourgeoisie*, or upper middle class, had come into its own, and fashion reflected this new reality. Clothing styles became more understated, moving away from the extravagant aristocratic luxury of the ancien régime. Yet the aristocracy did not entirely disappear from France, even after the revolutions of 1848, and women's fashion in particular continued to show their influence. The ability of Parisian clothing designers and dressmakers to balance and integrate bourgeois and aristocratic style would produce one of the greatest achievements of Paris fashion, haute couture.

Charles Worth and the Making of Haute Couture

While the idea and production of fashionable clothing has existed through-out much of human history, what the French call haute couture was a creation of nineteenth-century Paris. As we have seen, traditionally dressmakers had made high fashion clothing to order for their mainly aristocratic custom-ers, and the most prominent succeeded in affiliating themselves with royal courts. During the early nineteenth century Napoleon's First Empire inspired the Empire style, generally featuring a high waist, slender skirt, and strong neoclassical influences. The haute couture industry that developed in the mid-nineteenth century kept the emphasis on clothes made to order, but it also added some new developments. The new approach to fashion gave the dressmaker more power and autonomy, turning him or her (but primarily him) into a fashion authority. It also supplemented the custom-made dress with a designers' line of clothing, displayed by models at regular fashion shows. The designer could then tailor these clothes for customers, thus blurring the line between individual creations and ready-to-wear clothing.

In keeping with the transnational character of Parisian fashion, the founder of modern haute couture was not even French. Charles Frederick Worth was born in southern England in 1825 and grew up in London. At the age of thirteen he apprenticed with a draper's shop in Piccadilly Circus, at the time the center of British fashion. After finishing his apprenticeship he decided to move to the heart of the fashion world, Paris, obtaining a position with the leading firm of Gagelin. Worth began making dresses for Marie Vernet, his French girlfriend and model with the firm. When his elegant designs caught the eye of the firm's clientele, Worth persuaded Gagelin to give him his own department, turning out striking creations that not only pleased Gagelin's clientele but also won awards for the firm at the Crystal Palace Exhibition of 1851 and the Paris Exposition of 1855. Flush with these successes, Worth asked to join the Gagelin board of directors. When the firm refused, he left in 1858 to open his own dressmaking firm in the elegant rue de la Paix.

Charles Worth took a revolutionary approach to dressmaking, and in doing so created modern haute couture. Much more than earlier couturiers (dressmakers), he insisted on total control of the production process, not only designing the dress but also personally selecting the fabrics and ornaments to be used. He used lavish materials of the highest quality, and designed clothes that displayed the strengths of a given fabric to maximum advantage. Worth cultivated relationships with the textile manufacturers themselves, rather than just buying what was available at stores, and told them the kinds of materials he wanted. More generally, starting with Worth the Paris designer began to dictate taste and style to the consumer, rather than simply executing her wishes as had been traditional with clothing made to order. Worth would present several elegant designs to the client—she could choose among different fabrics and colors—but all based on Worth's designs. He therefore exercised an unprecedented level of control over the business of producing fine clothes.

This idea of presenting a clothing line became the signature characteristic of haute couture. Worth invented the idea of clothing labels, so that each of his creations bore his name. Eventually the label became a mark of great prestige, so that women could boast they wore a Worth original. Four times a year the *Maison Worth* would hold a fashion show, presenting the latest designs to the public. Not only would individual customers flock to these exhibitions to order clothing, but other couturiers and designers, both French and foreign, would also attend, drawing inspiration for their own creations. Charles Worth thus founded the modern idea of the Paris runway, or fashion show, which would henceforth become a classic Parisian attraction and symbol of the city.

Haute couture was in effect clothing for the *haute bourgeoisie*; it represented a transition between the aristocratic ideal of clothing made to individual order according to the customer's dictates, and ready-to-wear clothing for the masses. Nonetheless, to win the prestige he required to position himself at the top of the fashion world, Worth needed an aristocratic connection. In 1859 he approached Princess Pauline von Metternich, wife of the new Austrian ambassador, asking to design clothing for her. After initially refusing, the princess did finally deign to look at Worth's album, eventually deciding to buy two dresses. She wore one of them at an imperial ball, attracting the attention of Empress Eugénie, who then contacted Worth to learn more about his firm.

Empress Eugénie de Montijo represented European aristocracy at its most international. Like the Austrian Marie Antoinette, she was a foreigner whose lineage embraced several countries. Born in 1826 in Granada, Spain, the empress's father was a Spanish count, and her mother came from a mixture of Scottish, Belgian, and American stock. Her grandfather was born in Scotland but emigrated to America where he became a wine merchant and eventually a United States consul. She divided her childhood between France and Spain, and in 1853 married Emperor Napoleon III, becoming the Empress Eugénie of France. As empress she strongly supported the Catholic Church, but also advocated for women's rights, going so far as to demand (unsuccessfully) that the French Academy elect George Sand as its first female member. She also championed her husband's disastrous intervention in Mexico.

In particular, the Empress Eugénie established herself as a leader of fashion, both in France and abroad. She exemplified the style of the Second Empire, represented not just in clothing but in the renovations of Paris engineered by Baron Haussmann, and did so as a way of underscoring the power and modernity of the imperial regime. Widely regarded as one of the most beautiful women in Europe, she used fashion to impress and overawe the regime's subjects and its neighbors abroad. She also used her patronage to support and establish people in the fashion industry. In 1854, for example, she gave the struggling Parisian luggage maker Louis Vuitton an imperial appointment, opening doors for a company whose success has endured to the present day. Her meeting with Charles Worth went very well, and by 1864 Worth had become the leading dressmaker to the empress, enabling him to establish a position as the most prestigious and expensive couturier in Paris. Together the empress and the dressmaker would create and rule modern Parisian style.

This role as a court dressmaker hearkened back to an earlier era, one of craftsmen's appointments to royal courts. The connection with the French empress and the Austrian princess granted Worth access to the world of the European nobility, and soon aristocratic women across the continent wore his fashions. At the same time, the increasing globalization of the late nineteenth century made Worth, and Parisian haute couture in general, an industry that catered to the bourgeoisie in both France and abroad. The increased efficiency of rail and steamship transportation made it possible for clothes buyers and individual customers to travel to Paris in search of style. Worth and other couturiers also developed mail order businesses to cater to an increasingly international clientele. By the 1860s Parisian haute couture had become recognized globally as the height of high style, and Paris the center of the fashion world.

No group better symbolized this international prominence than the wealthy American women who began flocking to the French capital in search of the latest fashions. By the 1860s the time required to cross the Atlantic had been reduced to little more than a week, making it much easier for Americans to visit Europe. American women began coming to Paris in droves, drawn not only by the city's beauty and modernity but above all by haute couture. The most fashionable ladies in the United States prided themselves upon dressing in the latest Parisian styles. They soon gained a reputation, true of so many Americans in nineteenth-century Europe, of being big spenders. As Charles Worth himself commented,

> Some of the Americans are great spenders; all of them (all of them that I see, I mean) love dress, even if they are not extravagant over it. And I like to dress them, for, as I say occasionally, 'they have faith, figures, and francs,'—faith to believe in me, figures that I can put into shape, francs to pay my bills. Yes, I like to dress Americans.[7]

One of his American clients was Lillie Moulton, the wife of Mr. Charles Moulton, a wealthy American banker's son living in Paris. A gifted singer and active socialite, Mrs. Moulton lived in Paris during the Second Empire and became a frequent guest at the court of Emperor Napoleon III. In May 1863 she attended an elegant costume ball attended by the Emperor and Empress as well as prominent members of Second Empire society. It was a glittering affair, but Moulton mostly remembered her own costume.

> I must tell you about my dress. It was really one of the prettiest there. Worth said that he had put his whole soul on it. I thought that he had put a pretty good round price on his soul. A skirt of gold tissue, round the bottom of which was a band of silver, with all sorts of fantastic figures, such as dragons, owls, and so forth, embroidered in different colors under a skirt of white tulle with silver and gold spangles. The waist was a mass of spangles and false stones on a gold stuff; gold-embroidered bands came from the waist and fell in points over the skirt. I had wings of spangled silvery material, with great glass-colored beads sewed all over them. But the *chef-d'oeuvre* was the head-dress, which was a sort of helmet with gauze wings and the jewels of the family (Mrs. M.'s and mine) fastened on it. From the helmet flowed a mane of gold tinsel, which I curled in with my hair. The effect was very original, for it looked as though my head was on fire; in fact, I looked as if I was all on fire. Before I left home all the servants came to see me, and their *magnifique*, and *superbe*, and *étonnant* quite turned my head, even with the helmet on.[8]

When she paid a week's visit to the imperial residence in the Chateau de Compiègne, Mrs. Moulton brought twenty outfits, most of them designed by Charles Worth at a price that even her rich husband found excessive.

American designers also purchased Worth's creations, copying them for the wider mass market in the United States. Parisian haute couture was so popular that it attracted criticism from those who viewed the French capital as a den of iniquity. As one writer commented, "Let American and Christian women *blush*, at the character of their Parisian models of fashion!"[9] "When good Americans die they go to Paris," Oscar Wilde once commented, and the Maison Worth made it its business to ensure they were well dressed in the afterlife.

The influence of Parisian haute couture went well beyond dressing wealthy American women; it had an impact on modern art as well. The heyday of Charles Worth also witnessed the Impressionist revolution in French painting, and the two worlds frequently came into contact. In his celebrated 1863 essay, "The Painter of Modern Life," Baudelaire called upon modern painters to leave their studios, go out into the streets, and paint the world as they saw it. For many this meant painting fashionable women as representatives of the modern world. Works like Claude Monet's *The Woman in the Green Dress* (1866) and Edgar Degas's *The Milliners* (1898) portrayed different aspects of the world of fashion. Centered in Paris, modern art during the late nineteenth century was also a transnational movement, drawing painters from around the world to the French capital. One of these was the American Mary Cassatt, whose paintings such as *The Cup of Tea* (1879) and *The Fitting* (1891) illustrated the world of wealthy American women in Paris. In general, modern art and fashion together underscored the place of nineteenth-century Paris as what Walter Benjamin called the capital of modernity.

Charles Worth's transformation of haute couture made Paris the world's center of the fashion industry; as historian Diana de Marly has commented, "It was Worth who turned dressmaking into big business; he found Paris with a craft and left it with an industry."[10] Haute couture constituted the elegant extreme of a much larger phenomenon, the rise of the modern Paris garment industry. Spurred on by the popularization of the sewing machine after the 1850s, clothing manufacture mushroomed into the French capital's largest industry, employing nearly three hundred thousand workers by the turn of the century. The Maison Worth alone had twelve hundred employees by 1871. Most garment industry workers were women who labored over twelve hours per day for very low wages, in conditions light years removed from the elegance of the rue de la Paix. Jeanne Bouvier, a Parisian seamstress who later became a union activist and labor historian, described her life in the industry during the late nineteenth century:

> One day I was hired by a firm in the Rue Caumartin. I was still earning five francs a day. It was the practice in this firm to make us work very late, without allowing time to eat dinner. During the season that I spent in

that workshop, these late nights lasted until two in the morning nearly every day, and without our having eaten, except for a small loaf of bread and a bit of chocolate at four o'clock. They made us remain absolutely silent . . . It was simply hateful to make us work late in this manner, and in a terribly harsh winter, what is more!

The Seine was full of enormous blocks of ice, and great piles of snow swept along the quays. It took me three-quarters of an hour to make my way home, and this was at two in the morning, without having eaten dinner. When I got home, I did not have the energy to eat. After a season like that, I had to take to my bed and go to the hospital to have myself cared for.[11]

The worlds of women like Jeanne Bouvier and Lillie Moulton could not have been more different, yet both were essential to the garment industry of the French capital. Here, as in so many other facets of modern Parisian life, the boulevard and the barricade rubbed shoulders.

The Maison Worth continued to dominate Parisian haute couture through the late nineteenth century, its success spawning imitators and rivals like Jacques Doucet, Jeanne Paquin, and the Callot sisters, all of whom set up their own fashion houses in Paris. When Worth died in 1895, to be succeeded by his son Jean-Philippe Worth as director of the business, he had come from being a poor English immigrant to one of the dominant figures in the culture of modern Paris.

An industry founded by an Englishman and supported by European aristocrats and American millionaires, haute couture represented Parisian life at its most global. It drew heavily upon the city's local traditions of elegance, artistry, and public display, as well as its vast reservoir of skilled artisanal labor. At the same time, it would not have achieved such prominence without the rise of transnational networks of communication and transportation, not to mention cultures of modernity. Haute couture symbolized Paris as ground zero of modernity, the eternal source of new fashions and new ideas. It underscored the French capital's position as both a world city and the greatest representative of the universal nation. French taste owed much to many peoples and traditions, and the interaction of global and local traditions made it the aesthetic standard bearer of the modern world.

5

Universalism from the Margins
The Alliance Israélite Universelle

What happens when transnational people encounter a universal nation? Traditionally the Jews have constituted the world's classic diasporic community, united by religion, custom, and persecution, but scattered throughout the world. A key theme of modern Jewish history has been the nationalization of this people, either as minority citizens in various nations or through the construction of their own nation-state, Israel. As the first modern nation to emancipate the Jews and make them citizens, France played a key role in this process. At the same time, the seminal contributions of the Dreyfus Affair to both political antisemitism and Zionism constitute another, very different French influence on the nationalization of modern Jewry.

This essay will consider how Jews in France during the late nineteenth century both embraced the universalism of the French republic and at the same time gave it a distinctly Jewish cast. Although most histories of French Jews during the early Third Republic focus on the Dreyfus Affair and the rise of racial antisemitism, here we will consider the history of the Alliance Israélite Universelle, the Universal Jewish Alliance. Formed in 1860 by assimilated Parisian Jews, the AIU emphasized uplift of the Jewish masses, especially in North Africa and the Middle East, and their integration into modern civilization. An expression both of Jewish nationalism and of a profound belief in French culture as the road to enlightenment, the AIU's efforts on behalf of fellow Jews represented an important dimension of the rise of France as a transnational nation. At the same time, aspects of the AIU's outreach to and efforts on behalf of Jews abroad replicated tropes of French colonialism, especially the idea of the civilizing mission, underscoring another important aspect of the nation's universalist tradition.

In a recent study, Professor Maurice Samuels has considered the modern history of Jews in France as a way of defending the nation's universalist tradition. While not completely rejecting the critiques of French universalism posed by many contemporary scholars (especially American ones), Samuels nonetheless argues not only that universalism had room for Jewish community traditions but that French Jews could both embrace this ideology as a way of defending their own culture. He offers the AIU as an example to support this more positive perspective on French universalism.[1] In line with his argument I suggest in this essay that the French did not simply impose universalism on different peoples under their rule, but that those peoples selectively chose aspects of it, to the extent they had the power to do so, aspects that would benefit them and align with their own views of the world.

Universalism in modern France arose not just from the thoughts and efforts of the French elites who shaped its main outlines, but equally to the many different peoples inside and outside the hexagon who made use of it. Both those who rejected it, notably leaders of anticolonial movements, but also those who adapted to or even embraced it, are part of its history. In subtle ways, as the history of the AIU demonstrates, in altering their lives to fit universalist standards they changed not only themselves but French universalism, and France in general.

The Jews in France

The history of Jews in France goes back as far as the history of France itself. Jews originally came to what was then known as Gaul as citizens of the Roman Empire. By the second century AD, after the destruction of the Second Temple and the crushing of Jerusalem, Jews fleeing Palestine began moving to Gaul. Granted religious toleration in Roman Gaul, in spite of the often-hostile attitude of the Catholic Church, Jewish communities grew and prospered. By the sixth century Paris had a thriving Jewish population, and Jews lived in many other cities throughout the country. Jews succeeded in establishing strong positive relations with Charlemagne and the

Carolingian kings that followed him, and many worked as merchants and traders between France and the Muslim Middle East, especially Palestine.[2]

Although French Jews in the early Middle Ages mostly enjoyed economic prosperity and free status, the threat of antisemitism, inspired especially but not only by the church, was ever present. In medieval France both religious and royal authorities frequently persecuted and even expelled the Jewish population. In 1096, during the first Crusade, Christians attacked the Jewish community in Rouen before going on to massacre thousands of Jews in the Rhineland. French kings periodically expelled the Jews from the country, most notably Philip Augustus in 1182 and Philip the Fair in 1306. By the end of the fourteenth century Jews had largely disappeared from France, returning in significant numbers only after 1600.

While anti-Semitic oppression did not entirely disappear during the early modern era, Jewish communities grew and became a permanent part of France. In 1648 Louis XIV annexed Alsace-Lorraine, bringing into the kingdom a large new Jewish population of more than twenty thousand by the eighteenth century. A sizeable community of Portuguese origin also took root in Bordeaux. By the middle of the century roughly forty to fifty thousand Jews lived in France, out of a national population of twenty-five million. While French Jews remained outside the mainstream of national life and continued to suffer from discrimination, they were there to stay.

The Enlightenment brought new perspectives on the situation of Jews in France, and increased toleration of this religious minority. In general, the *philosophes* who led the movement approached the Jewish question with some ambivalence: while they did not particularly approve of Jewish culture and religion, they did advocate toleration of them and criticized religious antisemitism. Both Voltaire and Montesquieu, for example, wrote essays highly critical of the Jews while at the same time condemning persecution of them. Others, notably the Count Mirabeau and the Abbé Grégoire, took a more positive perspective on France's Jews, influenced in part by contacts with the Jewish Enlightenment led by Moses Mendelssohn in Germany. Above all, the Enlightenment's opposition to the Church and to what it saw as religious ignorance and intolerance led many of its writers to reject anti-Semitic intolerance and violence. In 1785 this new spirit of tolerance led to the abolition of the Jewish poll tax and of restrictions on the ability of Jews to live anywhere in France.

These changing attitudes helped produce the key event in modern French Jewish history, the emancipation of the Jews under the French Revolution and Napoleon. Jews petitioned for the right to take part in the elections to the Estates General in 1789, and some but not all were granted that right. At the end of 1789 members of the National Assembly debated the questions of Jewish citizenship, ultimately in January 1790 extending it to the Jews of Bordeaux and Avignon. This proved only a prelude, however. On September 27, 1791, members of the National Assembly voted, nearly unanimously, to extend the rights of citizenship to all Jews in the country. France became the first nation in the modern world to grant civic equality to its Jewish population.

These events, although they at first only affected the wealthiest individuals and families, were joyfully welcomed by France's Jews. As one Jewish leader, Berr Isaac Berr, commented the next day:

> The day has thus arrived when the veil that covered us with humiliation has been torn off, and we shall finally recuperate those rights that, for more than eighteen centuries, have been ravished from us. . . .
>
> The name of full Citizen that we have just obtained is without fear of contradiction, the dearest status that man can possess in a free empire. But it is not enough to have the status we must truly be in a position to carry out the duties. . . .
>
> I could not repeat often enough to you how indispensable it is to leave behind this "esprit de corps" or community spirit in the case of all civil and political parties, which are not inherent in our spiritual laws; in that realm, we must be absolutely nothing but individuals, Frenchmen concerned with true patriotism and with the general good of the nation.[3]

September 27, 1791, thus became for many French Jews the greatest date in their history, the day when France made its Jews free and equal citizens of the nation. On the first anniversary of the emancipation, for example, the Jewish community of Metz, in Alsace, gathered in the local synagogue to sing the *Marseillaise* in Hebrew.[4]

After the fall of the revolutionary republic France continued to liberate its Jews. In 1806 Napoleon called first an assembly of Jewish notables, followed by the convocation of the traditional Jewish body the Sanhedrin, to set forth structures to govern the community. He created the consistories, local organizations of both rabbis and lay people ruled over by the central consistory in Paris. Perhaps most important, Napoleon's tremendous military conquests spread Jewish liberation throughout Europe. Wherever the Napoleonic armies went they tore down ghetto walls and brought Jews into the political mainstream. In Trier, in the German Rhineland, young Herschel Marx was born the son of the local rabbi. Under Napoleonic rule he became a lawyer, but when the French defeat in 1815 renewed restrictions on the Jews he converted to Christianity and changed his name to Heinrich. A few years later he fathered his son, Karl Marx, who he baptized at birth. Even with the restoration of anti-Semitic measures in Europe after the fall of Napoleon, the tradition of France as the land that liberated the Jews remained powerful across the continent during the nineteenth century.

For Jews in France itself, the restoration of the monarchy reaffirmed rather than reversed the emancipation of their community. French Jews prospered during the first half of the nineteenth century. The size of the community doubled from forty thousand to eighty thousand between 1789 and 1861. It also became more geographically diverse: whereas 80 percent of French Jews lived in Alsace-Lorraine in 1808, only 63 percent did so in 1861. The loosening of traditional restrictions enabled some Jews to take advantage of increasing educational and economic opportunities, so by the mid-nineteenth century a substantial Jewish bourgeoisie had developed. This was especially true in Paris, which increasingly became the center of French Jewish life. Parisian Jews represented only 6 percent of the national population in 1811, but 26 percent in 1861. Jewish financiers, families such as the Oppenheims, the Pereires, and above all the French branch of the Rothschilds, became part of the national *haute bourgeoisie*. More generally, by the mid-nineteenth century France had a strong Jewish middle class, people concerned with and committed to continuing the uplift of their community.

It was this community of affluent Parisian Jews that created the Alliance Israélite Universelle during the Second Empire. Two key perspectives motivated the founders of the AIU, and this community in general. First was a powerful belief in (and gratitude to) French universalism and civilization which had, in their own eyes, made their successes possible. Second, and equally important, was a desire to extend to other Jews beyond France the same benefits they had been given, to create a new Jewish enlightenment based upon the liberal values of the French Revolution. As one historian has put it, "From the French people as 'saviors of the world' to French Jewry as saviors of the Jewish world, there was only one step."[5] A sense of successful integration into French life did not diminish the concern of these Jews for their less fortunate coreligionists; rather, it led them to apply French universalist principles to the salvation of their own people. In the words of historian Esther Benbassa, "the Jewish leadership of France, proud of its achievements, convinced of the superiority of a country so generous to its Jews, and filled with gratitude toward it, labored to bring about the Frenchification of fellow Jews in the East. It tried to impose upon them, from above, a voluntarist style of westernization with its own pattern of emancipation, and to give them a French-style education nourished by dreams of France."[6] On May 17, 1860, a small group of Jewish leaders gathered in a Parisian townhouse to found the AIU. Perhaps the most prominent was Adolphe Crémieux, a republican lawyer and activist. Born Isaac-Jacob Adolphe Crémieux in Nîmes in 1796, Crémieux came from a wealthy Jewish family, and spent most of his life advocating for liberal and Jewish causes in France and abroad. During the July Monarchy he campaigned for liberalization and against the Guizot regime, and after the revolution of 1848 he became minister of justice in the new provisional government. In this capacity he played a key role in abolishing slavery in the French colonies. At the same time Crémieux was very active in the Jewish community. He helped repeal discriminatory legislation in 1827, and in 1834 became vice president of the Central Consistory of French Jews, a position he held until his death in 1880. Crémieux is best known for the Crémieux decree of 1870, which made the Jews of colonial Algeria citizens of France. Crémieux played a central role in establishing the AIU, which elected him its president in 1864.

A desire to protect Jews throughout the world from oppression motivated those assembled; the immediate spark was the 1858 Mortara affair, which involved the baptism of an Italian Jewish child against the will of his parents, and his seizure by the Vatican. At the May 1860 meeting the leaders of the AIU published a manifesto outlining the organization's three essential goals. First, the manifesto emphasized the need to advocate for Jews and combat antisemitism. Since Jews did not have a state of their own, the AIU could play this role for them. Second, the AIU would raise awareness of the poor condition of Jewish communities among progressive forces in the West, striving to bring about the same emancipation that had so benefitted the Jews of France. The Alliance Israélite Universelle stood for worldwide Jewish solidarity, for the ability of the people everywhere to enjoy tolerance and justice.

People of Israel!

If, scattered to the four corners of the earth . . . you remain attached to the ancient religion of your fathers, no matter how weak the links that bind you; If you do not deny your faith, if you do not hide your religion . . .

If you despise the prejudices from which we still suffer, the reproaches made against us, the lies and slurs told about us, the denials of justice that are tolerated, the persecutions that are justified or excused . . .

If you believe that many of your co-religionaires, still crushed by twenty centuries of poverty, of abuse, of restrictions, can still achieve their dignity as human beings and as citizens;

If you believe we must reform and not condemn those who are corrupt; enlighten and not abandon those who are blind; lift up and not just complain about those who have been beaten down; defend and not be silent about those who have been slandered; everywhere support those who have been persecuted and not just complain about persecution . . .

If you believe that it would be an honor for your religion, a lesson for the peoples of the world, an achievement for humanity, a triumph for truth and universal reason, to bring together all the living forces of Judaism, small in number, large in the love of and desire for truth;

If, finally, you believe that the influence of the principles of [17]89 is all-powerful in the world, that the law arising from it is a law of justice, that hopefully its spirit will prevail everywhere, and that the example of peoples who enjoy absolute freedom of religion is a powerful force;

If you believe all these things, Jews of the world, come listen to our appeal, join us, work with us in a great and perhaps blessed endeavor:

We will found the Universal Jewish Alliance![7]

The third goal was perhaps the most central to the work of the AIU. Its leaders strongly believed that Jews must be ready intellectually and morally to take advantage of emancipation, that they must be educated about modern principles of civilization. One must, in short, learn to be free. This posed a problem, because when the assimilated and affluent Jews of France and other western European countries looked at the Jewish communities of eastern Europe and the Mediterranean basin, they often saw a people sunk in ignorance and superstition, unprepared to embrace the modern world. The Jewish version of France's *mission civilisatrice*, like the original model, often drew upon Orientalist stereotypes of the Other. In 1873 Baron Maurice de Hirsch, a wealthy financier who bankrolled the first railroads in the Ottoman Empire, observed:

> During my many and long stays in Turkey, I have been painfully struck by the ignorance and misery of the great majority of the Jews who inhabit this empire. There is progress everywhere in Turkey, but the Jews hardly profit from it because of their poverty and lack of enlightenment. To provide for the instruction and education of the youth is the most efficient remedy that one can bring to this evil . . . I have decided to create a foundation of one million francs in Constantinople designed specially to improve the situation of the Jews of the Ottoman Empire by instruction and education.[8]

The case of Algeria, and Algeria's Jews, played an especially important role in the development of the AIU's attitudes toward improving the quality of

Jewish life. Just as the French conquest of Alsace-Lorraine in the seventeenth century had brought a large population of Ashkenazim into the French kingdom, so did France's annexation of Algeria in 1830 bring a new Sephardic community into the nation. While Jews in France tended to regard those of Algeria through a haze of Orientalist perspectives, at the same time they felt uplifting them would benefit both France as a nation and the Jews as a people. This uplift must come from France, specifically from the French Jewish community which had undergone a similar process of modernization as a result of the Enlightenment and the Revolution. French Jews would thus extend to their brethren in colonial Algeria an understanding of the benefits offered by French rule and Jewish enlightenment.

During the late nineteenth century, therefore, the AIU engaged itself above all in creating and operating schools to educate the Jewish masses, primarily in the Middle East and North Africa. To a certain extent, the AIU's activities were part and parcel of the broader climate of western imperialism during this era. Not only did they at times share rather condescending attitudes about the need to uplift the "natives," but increased European influence in North Africa and the Middle East facilitated the ability of the AIU to bypass local opposition to its programs. However, this parallel only goes so far; in contrast to European colonialists in general, the AIU really did consider the education of "Eastern" Jews as its first priority. Thanks to the generosity of individuals such as Baron de Hirsch and many others, it established schools throughout the Middle East and North Africa.

What did these schools teach? First and foremost, all instruction was in French, which the members of the AIU regarded as *the* language of civilization. Some taught other languages, notably Spanish in Morocco where the Jewish population was mostly of Spanish origin. The schools tended to frown upon dialects, however, such as Judeo-Latino in North Africa or Yiddish in Eastern Europe. They also taught Hebrew and Jewish history, focusing on both the modern and the Biblical eras. European history—ancient, medieval, and modern—frequently figured in the curriculum, as did math and science. Some schools in addition taught vocational education, although this often proved less than popular with many Jewish families. Finally, the AIU created some of the first schools for Jewish girls in these areas, breaking with traditional patterns of patriarchy. In general, the Alliance Israélite Universelle saw education as the indispensable ticket to Jewish emancipation, its way of giving to their Eastern brethren what France had given to them.

Not all local Jews viewed the Alliance schools favorably. Many traditionalists, both rabbis and secular leaders, looked askance at the AIU's emphasis on modern ideas, seeing it as a threat to the culture that had sustained their communities for generations. Certain rabbis argued that Jewish boys should focus on religious, not secular, education. Some, like this group of Tunisian Jews writing in 1900, considered the activities of the Alliance an attempt to impose a foreign culture on their communities:

> The Alliance Israélite . . . in violation of the most basic rules of conduct, is seeking to impose the French spirit, embodied by the French national education system, on the Jewish population of Tunisia. While the Jews of France can still pride themselves on partaking to a certain degree in the national life of the French, they will surely not venture to believe that the same is true of Tunisian Jews, whose past has nothing to do with France or the French . . . In order to enlighten this population, to introduce it to modern life, one must not replace its traditions and historical memories by other traditions and other memories. One must not seek to replace one's own national spirit by that of another nation.[9]

The activities of the AIU in North Africa and the Middle East paralleled those of French colonialism in general, and the organization's vision of uplifting foreign Jews at times produced reactions similar to those of other peoples subject to European imperial domination in the late nineteenth century.

Yet many other Eastern Jews agreed with their French brethren, seeing modern secular education as a passport to emancipation and a better life. By 1900 Alliance schools enrolled thousands of students throughout the Middle East and North Africa, including Morocco, Algeria, Tunisia, Egypt, Turkey, and Persia. The majority were primary schools, but by the beginning of the twentieth century a network of AIU secondary schools had also developed. In some cases, such as the following 1867 appeal, local

Jewish communities petitioned the Alliance to start a school to educate their young people:

> We, the undersigned, directors of the Jewish school of Edirne [Turkey] called the *Talmud Torah'im derekh erez*, convinced of the necessity of giving a good French education to our students in order to introduce them to European civilization, we beg the very honorable Central Committee of the Alliance Israélite Universelle to give its valuable assistance by providing us with a suitable teacher for the teaching of the French language and of the elements of modern sciences.[10]

All in all, one must judge the AIU's efforts to give modern secular education to the Jews of North Africa and the Middle East a success. Occurring at the same time as the modernization of commerce, industry, and public administration in the region, it enabled many Jews to obtain positions as clerks, administrators, journalists, and other white-collar professionals. In Turkey, for example, much of the Jewish middle class by the beginnings of the twentieth century was AIU-trained and spoke French. One irony of the AIU's educational mission was that while Jewish emancipation led to integration into the French national community, this did not happen in the Middle East and North Africa. Few AIU schools taught local languages such as Arabic or Turkish, and their Jewish graduates usually spoke French better than the dominant languages around them. The Alliance's universal vision was thus very much made in France, its vision of civilization a quintessentially French one.

Finally, one must also consider the relationship of the Alliance to another transnational Jewish movement in the modern era, Zionism. As noted earlier, the experience of Jews in France had an important impact on the rise of Zionism: Zionist founder Theodor Herzl had witnessed the Dreyfus Affair as the Paris correspondent for the Viennese newspaper *Die Neue Freie Presse* during the 1890s, an experience that helped convince him that the Jews had no place in Europe and led him to publish the Zionist manifesto *The Jewish State* in 1896. Herzl's conclusions did not resemble those of most French Jews, however, and for the leaders of the AIU in particular Zionism had little appeal. This emerged very early on in its history. In the 1860s, for example, Jewish nationalists asked the AIU to support its proposal to the Turkish government to allow Jews to buy land and settle in Palestine, yet the AIU made it clear that emancipation, not nationalism, was its primary goal. As one AIU leader declared in 1862, "What Judaism calls messianic times is to be identified with what our modern thinkers, who have grown up on the principles of 1789, call progress and civilization."[11] For the AIU, Jewish integration into modern nations rather than the creation of a separate Jewish nation remained its primary goal.

Nevertheless, in the last analysis the visions of Zionism and the AIU had more than a little in common. Zionism, like the Alliance, represented the integration of Jewish communities into a modernist vision of national community, one that would build upon the emancipation of the Jews in Europe and overcome the inadequacies and contradictions of that process by creating a separate Jewish state, one where Jews could become full citizens and members of the modern era. Moreover, there is a distinct parallel between the AIU's interest in extending the principles of the French Enlightenment and Revolution to the Jews of North Africa and the Middle East, and the efforts of Israel, a state conceptualized and founded by European Ashkenazi Jews, to integrate the same Sephardic Jewish populations into its national community. In this regard both ideologies could claim some successes. After France's withdrawal from colonial North Africa in the 1950s and 1960s the Jews of Morocco and Tunisia moved overwhelmingly to Israel. The Jews of Algeria, however, whose possession of French citizenship represented one of the triumphs of the AIU, chose France instead, where their communities became major diasporic supporters of Israel. Today's Alliance Israélite Universelle actively embraces Zionism and the State of Israel, where it has a major branch, and remains committed to supporting Jewish and universalist values.

The history of the Alliance Israélite Universelle provides an interesting perspective on the transnational history of France in the late nineteenth century. It illustrates the fact that universalism was not just imposed from the center, but also embraced from the margins of national existence. It also suggests that one could embrace the universalist ideal without necessarily abandoning one's own culture and history; quite the contrary, one could use the former to strengthen the latter. Finally, even during the rising antisemitism of the Dreyfus Affair many French Jews clung to the ideals of the French Revolution as key to Jewish progress in the modern world; indeed, the positive outcome of the affair seemed to confirm this belief. The vision of France as a universal nation had many sources, and in general one must consider its ability to inspire efforts like the Alliance Israélite Universelle a key to its success.

6

Painter of Empire
The Life of Paul Gauguin

When we think of Paul Gauguin, or view his lush paintings of life in Tahiti, we think of the romance of empire and the desire to escape ordinary bourgeois existence for an exotic paradise. A closer examination of his life reveals the difficulties and suffering that lay behind this pretty fantasy, both for Gauguin himself and for the Tahitians he portrayed. The artistic work of Paul Gauguin is nonetheless crucial to the study of the republican empire, for what it reveals about those he painted as well as his own life as a French man in the late nineteenth century. Gauguin's biography illustrates the romance of colonial horizons and the many ties between empire and metropole under the Third Republic. It underscores the increasingly global reach of French life at the dawn of the twentieth century, illustrating some of the ways in which the colonies contributed to the making of modern France. Gauguin's romanticized images of Tahiti demonstrated the attractions of empire, and in doing so undergirded a colonial order that ultimately disempowered and oppressed that empire's residents.

The life of Paul Gauguin exemplifies the history of France not only as an imperial but also a transnational nation. Gauguin was born in Paris on June 7, 1848, to a French father, Clovis Gauguin, and a mother of French and Peruvian heritage, Aline Gauguin, whose mother was the famous feminist writer Flora Tristán. During her short life Tristán traveled and wrote widely, advocating tirelessly for working class emancipation. Her 1843 book, *The Workers' Union*, drew upon British and French Utopian Socialism, and was one of the first to link socialism and women's liberation. Gauguin could claim descent from Peru's last Spanish viceroy, who was Tristán's uncle, Pío de Tristán. Shortly after Gauguin's first birthday his parents, tired of the revolutionary turmoil in the capital, left France to settle in Peru. Gauguin and his mother arrived in Lima at the end of 1849 following a turbulent sea voyage that claimed his father's life. There the young Gauguin lived an idyllic childhood until he was seven, surrounded by his mother's family. His first language was Spanish, and his first exposure to art came from the pre-Columbian carvings collected by his mother; the image of her garbed in traditional Peruvian costume would remain vivid for Gauguin and influence his artistic vision as a grown man.[1]

When young Paul was seven his mother moved them back to France, spurred by impending civil war in Peru. They first settled in his father's hometown of Orléans, where Paul attended Catholic boarding school, then his mother moved them to Paris to work as a seamstress. There Aline became the friend (and most likely mistress) of Gustave Arosa, a wealthy and well-connected Spaniard who would become Paul's guardian and a major influence on his life. Arosa introduced the Gauguins to the neighborhood between the Opéra and Pigalle, south of Montmartre, where the painter would spend most of his life in Paris. The young Gauguin did not adjust easily to life in France, often feeling like an outsider, and when he turned seventeen chose to join the merchant marine as an ordinary sailor. In 1865 he made his first voyage to Rio de Janeiro (coincidentally the exact same trip made by fellow painter and aspiring sailor Edouard Manet seventeen years earlier), spending most of the next five years at sea. Until his early twenties, therefore, Gauguin had a complex relation to France, both a part of the nation's life and yet never completely fitting in.

After fulfilling his military service in the navy during the Franco-Prussian war, Gauguin returned in 1871 to a Paris shattered by the violence of the Commune. He settled back into the city's ninth arrondissement, and with the help of Arosa found steady employment in the Paris stock exchange. At this time the young man began painting, at first as a hobby. His neighborhood was full of young artists, including the studios of Edouard Manet, Edgar Degas, and Pierre Auguste Renoir, and the places where they congregated, such as the Nouvelle Athènes café in the Place Pigalle. The Arosa family introduced him to the work of prominent artists, notably Camille Pissarro, and he eagerly followed the debates about art that swirled around the *quartier*.

Gauguin thus found himself at the Parisian ground zero of one of the most important movements in the history of modern art, impressionism. The birth of impressionism in 1860s Paris signaled the advent of modern painting, and in important ways the modern era in general. Although the term "impressionism" did not come into existence until the 1870s (and even then many leaders of the movement rejected it), as an artistic school it began to coalesce in the last decade of the Second Empire, led by a few seminal artists. Like their realist predecessors, the impressionists rejected an emphasis on classical and Romantic themes, preferring instead to paint modern life with all its warts and imperfections. They differed sharply, however, in their opinion of what constituted reality. Abjuring a positivist, objective approach to daily life, they insisted instead on the importance of momentary impressions and feelings in structuring how the artist, and people in general, perceived the world. Moreover, in contrast to the dark tones and traditional representational styles of an artist such as Gustave Courbet, the impressionists for the most part gloried in bright colors and a more abstract approach. Their emphasis on inner feeling and subjectivity heralded the birth of modern art.[2]

The world first learned of the impressionist movement in 1863, at the annual Paris Salon. The Salon, originally created in the seventeenth century, was the nation's most prestigious art exhibition. To be chosen to exhibit at the Salon was to win recognition as a leading French artist. By the mid-nineteenth century the Salon had become known for aesthetic conservatism, its judges and juries favoring more conventional, academic works. A scandal erupted at the 1863 Salon when the judges rejected paintings by several artists, including Manet, Pissarro, and Paul Cézanne, who would come to be identified with the new movement. Many in the art world reacted with fury, so to appease Salon critics Napoleon III allowed those who had been turned down to organize their own exhibit, the Salon des Refusés (Salon of the Rejects), so that the public could judge for itself.

The Salon des Refusés became in effect the first modern art exhibit, and with it impressionism was born. During the 1860s the major artists of the school, including Pissarro, Manet, Degas, Renoir as well as Claude Monet, Berthe Morisot, and Paul Cézanne, came to know each other, to work and paint together, and to develop a common (if not identical) aesthetic. They did not hold their first formal exhibit until 1874, but impressionism had already become a coherent, and revolutionary, aesthetic movement in the waning years of the Second Empire.

The writers and artists of mid-century Paris produced works that had a major role in shaping the idea of modernity as a global phenomenon, and their ideas attracted fans and imitators around the world. But global influences went two ways, for much of Parisian avant-garde art and literature drew upon influences from abroad. For example, the painting of Dutch artists Rembrandt and Frans Hals had a major impact on Manet, and foreign artists such as James McNeil Whistler and Vincent Van Gogh made important contributions to the impressionist movement. One of impressionism's key influences was *japonisme*, the vogue for Japanese art and culture that swept mid-century France. Many impressionist painters admired and found inspiration in the *ukiyo-e*, or woodblock prints of Japanese artists, notably Hiroshige. Monet and Degas in particular drew inspiration from this artistic school. The Parisian artistic avant-garde of the late nineteenth century involved interactions between French and foreign artists, between domestic and global influences that made it both national and transnational.[3]

While becoming increasingly immersed in this new art world Gauguin was building his life as a young family and professional man, setting up conflicts between bourgeois and artistic imperatives that would haunt him for years to come. At the end of 1872 Gauguin met a young woman from Copenhagen, Mette-Sophie Gad. They fell in love and married a year later, producing five children over the next ten years; by his mid-twenties, Gauguin had to all appearances staked out a thoroughly bourgeois life. In 1875 the family even left the Pigalle area for a new apartment in the affluent west end of Paris, the sixteenth arrondissement. Yet appearances often deceive: beneath the façade of the middle-class businessman remained the Peruvian exile, adventurous sailor, and grandson of Flora Tristan. Gauguin continued to socialize with foreigners and radicals, notably the anarchist painter Pissarro. He and Mette began to quarrel about money matters and their increasingly divergent views of their life together. Most important, Gauguin devoted more and more time to his art, painting during his lunch hours and on weekends, frequenting the studios of fellow painters. In 1875 he succeeded in getting a painting accepted to the annual Salon, a considerable triumph but also one that placed him at odds with Pissarro and his other impressionist friends. Pissarro began consciously drawing the younger man into avant-garde circles, and by 1877—although he still had ties to the world of finance—Gauguin considered himself a full-time painter. Much to his wife's consternation he left his job as a stockbroker and moved the family across town to Montparnasse, a seamy area not yet noted as an artistic center. By the end of the decade he was presenting his work regularly in impressionist exhibits. This had a fatal impact on his family life: after briefly moving with his wife and five children to Copenhagen, Gauguin abandoned them to return to Paris in 1885. He would never live with his family again.

For the rest of his life Gauguin would devote himself to his art, ever searching for new inspiration and new horizons, ever worried about money and living on the edge. It is easy to view him as the classic refugee from bourgeois propriety, the bohemian who renounced home, family, and financial stability for creative inspiration. This has been a traditional perspective on Gauguin, encouraged by W. Somerset Maugham's great biographical novel *The Moon and Sixpence*. Yet one might more sensibly view Gauguin as typifying a different vision of French life, one who did not so much renounce middle class respectability as never fit into it in the first place. He had spent much of his childhood in Latin America and his early adult years as a sailor at sea before simultaneously pursuing both art and business, ultimately abandoning the latter for the former. With a wife and family in Denmark, Gauguin exemplified the interaction between France and the world, in particular how life beyond the nation's borders influenced what it meant to be French.

Gauguin's flight from conventional domesticity paralleled his evolution as an artist. By the late 1880s he and other Parisian painters, notably Cézanne, Van Gogh, and Henri de Toulouse-Lautrec, were moving away from impressionism to a new style that, twenty years later, British art critic Roger Fry would baptize "post-impressionism." It was by no means easy to define, especially because its major practitioners did not identify as belonging to a unified artistic school or even accept the term. In general, however, the artists noted above differed from their impressionist colleagues by focusing less on the purely visual and more on symbolism and emotion. One can contrast the diaphanous imagery of Monet's greatest paintings with the bold, vibrant colors of Van Gogh and Gauguin, colors that appealed to the heart as much as to the eye.[4]

Gauguin's new post-impressionist perspective developed in tandem with his increasing attraction to exoticism and empire. This went hand in hand with a new French interest in colonialism after 1870. The French people overthrew Napoleon III's Second Empire that year and replaced it with the Third Republic, but ironically the new republic would go on to build the greatest overseas empire in the nation's history. During the 1880s France significantly expanded its overseas holdings, conquering Annam and Tonkin to create the new colony of French Indochina while also carving out new colonial possessions in large parts of Africa. The contradictions of republican empire, of civilizing nonwhite natives by force of arms, became key to the Third Republic. In these years, empire represented what was new and dynamic about French life.

Seen from this perspective, it is not surprising that Gauguin would find himself drawn to *la France outre-mer*, overseas France. In his explorations of the French margins the painter moved, accidentally but with a certain underlying logic, from the provinces to colonies in the old and then the new empire; in doing so he replicated in his personal life the direction of republican imperialism in general, from the integration of the provinces to the conquest of colonies overseas. After struggling in Paris to provide for himself and his young son Clovis, whom he had brought with him from Copenhagen, Gauguin left the little boy in boarding school and relocated to Brittany in 1886. One of the poorest places in France, Celtic Brittany seemed in many ways a place apart from the mainstream of French life, a kind of internal colony. Settling in the picturesque little port of Pont-Aven, where American painters had founded an artists' colony earlier in the century, Gauguin spent several months painting charming landscapes and portraits of women in traditional Breton costumes.

He returned to Paris the following year, but both his sojourn in Brittany and his reading of writers such as Pierre Loti had ignited in him a desire for exotic locales, both as a source of artistic inspiration and as a comfortable place to live freely and cheaply. Madagascar, much in the news as the French busily established colonial rule there, was one object of his fantasies. A more realistic opportunity soon presented itself, however: since Gauguin's brother-in-law lived in Panama, he decided to go there and earn money by working on the canal. Setting sail in April 1887, he found the Panama Canal zone a pestilent hellhole and only lasted two weeks there, fleeing for the more welcoming shores of Martinique. There he lived for several months just outside Saint-Pierre, the vibrant and polyglot "Paris of the Caribbean." It was Gauguin's first exposure to a nonwhite colonial society, whose lush landscapes and beautiful Creole women fascinated him. As he later wrote, "I had a decisive experience on Martinique. It was only there that I felt like my real self."[5]

Illness forced Gauguin to return to France at the end of 1887, where he once again immersed himself in the world of the Parisian artistic avant-garde. Yet the romance of far horizons still beckoned powerfully. In the fall of 1888 Gauguin accepted an invitation from Van Gogh to live and paint with him Arles, the Provençal city where he had a studio and would do some of his most important work. The two great artists lived together for two months until the celebrated episode in which Van Gogh cut off his ear and gave it to a prostitute. Gauguin left immediately and the two never saw each other again, although they remained in touch until Van Gogh's death two years later.

Although he returned to Paris, for Gauguin the lure of empire he had first experienced in Martinique proved ever more powerful. He enthusiastically visited the 1889 Paris exposition, observing with relish the Cambodian sculptures and Javanese dancers. The painter's imagination also began to focus on Tahiti after reading Loti's autobiographical novel *The Marriage of Loti*; when a friend suggested moving there in 1890, he decided to do so. Gauguin made one final trip to Copenhagen to visit his wife and children—the last time he would ever see them—and then in the spring of 1891 boarded the ship *Océanien* in Marseilles, bound for the Pacific and a new life.

Far from an unspoiled new land, Tahiti in the late nineteenth century had been dealing with a variety of Europeans for well over a century. Polynesians first arrived in Tahiti in about 1000 AD, after a long series of ocean voyages from western Polynesia. There they established a society of separate clans ruled by individual chiefs. Although reports of Europeans sighting the country go back to the sixteenth century, the first sustained contacts occurred in the mid-eighteenth, primarily with British and French explorers. British captain James Wallis arrived in 1767, followed a year later by the famed voyagers Louis-Antoine de Bougainville of France and James Cook of Britain. Cook in particular returned several times to Tahiti over the next ten years. In 1788 the *HMS Bounty*, commanded by the infamous Captain William Bligh, arrived in the island and stayed there for several months, collecting breadfruit trees to transplant to Britain's slave colonies in the Caribbean. The famous mutiny took place a few weeks after the ship left Tahiti, and some of the mutineers returned there to settle permanently.[6]

By the beginning of the nineteenth century Europeans had established a permanent presence in the island. Tahiti became a regular port of call for whaling ships, whose crews introduced alcohol, venereal disease and other scourges to the local inhabitants. As a result, Tahiti experienced a demographic disaster during the first half of the nineteenth century, the population dropping by at least two thirds. Whalers, merchants, and other visiting Europeans also crafted the enduring image of Tahiti as an earthly paradise, blessed with lush green mountains, pristine beaches, and sensual, beautiful women. The other major group of Europeans that came to Tahiti in the early nineteenth century, missionaries, strongly opposed these libidinal fantasies. In 1797 representatives of the London Missionary Society arrived in Tahiti, and immediately set out trying to convert the country to Christianity.

The activities of both sailors and missionaries led first to the unification of the Tahitian islands, and ultimately to the imposition of French colonial rule. One of the leading families on the island managed to craft alliances with both the *Bounty* mutineers and the missionaries, enabling it to eventually rise to dominance as the Pomare dynasty. In 1790 tribal chief Tu declared himself King Pomare I, and he and his descendants began extending their rule across Tahiti and the other neighboring islands. His son, Pomare II, succeeded him in 1803 and began working closely with the British missionaries, who converted him to Protestantism in 1812. Members of the London Missionary Society went on to found the Tahitian capital of Papeete in 1812 and convert the entire country to Christianity in 1820.

The increasing influence of British missionaries soon brought trouble with the French. In 1838 the French launched a punitive naval expedition against the islands after Queen Pomare IV expelled two French Catholic priests. Four years later, after chiefly negotiating with families hostile to the Pomare dynasty, France established a protectorate over the Tahitian islands. This precipitated a war between the French and the Pomares which France won, using its victory further to increase its power over the country. In 1877 Queen Pomare IV died after fifty years in power, and the French persuaded her son to abdicate in favor of French rule. Tahiti thus became a formal colony of France in 1880, and has remained a part of the French nation ever since.

This was the land that welcomed the great painter seeking far horizons. Paul Gauguin arrived in Tahiti on June 7, 1891, his forty-third birthday. He moved into lodgings in the capital city of Papeete and began immersing himself in local life, searching for artistic inspiration and exotic adventure. In a letter to his wife Mette he described his first impressions:

> Such a beautiful night it is. Thousands of persons are doing the same as I do this night; abandon themselves to sheer living, leaving their children to grow up quite alone. All these people roam about everywhere, no matter into what village, no matter by what road, sleeping in any house, eating, etc., without even returning thanks, being equally ready to reciprocate. And these people are called savages! . . . They sing; they never steal; my door is never closed; they do not kill . . . and they are called savages! I heard of the death of King Pomare with keen regret. The Tahitian soil is becoming quite French, and the old order is gradually disappearing.[7] [letter of July 1891, cited in Malingue, 163]

In his paean to traditional Tahitian life, Gauguin failed to recognize his own role in its decline, and in the French colonial enterprise there.

It soon became clear that there was more to the islands than his image of an unspoiled natural paradise. Shortly after Gauguin's arrival Tahiti held the funeral of its last king, Pomare V, who had abdicated a decade earlier and surrendered to French rule. Although blessed with undeniable physical beauty, the new colony had few natural resources and a dramatically declining population. Papeete itself was a small tropical port with a few thousand people, dominated by a white elite of mostly British, American, and German origin. Most French residents lived in the capital, and many struggled to survive, at times embodying the stereotype of the poor white man down on his luck in the colonies.

Gauguin embraced life in Tahiti enthusiastically. He circulated widely in local society, went to parties, especially the Bastille Day celebration on July 14, and initiated sexual liaisons with young Tahitian women. His bohemian lifestyle and flouting of social conventions, above all his open affairs with *vahines*, Indigenous women, soon scandalized white colonial society. This had serious financial implications for Gauguin, since it meant local people with money would not pay him to paint their portraits. Moreover, he fell afoul of the colonial governor, Théodore Lacascade, a mixed-race man from Guadeloupe whom Gauguin constantly referred to as "the negro Lascascade." For Gauguin Papeete seemed too European (and expensive), not the romantic Tahiti he had crossed the world to find. He therefore moved out of the city into a house in the beautiful seaside village of Mataiea, a place that to him seemed to embody authentic Tahitian culture.[8]

The journey that brought Gauguin from Paris to Tahiti via Brittany, Provence, and Martinique took place in the context of the broader relationship between art, empire, and the avant-garde in modern France. During the early nineteenth century French interest in the Middle East, especially after Napoleon's invasion of Egypt, helped fuel the orientalist school of art. Paintings like Théodore Géricault *The Raft of the Medusa* (1819) and Eugène Délacroix *The Massacre at Chios* (1824) depicted North African subjects and landscapes in vibrant, lurid colors, exemplifying a European fascination with the oriental "other." Orientalism was a major influence in

French art during the early nineteenth century, depicting North Africa and the Middle East as exotic and sensual, and forming a key aesthetic backdrop for the nation's conquest of Algeria in 1830.

The 1880s witnessed the rise of a new French art movement, symbolism, that would also feed into a fascination with empire and the exotic. In 1886 poet Jean Moréas published the symbolist manifesto in *Le Figaro*, launching a movement that spread across the art world, enlisting members such as Edvard Munch in Norway and Gustav Klimt in Austria. Beginning as a literary movement, symbolism embraced subjectivity and idealism, rejecting naturalism in favor of neo-Romanticism's emphasis on emotion and the dreamscape. Not surprisingly many abstract artists embraced symbolism, turning against realism to underscore the links between the exterior world and the artist's inner vision. Gauguin's emphasis on primitivist art and the exotic soon became seen as a major representative of symbolist art; for him, escape from the artificiality of Western civilization lay in the discovery of the more authentic cultures of the colonial world. Gauguin's own work thus rested upon a long-standing French fascination with exotic imagery and with the world of modern empire.

For the next two years Gauguin lived and painted in Mataiea, creating some of his most memorable and famous works. Paintings such as *Tahitian Women on the Beach* and *Woman with a Flower* (both 1891) used vibrant colors to give a lush, sensual portrayal of the people of Tahiti. In Tahiti Gauguin became a pioneer of primitivist art, the celebration of non-Western artistic styles and motifs that would become extremely popular in Parisian art circles during the early twentieth century, especially after World War I. Gauguin's Tahitian paintings reveal an often exoticist's vision of the islands as a place dominated by nature, spirituality, and sexual freedom, a sharp contrast to the Europe the painter had left behind. He saw himself as celebrating an authentic Tahitian culture, although his emphasis on female sexuality went together with the frequently exploitative nature of his relationships with very young (often adolescent) women. Moreover, Gauguin's focus on the picturesque and exotic masked the damage to the culture and people he celebrated by the French colonial rule that made his own presence there possible.

Gauguin's own life in Tahiti was in many ways anything but idyllic. By 1892 he had contracted syphilis, and his health began to decline. In spite of his dreams of living off tropical fruit and fish he found it cost money to survive in Tahiti, and at times he was so poor he was reduced to selling his paintings for food to local shopkeepers. Ironically, for a man who had sought to escape the artificiality of French life, he depended utterly upon the mail boats from France that brought news of family and friends, and in particular funds from the sale of his paintings there. Largely rejected by the local European community as a classic example of the degenerate white man in the tropics, Gauguin at one point attempted to take his own life.

Yet Tahiti also gave Paul Gauguin the freedom to pursue his own creativity in a setting of matchless physical beauty, and while he may at times have regretted his exile there, in the end he stood by it. In 1893 Gauguin returned to France, arriving in Marseilles in August and plunging himself back into the life of the art world. In November he held a major exhibition of his work at a Parisian gallery. Some critics praised the beauty and innovative style of Gauguin's work, while others considered it exoticizing and exploitative. By the beginning of 1895 Gauguin had enough of Paris and returned to Tahiti for good. He moved into a hut in the small village of Punaauia, outside Papeete, began an affair with a young Tahitian woman named Pau'ura, and started painting again. However, his physical condition continued to deteriorate, and he gradually sank into despair. In 1901, no longer able to support himself, Gauguin sold his hut and moved to the Marquesas, a remote island chain part of French Polynesia where he hoped once more to find authentic Tahitian culture. There in a small village he built his last home, which he called "The House of Pleasure" (*la maison du jouir*) and spent his final days painting and feuding with the colonial authorities. Poor and alone, Paul Gauguin died on May 8, 1903, at the young age of fifty-four.

Ever since his death, Paul Gauguin's Tahitian painting has remained both highly desirable and deeply controversial. Many art historians have condemned him as sexist, racist, and exoticist, while others have emphasized his advocacy for the cultures he portrayed in his brilliant works of art. In the introduction to a recent book of scholarship about Gauguin, the feminist art historian Norma Broude asked: "Was Gauguin's appetite for difference and the diversity of 'others' a prescient and creative expansion of his own identity and point of view as an already multicultural Frenchman, constituting a legitimate chapter in the history of French and world art? Or should his art be seen instead as a misguided and insufficiently informed translation of Indigenous cultures that were not his own, a cross-cultural appropriation and commodification that failed to enrich the cultural content or to respect the point of view of its traditional sources?"[9] I would argue that both perspectives have some merit; in many ways Gauguin approached Tahiti as an elitist Frenchman and citizen of empire, while at the same time Tahitian visions of art and culture spoke to his own sense of liminality in France.

Of Peruvian descent, with a Danish wife, French and Tahitian mistresses, and children in several countries, Paul Gauguin led a life both French and transnational at the same time. While in many ways he rejected the ideal of republican empire, seeking in Tahiti a place that remained immune from it, at the same time he not only represented but powerfully contributed to its appeal, both in his art and his life. In particular, the image of Tahitian women as sensual, alluring, and exotic constructed empire as a space for the gratification of European male desire, an escape from bourgeois domesticity at home. His exotic, primitivist vision of Tahiti helped shape life in those islands during the years to come, while conversely exercising an important influence on avant-garde French culture. Gauguin exemplified the two-way interaction between metropole and colony under the Third Republic, the global reach of French culture and the many influences from throughout the world that shaped it. He also underscored the importance of a particular locality, French colonial Tahiti, in illustrating the interactions between France and the world. In both respects Gauguin portrayed modern France as a transnational nation.

Part 3

Transnational France in the

Era of the World Wars

No period of modern history more clearly reveals the transnational character of life in France than the world wars of the early twentieth century. As the nation engaged in them as both participant and battleground, the French people experienced firsthand the challenges and horrors of global warfare. World Wars I and II transformed France, first straining and ultimately breaking the Third Republic. They reframed its relationships with its European neighbors, its overseas empire, and its great American republican ally. In 1944 France emerged from the era of the two world wars damaged and weakened, into a world forever changed. The grand nation had survived and would go on to enjoy unprecedented prosperity in the postwar era, but its integration into global networks would play a greater role than ever in its national life.

The era of the world wars would test the Third Republic like never before. When the First World War broke out in 1914 the republic had survived several major challenges, having already attained a greater age than any French regime since the Bourbon monarchy of the eighteenth century. The Great War would illustrate the deep roots it had sunk into French society, enabling it to survive a conflict that would topple regimes all over Europe. The war would also, however, reveal challenges to the Third Republic that would only increase during the interwar years, ultimately leaving it vulnerable to the new challenge posed by a powerful and vengeful Nazi Germany. The struggle against conquest and occupation would test French society to the utmost, exemplifying both the national will and the impact of the global war against fascism. During the early twentieth century, therefore, France's struggle for national survival would assume a definite transnational dimension.

France and the World during the Great War

The years before the outbreak of the first World War, known in hindsight as the belle epoque, witnessed the zenith of Europe's global power and prosperity. The era seemed to be a golden age, one that had known no major wars since 1871 and was blessed with an ever-growing economy following the 1890s depression. European empires covered the globe, and even though most citizens of Britain, France, and other European nations would never see the colonies they could take comfort and pride in the global superiority of their homelands. The peoples of Europe enjoyed better material conditions, such as food and shelter, than ever before. The boundless optimism of the age led many to assume that progress and prosperity would only continue into the indeterminate future.

A closer inspection of the world's condition at the dawn of the twentieth century illustrates the instability and ultimately unviability of this rosy portrait. In most parts of Europe, the middle classes still struggled for political representation; France remained the only republic in Europe, while kings and emperors ruled much of the continent. As Europe's working class grew it frequently felt marginalized and excluded from the general prosperity, often turning to radical social and political activism. The dawn of the twentieth century saw the formation of mass-based labor unions and socialist parties, often clamoring not just for higher wages and better working conditions but also for the overthrow of the capitalist system in general. Moreover, the idea that Europeans no longer went to war in the belle epoque was an illusion; European states had largely succeeded in consigning national rivalries to the colonial peripheries of Asia and Africa. When war did come to Europe, it did so as a result of great power competition and nationalist challenges to imperial rule in the semi-colonial zone of the Balkans. The famous "powder keg of Europe," the region produced numerous conflicts during the early twentieth century, but thanks to the interlocking series of great power alliances they spilled over into what became the First World War.

Although France lay on the other side of Europe from the Balkans, its alliance with other European powers, and its rivalry with Germany, gave it a central role in the impending conflict. France and Germany had never resolved the Franco-Prussian war, especially the German annexation of Alsace-Lorraine, and the alliance system of the belle epoque had largely developed around their continued enmity. By the early twentieth century the French had secured alliances with Russia and Britain, thus confronting Germany with the prospect of a two-front war, while the Germans had allied with Austria-Hungary and the Ottoman Empire. When the Balkan crisis broke with the Serb nationalist assassination of Austrian Archduke Francis Ferdinand in June 1914, a chain of events unfolded leading inexorably to war. The Russians mobilized their armies to defend Serbia against the Austrians, which led Germany to prepare for war against Russia and its ally France. On August 3 Germany declared war on France, and the next day its armies invaded Belgium, heading for Paris. The war to end all wars had begun.

With the signal exception of civil wars, modern warfare is by definition a transnational event, pitting one people against another. For the French, World War I went beyond the specific conflict with Germany to assume a global character. After the failure of the German offensive in the fall of 1914, the war settled down into the agonizing stalemate of trench warfare, a bloody standoff that would produce millions of casualties and no military progress whatsoever. Germany had succeeded in occupying roughly 10 percent of France, the northeast of the country, so that the frontier between the two sides in the West ran right through French territory. As first the British and their dominions and then the United States sent their armies to the war, they deployed them in France. The French government also imported more than half a million colonial subjects to fight on its battlefields and work in its war plants; it even imported thousands of laborers from China. Paris became a meeting place for people from a variety of countries, its spectacular diversity a concrete example of a world at war. The famous Christmas truces of 1914, when British and German soldiers in France spontaneously fraternized to celebrate the holiday, demonstrated that the encounters of peoples brought together in the global conflict could at times take strange and unexpected forms.

France thus served as the great battlefield of World War I, the place where armies from Europe and America fought for victory and global supremacy. Ultimately those forces, not France itself, determined the outcome of the war. In March 1917 revolutionaries overthrew the czarist empire in Russia, setting in motion a chain of events that led to the Bolshevik seizure of power in November and the new Soviet regime's withdrawal from the war the following January. This freed up German forces to stage a new offensive into France during that spring, right when American troops were beginning to arrive in force on the battlefields of the Western Front. It came down to a race between the Germans and the Americans, one which America won thanks to its massive supply of fresh manpower. Although at first the German offensive carried all before it, threatening Paris as it had in 1914, by the end of the spring it had clearly failed, and a massive French counterattack in July spelled its doom. Germany soon began negotiating for an end to the war, a process that took several months. In the first week of November revolution broke out in Germany, overthrowing the imperial regime. A few days later, on November 11, 1918, German delegates signed an armistice ending hostilities. After more than four years of war, and well more than one million combat deaths, France and its allies had at last won the Great War.

It remained to make the peace. On January 18, 1919, the formal peace conference opened in Paris. Similar to the Congress of Vienna a century earlier, the Paris peace conference set out both to finalize the end of hostilities and to remake the world, but on a much greater scale. The Paris Peace Conference was a truly global event, and it represented one of the most spectacular transnational moments in the history of modern France. Not only did all the belligerent powers take part, but delegations from many colonies in Asia and Africa attended with the hope of winning greater autonomy or even independence for their peoples. Delegates from Africa and the Americas held a global Pan-African Congress in the city, whereas the British refusal to allow an Egyptian delegation to attend the peace conference sparked the Wafd revolution in that country. For a few months in 1919, Paris became the capital of the world.

The Paris Peace Conference formalized and underscored France's victory in World War I, but it also revealed some of the challenges facing the nation in the new century. The Treaty of Versailles made France the strongest power on the European continent, and its division of the German colonies among the victorious powers made the French empire larger than ever. Yet this new predominance rested upon situations that would not last: the defeat and humiliation of imperial Germany, and the collapse of revolutionary Russia into civil war. The two largest and potentially most powerful countries in Europe, both nations would soon recover, posing new challenges to French superiority on the continent. Moreover, France's alliances with the new states of eastern Europe, like Poland and Czechoslovakia, created out of the ruins of the German and Russian empires, would commit it to the ultimately hopeless task of defending the Versailles order against bigger and stronger powers.

At home France had to deal with the impact of more than one million dead and many more permanently disabled young men, and the need to rebuild the regions devastated by war and German occupation. The French establishment had easily defeated the threat of insurrection that swept so much of Europe in 1919, but the creation of the new French Communist Party a year later in alliance with the Soviet Union served as a reminder that not all in France accepted the capitalist order. During the interwar years the French birth rate continued the steady decline begun in the nineteenth century, approaching zero population growth by the 1930s and making France only the fifth largest nation in Europe. The empire was larger than ever, but the interwar years also brought the rise of anti-colonial movements, especially in Indochina.

For many in France, the 1920s and 1930s represented a period of anxiety. The nation experienced some prosperity and many intellectual and cultural achievements, yet the uncertain international situation often overshadowed them. During the decade after the armistice the French economy made significant progress, and France began to adopt the kind of mass production, exemplified by the gigantic Renault and Citroën auto plants, that had made America an industrial giant. Not all benefitted from this, however;

working class wages did not rise significantly, and many members of the middle classes who had depended on investments and annuities saw them disappear in the postwar era. Although the effort to pass female suffrage failed in 1919, French women became more and more prominent in the workforce, stoking conservative fears about the dangers posed by feminism to the national birth rate.

During the interwar years France became more than ever a transnational nation; global influences played a central role in national life, for good and for ill. The turmoil of postwar central and eastern Europe generated large numbers of refugees, many of whom sought shelter in France. White Russians, representatives of the losing side in the Russian Civil War, became a fixture in Paris, running nightclubs and driving taxicabs. Many others fleeing their homelands in search of a better life came to France. In 1924 the United States passed the Johnson-Reed Act, sharply limiting immigration from eastern Europe. With the closing of the gateway to America, France emerged in the 1920s as the largest immigrant nation in the world. Most of the new arrivals ended up in working class jobs such as steel manufacturing and the garment industry, but some also worked in agriculture.

At the same time, France and Paris in particular played host to a burgeoning number of tourists, especially but not only Americans. An illustrious colony of expatriate American writers and artists, including Gertrude Stein, Ernest Hemingway, and F. Scott Fitzgerald, settled on the Left Bank of Paris, enjoying both intellectual stimulation and cheap rent. Another settlement of Americans, primarily Black musicians catering to the tremendous popularity of jazz in Paris, took root in Montmartre, on the other side of the river. For these people, Paris was a place of endless amusements, in Hemingway's words "a moveable feast."

In contrast, many others came to France not in search of good times but out of desperation. The rise of fascism in Germany and elsewhere during the 1930s brought a new flood of refugees; as the number of democracies dwindled in Europe, France increasingly became the destination for those who had nowhere else to go. Penniless outsiders clustered in cheap hotels and cafes in Parisian neighborhoods such as the Marais, searching for any kind of work they could do without papers and hoping against hope for better days. A small colony of German antifascist intellectuals, including illustrious names such as Thomas Mann and Bertolt Brecht, settled in Mediterranean port of Sanary-sur-Mer. By the end of the decade it seemed the universal nation had become the universal refuge.

Tragically and all too often fatally for many of these desperate people, France in the end would prove no safe harbor from the rising tide of European fascism during the 1930s. The Depression came late to France, not seriously affecting the national economy until 1931, but once in place it endured for the rest of the decade. Although the failure of successive French governments to cope with the crisis did not destroy democracy, as it did in Germany and elsewhere, nonetheless weakened the republican consensus in France. Especially compared with the economic dynamism of Nazi Germany, which brought that nation out of the depression in two years, the Third Republic seemed listless and ineffectual. The successes of fascism abroad inspired imitators at home, which by 1934 had become powerful enough to pose a direct threat to the regime. That year, in response to fascist rioting in Paris, the main parties of the French Left came together in an alliance called the Popular Front, dedicated to preserving the republic. In 1936 the coalition of Socialists, Communists, and Radicals won the national elections, electing the Jewish Socialist Léon Blum prime minister of France. In the dark days of the 1930s in Europe, the France of the Popular Front stood out as a beacon of hope, isolated but resolute nonetheless.

Hope in the Popular Front proved vain. The regime only lasted until 1938, prey both to internal dissension and to the determined opposition of the French Right, many of whom embraced the bitter belief "Better Hitler than Blum." At the same time, while the French struggled with their internal divisions Nazi Germany increasingly challenged the postwar order in Europe. Since its wartime allies Britain and America showed little interest in European affairs, France largely had to confront this threat on its own. The Nazis began rearming Germany soon after they came to power, and in March 1936 openly defied the Versailles Treaty by marching troops into the Rhineland, the area between the Rhine River and the French border that had been demilitarized as part of the peace settlement. Paris and London did nothing to stop Nazi Germany, which scored its first major foreign policy success.

The failure of France and the Western allies to protest this action effectively gave Nazi Germany a green light to pursue its expansionist policies. A few months later civil war broke out in Spain as conservative forces led by General Francisco Franco attacked Spain's ruling Popular Front government. While Nazi Germany and Fascist Italy strongly aided Franco's forces, leading to their victory in early 1939, France and Britain effectively did nothing to prevent another country from falling to fascism. In March 1938 Germany occupied Austria, again in defiance of Versailles, again without effective protest from France and the West. That fall the Germans forced another crisis, this time over Czechoslovakia as they demanded the right to annex the country's German-speaking Sudetenland region. Czechoslovakia had been one of France's strongest allies in Eastern Europe, yet in the Munich conference that brought the parties together to deal with the crisis (excluding the Soviet Union and Czechoslovakia itself) Hitler prevailed, and Germany was able to annex the wealthiest part of the country. Munich would go on to become an infamous symbol of appeasement, but at the time massive crowds in London and Paris cheered their leaders' ability to keep the peace in Europe.

It soon became evident this was just a stay of execution rather than a true conversion of swords to plowshares. In March 1939 Czechoslovakia collapsed; Slovakia declared independence while Hitler's troops occupied Prague and the rest of the country. This signaled to the French that a peaceful settlement was ultimately impossible, and the nation redoubled its belated efforts to rearm in the face of the ever-more imminent threat from Nazi Germany. Germany's subsequent action underscored the urgency of this. Ignoring the outraged protests from the West, Hitler now set his sights on a new victim, Poland. In the face of this threat, France and Britain pledged to Warsaw to go to war if Germany attacked, hoping to deter Berlin.

In the face of this threat, however, Hitler played a trump card that would shock the world. Horrified by the Nazis' destruction of the once-powerful German Communist Party, after 1933 the Soviets sought alliances with the

Western Allies and encouraged the Popular Front strategy. In 1936 Paris and Moscow signed a formal alliance. However, Stalin felt betrayed by the Munich agreement and secretly began to explore a possible alliance with Germany. On August 23, 1939, Berlin and Moscow announced they had signed a nonaggression pact. The news stunned France and the Western allies, making it clear that the French could no longer count on Russian support in the east against Hitler. A week later, on September 1, German forces launched a massive invasion of Poland. France and Britain responded by declaring war against Germany on September 3. World War II had begun.

While Germany launched the dreaded Blitzkrieg, or lightning war, against Poland, crushing Polish resistance in three weeks, France and Britain essentially did nothing. The French hoped they could withstand a German attack by sheltering behind the Maginot Line, a massive series of fortifications built along the border with Germany during the 1930s. In France people spoke of *le drôle de guerre*, the phony war. In response to the Nazi-Soviet alliance the government banned the French Communist Party, driving it underground; unlike in 1914, France entered the Second World War politically divided. For several months the nation anxiously awaited the next phase of the war. On May 10, 1940, the long-awaited storm finally broke. Germany invaded the Low Countries, overwhelming them in little more than a week, and then sent its forces storming into France. Britain quickly dispatched forces to France to aid its ally, but in vain. In contrast to 1914, when the thrust of the German invasion went through Belgium, in 1940 Germany attacked further south, through the rugged (and consequently lightly defended) Ardennes Forest.

The speed and power of the German attack—led by the heavily armored Panzer tanks and powerfully supported by the dive bombers of the Luftwaffe, Germany's air force—soon shattered French resistance. By the beginning of June France had clearly lost the war; the French government evacuated Paris for Bordeaux, and millions of people in northern France abandoned their homes and fled south ahead of the advancing German armies. On June 14 the German armies entered Paris as they had nearly seventy years earlier during the Franco-Prussian War, staging a spectacular and heartbreaking march down the Champs-Élysées. This time, however, they had come to stay.

The next four years represented the strangest and most tragic period of modern French history. Not only had France suffered one of its greatest military defeats, it now lay under the complete control of an exceptionally brutal and vengeful enemy. Two days after German troops marched victoriously through Paris the French government sued for peace, signing the armistice agreement with Nazi Germany on June 22. Under its terms Germany would annex Alsace-Lorraine, occupy the majority of the country including the Atlantic Coast, Paris, and everything north of the Loire River, and force France to pay the costs of the occupation. Otherwise, what remained of the country could govern itself in alliance with Berlin, and could retain the French empire.

France soon took advantage of this. During the German invasion the French government had brought Marshal Philippe Pétain, the great military leader of World War I, out of retirement to help cope with the crisis. Pétain soon recognized that the war was lost, and France had to make the best deal it could with the victorious Germans. Appointed prime minister on June 16, he led the negotiations that produced the armistice, and then moved to create a new regime out of the ashes of defeat. On July 1 he moved the government from Bordeaux to the spa town of Vichy in central France. There on July 10 the assembled legislators voted to award full powers to Marshal Pétain, granting him the ability to write a new constitution for a new regime. As in 1870, conquest by Germany led to revolution in France. After seventy years, the Third Republic was no more.

From 1940 to 1944 the people of France had to adjust both to foreign military occupation and to a political revolution that created a new French regime, the Vichy state. Rarely in the nation's history had national and transnational factors interacted so intimately; ever since 1944, historians have debated whether Vichy's "National Revolution" came from Berlin or arose out of French society, and if one could consider it fascist or more generally authoritarian. These are of course very complicated questions: in general, one can say that while the specific outlines of Vichy policy came very much out of the French right's hostility to republican democracy, at the same time Vichy would never have happened without the defeat of 1940 and the support of Nazi Germany. In the broader context of the greatest war the world had ever seen, occupied France struggled to define and redefine itself as a nation.

Vichy's concept of the National Revolution represented a straightforward rejection not only of the Third Republic's liberal democracy but even of the French Revolution itself, going so far as to replace the revolutionary slogan "Liberty, Equality, Fraternity," with "Labor, Fatherland, Family." It adopted the model of the traditional family, with Marshal Pétain as the benevolent, authoritarian father figure. Vichy promoted a more traditional vision of education, firing "leftist" schoolteachers and reintroducing religion into the public school curriculum. It abolished independent labor unions and banned strikes. It also took a strong stance against feminism, emphasizing the role of French women as mothers above all and taking steps to improve the nation's birthrate. Germany required none of these policies, and yet in adapting them Vichy adapted to what it felt the Nazi New Order in Europe called for.

The tragic history of France's Jews during the German occupation offers some important insights into the balance between national and transnational considerations. In 1940 France had some 330,000 Jewish residents, the majority of whom were French citizens. In the modern era France played a complex role in Jewish history: although Napoleon's France was the first nation in Europe to grant Jews citizenship en masse, the Dreyfus Affair played a major role in the birth of modern antisemitism. While the forces in favor of Dreyfus and the republic had triumphed at the turn of the century, Vichy represented in part the revenge of the anti-Dreyfusards. Within months after the armistice of 1940, without any prompting from the occupation authorities, the Vichy regime established its first anti-Semitic legislation, banning Jews from certain positions in industry, civil service, and the professions. By the spring of 1941 the Nazis began rounding up Jews in France and placing them in internment camps. Faced with this increased pressure, Vichy worked out a deal with the Germans: it would help round up and deport foreign Jews if the Nazis left Jews with French citizenship alone. By 1942, after the Germans had decided on the Final Solution, Vichy authorities helped collect Jews for deportation to the East, most notably in the July 1942 roundup of thirteen thousand Parisian Jews. Ultimately some seventy-five thousand Jews in France, roughly one quarter of the entire population, were murdered in the concentration camps of the Nazi regime. Their deaths, and the fact that three quarters of the Jewish population in France survived the war, illustrated the intricate interactions between national and foreign perspectives on antisemitism.

If part of France collaborated with the Nazi occupiers, another part resisted them, and this aspect of French life during the occupation also had an important transnational character. From its beginnings the French resistance took two forms, one outside of metropolitan France, and one inside. On June 18, 1940, Charles de Gaulle, the youngest general in France, broadcast a radio appeal to the French nation from his exile in London appealing for continued resistance to the invader. Although de Gaulle meant above all military resistance, not guerrilla warfare, his radio broadcast launched the idea of the resistance to the Nazi occupation. Winning the loyalty of the thousands of French who fled to Britain during the summer of 1940, de Gaulle secured the recognition of the British government as representative of Free France.

This was all well and good, but it meant little to the people of France, most of whom hadn't even heard his radio broadcast and strongly supported Pétain. Moreover, de Gaulle's residence in London and sponsorship by Britain did not help his claim to be the legitimate leader of France, especially after the British navy sunk the French Mediterranean fleet at Mers-el-Kébir to prevent it from joining the Axis. The solution came from the French empire. In the armistice of 1940 Germany had allowed France to maintain control of its colonies, most of which rallied to Vichy. In Chad, however, Félix Éboué declared his support for de Gaulle in August, and over the next few months rallied French Equatorial Africa in general to the cause. The city of Brazzaville became the first capital of Free France. By the end of the year Tahiti and New Caledonia also declared for de Gaulle. At times the struggle against Vichy merged with anticolonial activism, most notably in Indochina. In 1941 Ho Chi Minh and other Vietnamese revolutionaries founded the Viet Minh, which took up arms against the Japanese occupation but also made it clear it was fighting for national independence from French colonial rule. In 1942 American and British forces invaded North Africa, overwhelming the Vichy forces there. De Gaulle moved from London to establish himself in triumph on "French" soil and began recruiting an army to help in the invasion of France. Ultimately most Free French soldiers would come from the empire. More than ever before, during World War II the colonies thus moved from the margins to the center of French life.

The anti-Nazi resistance inside France itself also illustrated the transnational character of French life during World War II. The resistance began haphazardly, as French people adjusted to the shock of defeat and began looking for ways to challenge German rule. To take part in resistance activities, ranging from distributing leaflets to attacking Vichy and German officials, meant putting one's life, and potentially the lives of one's family, at risk. People who did not have significant social ties could do this more easily, walking away from their own lives into an underground existence. For immigrants, many of whom were already isolated from the mainstream of French society, this came easier. As a result, foreigners played a preponderant role in the French resistance.

For all its heroism, the resistance could not defeat Vichy, let alone Nazi Germany; only the Allies could do that. When the Liberation came in 1944, it did so in the context of complex negotiations between de Gaulle's Free French and the American and British military commands. Although the Allies did not inform de Gaulle of the D-Day landings until their troops were already on the ground, he did eventually get them to agree that any liberated territory in France would be placed under the command of his provisional government. In particular, de Gaulle won the right of Free French troops to liberate Paris, thus underscoring his legitimate rule over the nation as a whole.

Charles de Gaulle flew into Paris the day of the Liberation and led a triumphant march of one million Parisians down the Champs-Élysées as the bells of Notre Dame and other churches pealed in jubilation. By the spring of 1945 Allied and Free French troops completed the liberation of France, and a month later the war in Europe ended with the unconditional surrender of Nazi Germany. The nation had been freed, but not necessarily by its own efforts. The meaning of national liberty in an increasingly globalized world remained to be seen.

7

Lafayette, We Are Here!
France and the Americans during the Great War

A major feature of French life during the twentieth century has been the influence of the United States. The often turbulent relationship between the two great republics, both strongly attached to ideas of liberty and universalism, has not only helped shaped each but has in many ways contributed to defining transnational modernity. Although the American presence in France goes back to the beginnings of the United States, no period was more crucial in establishing this relationship than World War I. Some two million American soldiers crossed the Atlantic during the war, by far the largest group of Americans to leave home up to that time. They played a crucial role in winning the war and, moreover, had a tremendous impact on the French soldiers and civilians they encountered. The First World War marked America's initial steps toward becoming a dominant world power, and it is perhaps only appropriate that it took these steps in France.[1]

Americans have been going to and living in France since there was an America. During the Revolutionary War Benjamin Franklin led a delegation to the French capital; that is where they won American independence into being with the 1783 Treaty of Paris. During the nineteenth century a steady stream of young American men traveled to France to study art and literature, including Black and mixed-race Creoles from Louisiana who went to Paris to pursue studies forbidden to them in the slave South. Americans witnessed firsthand many of the great events of nineteenth century French history, notably the siege and Commune of 1870–1871. But nothing in American history compared with the massive influx of U.S. citizens, soldiers and others during the Great War, an experience that would leave a lasting mark on the peoples of both nations.[2]

For France, World War I was one of the great transnational moments in its modern history. It brought together on French soil the three major influences in its global history—Europe, the French empire, and the United States. In particular, the encounter with America and the Americans had a major impact on the French people: even though the American military presence in France only lasted a couple of years, following which the United States withdrew from active participation in European politics and diplomacy for a generation, the experience of World War I would nonetheless make America and the Americans an enduring part of life in twentieth-century France.

America at War

Well before the United States entered the conflict, individual American citizens volunteered their services in support of France's war effort. As soon as World War I broke out in August 1914 members of the American colony in Paris organized a volunteer ambulance service, enabling U.S. citizens to help at the front in a strictly noncombatant role. Early in 1915 they founded the American Field Service, which for the rest of the war would recruit ambulance drivers and deploy them on the front lines, not only in France but Italy and other parts of the European theater.

The ambulance drivers were some of the first Americans to see action in France during the war. Such work appealed to those who wanted to see action without actually joining the army, in particular college students and intellectuals—entire groups joined from top universities such as Harvard and Stanford. Some of America's most prominent writers of the future, including Ernest Hemingway, John Dos Passos, Archibald MacLeish, E.E. Cummings, and Harry Crosby, got their first glimpse of France during the war and would become central figures in the American expatriate community of Paris during the 1920s. Other Americans, such as Walt Disney and Ray Kroc, the future founder of McDonalds, also drove ambulances in France. In early 1916 Americans living in France convinced the French government to form the Lafayette Escadrille, a unit of American volunteer pilots fighting for the French, that would go on to take part in the great battle of Verdun later that year.[3]

Such Americans constituted, for the most part, the exception that proved the rule during the first years of World War I. Most of their compatriots seemed more than happy to let things take their course in Europe without engaging in the war directly. America's decision to intervene in the First World War was more than a little surprising, representing a major departure from its history. The United States did nonetheless join the war on the side of the Entente, thanks in large part to a series of military and diplomatic errors by Berlin that ultimately cost Germany the war. In 1915, in reaction to the Entente's naval blockade of the Central Powers, Germany began using its U-boats, or submarines to attack British and French shipping—not just naval ships but commercial vessels as well. On May 7, 1915, a German U-boat sank the *Lusitania*, a large British ocean liner, killing 128 American citizens. This created a furor in the United States, leading Germany to abandon the policy for the time being. In January 1917, however, Berlin decided to resume the policy of unrestricted submarine warfare, calculating that even if it led to American intervention, its forces would be triumphant in the west before the United States could mobilize its troops and get them across the Atlantic.

A week later the Germans committed a colossal diplomatic blunder: the German foreign secretary sent a secret telegram to the Mexican government, at the time facing invasion by the American Expeditionary Force under General John J. Pershing, proposing an alliance against the United States that could ultimately return Texas, New Mexico, and Arizona to Mexico. Intercepted and decoded by British intelligence and then leaked to the American press, the Zimmerman telegraph caused an uproar in the United States, revealing what many newspapers termed "the Prussian Invasion Plot." Together with the attacks on American shipping by German submarines it overwhelmed neutral anti-interventionism. On April 2, 1917, President Woodrow Wilson appeared before Congress to request authorization to go to war, and on April 6 the United States formally declared war against the Central Powers.

America chose to enter the war at a turning point in that great conflict. A month earlier revolution had broken out in Russia, largely in response to popular despair over the course of the war, and had overthrown Czar Nicholas II. Although the new provisional government pledged to continue the war effort, many demanded an immediate peace and a more radical regime. On April 16 Bolshevik leader Vladimir Lenin arrived from exile at Petrograd's Finland station, proclaiming his party's intention to push the revolution forward and setting in motion a chain of events that would lead to the establishment of the world's first Communist state that November. Also, in April Germany's powerful Social Democratic Party split in two, the dissidents forming a new antiwar party and beginning to organize among the nation's increasingly restive factory workers. The same month mutinies broke out in the French army, as across the Western Front soldiers refused to obey orders for yet another offensive that would only lead to more pointless slaughter. French workers also began a series of strikes, starting with women in the Parisian garment industry, that increasingly challenged the nation's commitment to the war effort. Across Europe, more and more people questioned the commitment to a conflict that seemed to produce nothing but more corpses, their discontent threatening not only the war effort but the established order in general.[4]

For the French, America's decision to enter the war, coming as it did right when the nation seemed to be at its last gasp, represented an incredibly bright spot in an otherwise dismal spring. For years French diplomats, politicians, and others had labored to convince the United States to join their alliance. Even the fashion industry got involved, its leaders claiming that if Germany crushed France Parisian haute couture might no longer be available to wealthy American women. In late April and early May France sent a high-powered delegation, led by Prime Minister Réné Viviani and Marshall Joseph Joffre, to tour the United States. Everywhere the delegation encountered huge enthusiastic crowds that welcomed it to America and cheered the new alliance.

On June 13 the first detachment of the American Expeditionary Force, led by General Pershing, arrived in Paris. Accompanied by General Joffre and War Minister Painlevé, the two hundred Americans marched in triumph through the French capital, acclaimed by huge throngs of cheering and weeping Parisians. A similarly rapturous welcome greeted the Americans when on July 4, 1917, the next AEF detachments marched through Paris in celebration of America's Independence Day, ending up at the tomb of the Marquis de Lafayette. There Lieutenant Colonel Stanton proclaimed to the listening crowds, "*Nous voilà, Lafayette* [Lafayette, we are here]!"

The benefits of the American alliance were obvious: in 1917 the United States not only had a population over twice that of France, but also the most powerful economy in the world. At the same time, however, it had a very small standing army; not only would it have to quickly enlist a huge number of new soldiers, but also transport them thousands of watery miles to Europe and the Western Front. The American government thus immediately embarked upon the monumental task of enlisting and training millions of young men, many of whom had rarely ventured far beyond their hometowns and nearly a third of whom were illiterate. French excitement about the powerful new ally soon turned to grumbling about the slow pace of the AEF's deployment to the battlefields of France. The first American detachments did not see battle until October, and the bulk of the U.S. armed forces arrived in the spring and summer of 1918.

The Franco-American encounter of the First World War was generally a positive one, but not without its difficulties. Most American soldiers saw little of France; after landing in ports such as Brest or St. Nazaire they generally traveled to training camps or the front lines. Lorraine in particular became the AEF's main staging ground during the war. Often, they were lodged with French families in small villages or farms, whose conditions often came as a shock to soldiers from New York or Chicago. For the French, they had to adjust to hosting large numbers of young men far from home who spoke no French, and who knew nothing of their lives and customs. Inevitably, perhaps, conflicts and misunderstandings arose, often over property damages and American suspicions that they were being overcharged by French peasants whose lives they had come to protect.[5]

Most French people were very impressed by the American soldiers they met. They commented on their impressive physical appearance, describing Americans as tall, well-built, and handsome, in general pleasing to the eye, especially the female eye. In a nation whose own young men were off at war, or who had frequently returned from combat disabled and shattered (if they returned at all), the presence of a seemingly endless supply of healthy youthful soldiers had a striking impact. Americans were also seen as wealthy and free-spending, and while many admired their affluence it also caused problems. The AEF tended to pay very high prices for goods it requisitioned, so its presence in a small French village usually brought a major infusion of cash. This was great for farmers and shopkeepers, but because the presence of the U.S. military often prompted a general rise in prices, it hurt French consumers. Many Americans, in contrast, resented what they saw as overcharging by their French hosts.

Alcohol use and sexual mores also distinguished the two groups during the war. In the United States France had long had a reputation as a land of license, and American authorities worried about the impact of different cultural practices on their soldiers. Not only did France have some of the highest drinking and alcoholism rates in the world during the early twentieth century, but its government issued soldiers a daily ration of red wine. The sight of young American soldiers—unused to alcohol, drunk and disorderly in French cafes—became a frequent occurrence during the war, especially in Parisian neighborhoods like Montmartre. Sexual adventurism was an even greater concern for the AEF command. America's doughboys, as U.S. soldiers were known during the war, left a highly puritanical country for one where prostitution was semi-legal and venereal disease rampant: the French army had counted a million cases of sexually transmitted maladies since the start of the war. President Georges Clemenceau shocked the Americans by suggesting the U.S. Army open official brothels for its soldiers at the front, just as the French had done.

American soldiers often found it easiest to make friends with the children in the towns and villages they passed through. The big, strange soldiers from far away frequently fascinated French boys and girls, who would often try to imitate their marching drills and their ways of speaking, even at times copying American profanities whose meanings they fortunately did not understand. The soldiers' lack of a common language frequently proved less of a barrier to communicating with the children than it did with their parents, especially when the Americans bought gifts for them. At Christmastime in particular, American soldiers would dress up as Santa

Claus and distribute presents to the young people of the village or urban neighborhood where they were stationed. Such positive encounters went a long way toward creating good relations between American soldiers and French civilians, ensuring that as the children grew older they had fond memories of *le temps américain.*

Finally, issues of American race relations also crossed the Atlantic. Some two hundred thousand African Americans served in France during the Great War, most in labor battalions rather than as combatants.[6] All served in racially segregated units. The AEF command was highly distrustful and contemptuous of Black soldiers, regarding them as inferior in general, so when the French called for more military manpower it responded by transferring entire African American units to French military command. The French were grateful for the support and treated the Black soldiers well, who in return were amazed that white people could approach them with dignity and respect. As one army officer noted, "The French soldiers have not the slightest prejudice or feeling. The *poilus* and my boys are great chums, eat, dance, sing, march and fight together in absolute accord."[7]

African American soldiers also found a warm welcome among the French civilian population. This kind and welcoming treatment prompted one soldier to write his mother, "These French people don't bother with no color line business. They treat us so good that the only time I ever know I'm colored is when I look in the glass."[8] French civilians also gradually learned about racial discrimination in the United States, at times noting their surprise at the racist attitudes of white American soldiers and officers. As one French woman wrote to an African American soldier: "Thank you for your friendship, I am happy to give you mine in exchange, because I know now what is your hard condition. I have spoken to white men, and always I have seen the same flash (lightning) in their angry eyes, when I have spoken them of colored men. But I do not fear them for myself; I am afraid of them for you, because they have said me the horrible punishment of colored men in America."[9] Most notably, Black American soldiers introduced jazz to France during the war; in early 1918 a U.S. army band made up of Harlem's finest jazz performers made a triumphal tour of the French countryside, and the new music immediately became a runaway sensation.

The popularity of African American soldiers at times worried the AEF command, which issued warnings to prevent fraternization with local civilians, especially white women. This attitude at times led to conflicts with French authorities, although they of course often pursued similar policies with regard to their own colonial soldiers and workers. The experience of African American soldiers and workers in France during World War I generated a powerful belief that the French did not accept or practice racism, in contrast to white Americans, and would prompt many Blacks to leave the United States for life in Paris after the war.

African Americans were not the only nonwhites to serve in France during the war. The French government also drew heavily upon the manpower resources of its empire, bringing them to serve the national war effort both in its military and its armaments factories. Hundreds of thousands of colonial soldiers, notably the famous *tirailleurs sénégalais*, or African rifles, helped defend France against the Germans, taking part in battles including Verdun and the Somme. Colonial soldiers from North Africa, Indochina, and the Caribbean also served on the battlefields of France. In addition the country also recruited laborers from the empire as well as China to work in war plants, frequently working alongside French women, the other major source of labor in a country whose men had mostly gone off to the front. Whereas the French generally welcomed colonial soldiers like Black Americans, in contrast colonial soldiers often encountered hostility and racist treatment. The different treatment of these peoples of color underscored the complexity of racial attitudes in France at the dawn of the twentieth century.[10]

In general, American soldiers were warmly welcomed in France as vital (if perhaps tardy) allies in the struggle against Germany and for civilization. At one point during the war the West Virginia mother of a soldier fighting in France received a letter from a French woman:

Madame:

Doubtless you are going to be very much surprised on receiving this letter for we do not know each other. I know only, that like me, you are the mother of a soldier for I have had the pleasure, quite recently of lodging your son, Capt. Roberts . . . Your son is truly charming Madam, and it is with great pleasure that we have welcomed him at our fireside, where for a few days he has taken the place of my eldest son, also an officer, who fell for France last year.

Believe me, Madam, that it is with our whole hearts that we welcome your children and receive them, for do they not come to avenge ours, and aid them in liberating our country? . . . We will not forget either that he has been the first of the Allies who has sat at our fireside and that he has made us know your country.[11]

By the spring of 1918 the AEF's troops were numerous enough to make a difference on the Western Front. French tendencies to patronize American soldiers and officers as inexperienced latecomers began to recede as their new allies began winning battles by themselves. When the Germans launched their spring offensive, Marshall Ferdinand Foch could count on more and more doughboys to support French troops. In early June the U.S. Marines fought and won the bloody battle of Belleau Wood, helping to block the German advance on Paris. By the late summer the Americans were fighting more and more battles on their own, and each month landing 250,000 new U.S. troops in French ports. The experience of battle, which their French compatriots had known for years, often came as a shock to the new soldiers; as Captain Frank Tiebaut of the 305th Infantry wrote the Argonne battle of September 1918:

Could anyone who was there ever forget . . . the anxious consultation of watches; the thrill of the take-off; the labored advance over a No Man's Land so barren, churned, pitted and snarled as to defy description; the towering billow of rusty, clinging wire; the flaming signal rockets that sprayed the heavens; the choking, blinding smoke and fog and gas that drenched the valleys, and then—one's utter amazement at finding himself at last within the German stronghold which during four years had been thought impregnable! This was certainly a long way from New York![12]

Ultimately more than one million American soldiers took part in the 1918 counteroffensive that broke the back of the German army and forced Berlin to sue for an armistice.

America also increasingly took the lead in diplomacy during the war. President Wilson was an idealist who had tried to broker a compromise solution before the United States intervened in the conflict, and even afterward he remained committed to the idea that America and its allies should fight not just for territorial gain, but for a resolution that would emphasize international peace and reconciliation rather than national victory. In January 1918 President Wilson announced his vision for peace, encapsulated in his famous Fourteen Points. Emphasizing democracy, national self-determination, and open diplomacy as key to the peaceful resolution of conflicts, the Fourteen Points struck many French leaders as naïve and even arrogant (supposedly President Clemenceau commented "The good Lord had only ten!"). But they proved tremendously popular among a French population weary of war. The Germans negotiated the armistice with the understanding that the final peace treaty would be based on the Fourteen Points. Although the French could justifiably claim they had done the most to win the war, by the end of 1918 it seemed quite possible that America would win the peace.

In 1919 diplomats, political leaders, and others gathered in Paris to negotiate and write the peace treaty that would bring World War I to an end. The Paris Peace Conference, far more than any other event in history up to that point, marked the creation of a united world, and France lay at its center. At no other time in its modern history has France been more transnational, its national experience more universal. Germany was defeated, but other global conflicts had arisen that the peace delegates tried to resolve. In eastern Europe the infant Soviet Union fought for its life, calling for a world revolution to overthrow the capitalist order. Although its representatives did not come to Paris, the delegates there saw it as a major threat to the new world they wished to bring into being and considered ways of suppressing or at least forestalling it. A range of representatives from Europe's colonies did travel to the peace conference, demanding that the democratic order the victorious allies planned for Europe be extended to the imperial world as well. French politics mirrored these global conflicts. Many on the French working class left admired and supported the Soviet experiment, and May Day (May 1) 1919 saw violent demonstrations in Paris calling for a new socialist order. Delegates from France's colonies, including as we shall see in the next chapter the young Ho Chi Minh, also came to the peace conference to demand colonial independence. In 1919 all the world's major conflicts, North vs. South, East vs. West, ran through Paris.

The Paris Peace Conference of 1919 both confirmed and ultimately contradicted America's new leading role in world affairs. In December 1918 Wilson journeyed to Paris, where the French and many others received him enthusiastically as a conquering hero. Nations and peoples throughout the world sent delegations to the conference, which brought the peoples of the world together as never before in history. Wilson's and America's emphasis on a peace and a new world order that focused on democracy, popular sovereignty, and an amicable end to the war appealed to many, but it also encountered resistance among leaders of the other Allied nations who wanted above all to punish Germany and prevent that nation from ever again threatening the established order. The Versailles Treaty that formally ended the war on June 28, 1919, reflected these differences, and has been criticized ever since by diplomatic historians as a bad compromise. In spite of his best efforts Wilson failed to sell the treaty to the American Congress, which refused to ratify it, and during the 1920s America once again embraced isolationism, keeping its distance from the troubles of Europe.

This political retreat did not, however, end the many interactions between America and France that had blossomed during the Great War. American tourism to France reached new heights during the 1920s, spurred both by wartime memories and the strength of the dollar against the franc. The interwar years also saw the birth of a dynamic new American expatriate community of writers and artists in Paris, centered in the Left Bank neighborhood of Saint-Germain-des-Prés. After serving as an ambulance driver in Italy during the war, for example, Ernest Hemingway returned to Europe in 1921. He settled in Paris, then home to an American intellectual community that included Gertrude Stein, F. Scott Fitzgerald, John Dos Passos, and Ezra Pound. There he published his first novel, *The Sun Also Rises*, before leaving the city for Key West in 1928. African Americans developed their own expatriate community, dominated by jazz musicians and centered in the bohemian neighborhood of Montmartre. In 1925 the young singer

Josephine Baker made a spectacular debut in the city, becoming one of France's greatest musical stars and spending the rest of her life in France. After the Armistice Paris became a center of some of the finest music and literature America had to offer during the Jazz Age of the 1920s.

World War I thus brought the world's two great republics, both with powerful and at times competing universal visions, together. In some ways this was temporary, but in others not. Within a year after the armistice the doughboys had gone home, but some who had seen France in wartime came back to visit or live. Exposure to France, especially Paris, reinforced urbanity and modernity back in America: as the 1918 song went, "How 'Ya gonna keep 'em down on the farm? (after they've seen Paree)." For the French as well, wartime contacts with Americans were reinforced by the popularity of American culture, ranging from jazz to Hollywood movies, in the interwar years. The Great War both created and underscored a powerful mutual fascination between the two nations that would play a major role in making France a transnational nation during the twentieth century.

LANDING OF THE "FRENCH 500"—OCTOBER 17, 1790

Fig. 1. *Landing of the "French 500,"* October 17, 1790. Courtesy of Gallia County Historical Society.

Fig. 2. Plaque in Gallipolis commemorating the Marquis de Lafayette and French contributions to America. Courtesy of Gallia County Historical Society.

Fig. 3. Karl Marx and Friedrich Engels, Paris 1844. Alamy DYEJEE.

Fig. 4. *The Execution of Emperor Maximilian of Mexico*. Library of Congress, LC-USZ62-62808.

Fig. 5. Charles Worth working in his Paris salon. Alamy 2BTYOWB.

Fig. 6. Alliance Israélite Universelle looms workshop, 1918. Library of Congress, LC-DIG-anrc-02142.

Fig. 7. *Mauru*. Painting of Tahiti by Paul Gauguin. Library of Congress, LC-USZ62-72244.

Fig. 8. *Our Boys in France*, American Soldiers during World War I. Library of Congress, LC-DIG-ggbain-27879.

Fig. 9. Ho Chi Minh (*foreground*), Moscow 1924. Alamy B9PPJ9.

Fig. 10. Nazi propaganda poster, "Red Poster," mocking the Manouchian group. Alamy RAORT6.

Fig. 11. Josephine Baker with her children. Alamy BPTY6N.

Fig. 12. Street artist performing hip hop in front of the Eiffel Tower. Alamy F093H3.

8

Colonial and Global Revolutionary
The Apprenticeship of Ho Chi Minh

On June 5, 1911, the French ship *Amiral Latouche-Tréville* left Saigon for France, arriving in Marseilles several weeks later. One of the passengers who disembarked in the great Provençal port was a young man from Annam, Nguyen Tat Thanh, seeing the world outside Vietnam for the first time. During his brief stay Thanh remembered having coffee in a café on the Canebière (and being called *monsieur* for the first time in his life) as well as seeing the human misery and prostitution of the dockside areas. At one point he commented to a friend, "Why don't the French civilize their compatriots before doing it to us?" Thanh's initial view of Marseilles, and of France, marked the beginning of his transformation from a young Vietnamese intellectual into a world revolutionary, a transformation he would mark by changing his name from Nguyen Tat Thanh to Nguyen Ai Quoc and ultimately Ho Chi Minh.[1]

As we have seen in this book, France in general and Paris in particular have often been destinations for immigrants and revolutionaries during the modern era. Like Karl Marx before him, the young Ho Chi Minh would settle in Paris for a few years—attracted by the presence of a community from his homeland—and during his life there would mature into a seasoned revolutionary before leaving France to undertake new challenges and opportunities. Unlike Marx, however, Ho Chi Minh arrived as a French subject, part of a colonial migration neither internal nor external but a mixture of both. Moreover, the young Vietnamese revolutionary would negotiate two different visions of universalism during his years abroad: those of the aging

Third Republic and of the young Soviet Union. In France he developed a systematic critique of the contradictions of French universalism before leaving to study in the citadel of world revolution. In more subtle ways he would also challenge Soviet universalism while at the same time embracing its global vision. Ultimately his years abroad would enable Ho Chi Minh to develop a specifically Vietnamese perspective on world revolution.

The land that would produce this great revolutionary leader had been targeted by the French for decades before his birth. During the eighteenth and nineteenth centuries Jesuit missionaries from France had practiced and proselytized their faith widely in Vietnam, and their presence had increasingly prompted the French government to intervene more directly in local affairs. France began its conquest of Vietnam in the 1850s under the Second Empire of Napoleon III. In 1858 the emperor dispatched a major fleet to the area, conquering the city of Saigon a year later. By the time the imperial regime collapsed in Paris in 1870, the French had taken control of large parts of southern Vietnam and Cambodia. In the early 1870s French forces captured Hanoi and seized control of the Vietnamese provinces of Tonkin and Annam, only to be forced out by the Black Flags, an army from China. France returned ten years later, waging a major war against the Chinese as well as Tonkin, and in 1887 formally established the new colony of French Indochina, which would ultimately include Laos as well as Cambodia and Vietnam.

The French ruled Indochina for nearly seventy years, and during that time they made important changes in the life of the region. In Vietnam in particular they confronted a complex series of local cultures—shaped by Confucianism and strongly influenced by China—and tried to impose Western values and administrative practices on them. Although small French colonies developed in cities such as Saigon and Hanoi, relatively few whites chose to leave Europe for colonial Indochina. Instead, the colony became important for its strategic and economic resources, and during the colonial era Saigon became one of the biggest ports in the eastern Pacific. The French also developed a thriving rubber industry there during the early twentieth century, centered in the great rubber plantations of southern Vietnam. Both hostility to French rule and the social changes produced by

French investment in education and industry created a variety of nationalist and anticolonial movements in colonial Vietnam, which would have an important influence on the young revolutionary.[2]

Ho Chi Minh was born in 1890 in Annam as Nguyen Sinh Cung, the first of several names he would bear during his life. His father was an educated man and public official who made sure to educate his son in both the Confucian classics and in French scholarship. The boy thrived at his studies, and at the age of ten his father gave him a new name, Nguyen Tat Thanh ("Nguyen the Accomplished"). In his adolescence Thanh attended a French *lycée* in the imperial capital of Hué, where he first got involved in protests against colonial rule. Rather than continue his education he decided to go abroad, seeking an international perspective on French colonialism. As he commented later in an interview, "The people of Vietnam, including my own father, often wondered who would help them to remove the yoke of French control. Some said Japan, others Great Britain, and some said the United States. I saw that I must go abroad to see for myself. After I had found out how they lived, I would return to help my countrymen."[3]

For the next several years Thanh traveled the world. Upon arrival in Marseilles he applied for admission to France's *Ecole Coloniale*, a training academy for colonial administrators that offered some scholarships to Vietnamese students. The school rejected his application, largely because he had no recommendation from the Governor General of Indochina. Therefore, after a brief sojourn in Le Havre where he worked as a gardener, Thanh signed on with a French shipping company and spent the next several years sailing throughout Africa and the Americas. The details of his early life abroad are hazy, but he seems to have spent several months living in New York, where he attended meetings of Marcus Garvey's Universal Negro Improvement Association in Harlem. By the time World War I erupted Thanh had settled in London. He worked on mastering his English and also involved himself in radical politics, including his first exposure to the writings of Karl Marx. According to his later testimony, these years of travel only increased his hatred of French colonialism. "The French in France are all good. But the French colonialists are very cruel and inhumane. It is the same everywhere ... To the colonialists, the life of an Asian or an African is not worth a penny."[4]

At the end of 1917 Thanh left London for Paris, where he would spend the next six years. The man who returned to France had grown a lot since his first visit to the country. His years at sea had radicalized him, imbuing in the young Vietnamese a life-long opposition to colonialism and a commitment to revolutionary politics. In both America and Britain he had come into contact with anti-colonial activists and gained an appreciation of the struggle against empire as a global phenomenon. For Thanh, France now more than ever represented the imperial overlord and a place where he could both learn more about colonialism and work to overthrow it. After his years in New York and London the young sailor had become a seasoned revolutionary.

Not only Thanh but the French had also changed during his absence. He returned to a France at war, engaged since the summer of 1914 in a bitter struggle for national survival. Desperate for manpower as World War I dragged on, the French brought large numbers of colonial subjects to the metropole to fight in its armies and work in its factories and fields. During the war tens of thousands of Vietnamese traveled to France as both soldiers and workers, creating an expatriate community that attracted the young revolutionary. France brought in nearly one hundred thousand workers and soldiers from colonial Indochina during the war, and while the French government repatriated most of them in the year after the armistice, a substantial number remained. Most Vietnamese worked in industry, but some also came to study in universities, creating small communities of expatriate intellectuals in Paris and other cities.

The year 1917 was also a revolutionary year, and the prospect of radical change also attracted the young Vietnamese to France. During the spring antiwar mutinies had broken out in the French Army, while workers in factories throughout the country began to go on strike not only for higher wages but also for an end to the war. This radical antiwar activism increased during the summer and fall, with more and more people in France believing the war could end in revolution. Thanh arrived in Paris shortly after the Bolshevik seizure of power in Russia, and resonated powerfully with the new Soviet regime's call for the overthrow of global capitalism. In Paris Thanh soon established connections with members of the Vietnamese community—notably leaders such as Phan Chu Trinh and Phan Van Truong—and with journalists and militants of the French Left. Trinh and Truong had both come to France shortly before the war, and while their political activities were modest in scope, the French government arrested them shortly after the beginning of hostilities on suspicion of plotting to overthrow the colonial regime in Vietnam. They were both soon released, but this experience led them to deemphasize radical political activism in France. Trinh gave Thanh a job working in his photography studio, enabling him to live modestly. Settling in a cheap hotel in Montmartre, Thanh attended meetings of the French Socialist Party (SFIO) as well as spending time reading in the Bibliothèque Nationale.[5]

By 1919 Thanh had thrown himself fully into political activism. He could hardly have chosen a more important, central spot to do so than Paris. During the first half of 1919 the French capital hosted the peace conference to bring an end to World War I. As we saw in the previous chapter, leaders of the major belligerent nations, headed by U.S. President Woodrow Wilson, traveled to the city to take part in the negotiations. Moreover, delegates from nations and peoples throughout the world attended the conference to plead their own cases. The victorious powers had to deal not only with making a treaty with Germany but also the threat to the global order posed by the infant Soviet Union, locked in its own brutal civil war. At the same time many colonial and oppressed peoples sent representatives to Paris to petition for autonomy or even independence, often in response to President Wilson's call for national self-determination as a key principle of the postwar international order. More than ever before in its history, during 1919 Paris became the center of the world.[6]

By the early 1920s a small Vietnamese community had developed in the French capital. Its members lived in places across the city, rather than being concentrated in a Vietnamese version of a Chinatown. The most important community institutions, the ones which brought countrymen from throughout the city together, were the Vietnamese restaurants that began springing up in the city after the end of the war. Some Vietnamese had migrated to Paris with their French employers who served in the French colonial administration. In 1923 they formed an Association of Vietnamese

Cooks in the city, which took the lead in aiding Vietnamese in Paris and organizing cultural celebrations such as Tet, the Vietnamese New Year's celebration.

In particular, the French capital was an epicenter for anticolonial activism in the years after World War I. During the early 1920s thousands of North Africans settled in Paris, as did people from Vietnam, colonial sub-Saharan Africa, and the Caribbean. Expatriates from the Americas settled there as well. Some fifteen thousand Latin American expatriates lived in Paris during these years, as did a substantial population of African Americans. Like Thanh, some of these Parisian colonial exiles would later become leaders in their own countries: in 1928, Leopold Senghor, future president of Senegal, would arrive in France to begin his studies at the Sorbonne. At one point in the early twenties Thanh lived in Paris just a few blocks away from Chinese activist Zhou en Lai, who would go on to become the premier of the People's Republic of China. Thanks to Thanh and other colonial activists, interwar Paris was a place of Global South activities.[7]

In this heady atmosphere, Thanh found himself at the center of efforts to combat French colonialism in Vietnam. That summer he helped found a new organization, the Association of Annamite Patriots, to organize Vietnamese workers in France. Although led by Trinh and Truong, it was Thanh who provided much of the energy behind the new group, and in particular he helped reach out beyond a narrow circle of intellectuals to recruit Vietnamese workers in Paris and throughout France. Inspired by the many other colonial groups lobbying the leaders of the Paris Peace Conference, in June Thanh's group decided to make its own appeal. On June 18 it submitted a petition, *Revendications en huit points du peuple annamite* (The Eight-Point Demands of the Annamite People), to the conference calling for the reform of French colonialism in Vietnam and the application there of Wilsonian principles of justice and self-determination.

The document took a fairly moderate tone: it did not ask for national independence, for example, instead focusing on issues such as civil liberties in Vietnam, amnesty for political prisoners, and equal treatment of the Vietnamese and French citizens in colonial Indochina. It was signed "Nguyen Ai Quoc" ("Nguyen the Patriot"). In taking up a new name, Thanh both illustrated his own revolutionary evolution and sought to confuse the French police, who first began to take notice of the Vietnamese revolutionary. Although ignored by the peace conference, the petition had a sizeable influence both in France and in Vietnam, where copies soon appeared in Hanoi. It energized the Vietnamese community in Paris as well as giving Quoc new visibility among the leaders of the SFIO. It also alarmed French officials in the Ministry of Colonies, leading them to call Quoc in for an interview in early September and to assign police agents to follow him. All this brought new prominence to Nguyen Ai Quoc, making him one of the leaders of the Vietnamese expatriates in France.

In July Quoc moved in with Phan Chu Trinh in a spacious apartment in the Gobelins area of the Left Bank, definitely a step up from his lodgings in Montmartre. Now under constant police surveillance, Quoc began publishing articles critical of French colonialism in *Humanité* and other leftist publications. Increasingly he began challenging the more moderate views of Trinh and others, arguing that French rule offered nothing good to the Vietnamese, and the only appropriate approach to it was resistance.

Already a convinced anti-colonial activist, during 1920 Quoc came to learn about and embrace Marxism, which became the other major theoretical and political commitment of his life. He began to attend meetings of both the SFIO and the main trade union confederation, the General Confederation of Labor (CGT). Quoc discovered there was a whole world of radical politics about which he knew very little, and that many French socialists considered anticolonialism of relatively little importance compared to the imminence of world revolution. At the advice of French colleagues he began reading Karl Marx's *Capital* along with other works, learning the basics of Marxist theory and politics.

In the summer of 1920 Quoc read Vladimir Lenin's "Theses on the National and Colonial Question," which the great Soviet leader had just presented to the Second Congress of the Comintern. In this famous essay Lenin clearly identified the struggle against imperialism as a key part of the movement to world revolution, and called for Communists to support colonial nationalist movements even though they were generally led by bourgeois forces. For Quoc, Lenin's statements about anticolonialism came as a revelation: "What emotion, enthusiasm, clear-sightedness, and confidence it instilled in me! I was overjoyed to tears. Though sitting alone in my room, I shouted aloud as if addressing large crowds: Dear martyrs, compatriots! This is what we need, this is the path to our liberation."[8] Lenin's unification of anticapitalism and anticolonialism left a permanent imprint on Quoc. He now saw Communist revolution as the key to the liberation of Vietnam from French rule, and after 1920 he never looked back.

In December 1920 Quoc took part in the SFIO's national congress at Tours, where members debated whether or not to affiliate with the Third International. He spoke briefly at the meeting, attacking French colonialism in Indochina and calling on French Socialists to oppose colonial oppression. Quoc voted with the majority to support adhesion to the Comintern, becoming one of the founding members of the new French Communist Party (PCF), and ensuring that right from its birth the Communists would have to deal with the colonial question; his intervention at Tours underscored the centrality of empire and the colonies to modern French politics in general. With his vote to join the new PCF Quoc thus began a political commitment that would last the rest of his life.

This new affiliation both arose out of and marked Quoc's increasingly radical orientation. In July 1921—after being beaten by the Paris police at Père Lachaise cemetery during a march to honor the fiftieth anniversary of the Paris Commune—Quoc had a major political fight with Trinh, who accused him of being too militant. He ended up moving out of their apartment into much more spartan quarters in northern Paris. At the same time he helped organize a new group, the Intercolonial Union, bringing together workers from Madagascar, Vietnam, and other French colonies. In addition, Quoc began editing a new journal, *Le Paria*, to represent the interests of all France's imperial subjects. The journal circulated widely in France, although the French government viewed it as subversive and threatened to deport those caught reading it. It was officially banned from the colonies, at one-point leading Quoc and his associates to smuggle it overseas inside toy clocks.

Quoc engaged in these activities as a representative of the PCF, quickly becoming its leading expert on colonialism. At the same time, however, he became increasingly disenchanted with the failure of Communists in France to make anticolonialism a priority. He felt that as a result the party often failed to address working class racism, or to show how anticolonial struggles were central to the fight for socialist revolution. During 1922 and 1923 the tone of his articles became more and more hostile to France in general; at one point he called himself Nguyen o Phap, or "Nguyen Who Detests the French."[9] He had moved from pointing out the contradictions in French universalism as it applied to the colonies to seeing the French as the enemies of the Vietnamese in general.

In 1923 a new opportunity presented itself to Quoc. A Soviet official, Dimitri Manuilsky, who had met Quoc at a PCF meeting the previous October, invited him to the Soviet Union to help him prepare a report on colonial questions for the upcoming Fifth Congress of the Comintern. During the early 1920s a number of French Communists made pilgrimages to Russia to see the revolution first-hand, and this was Quoc's opportunity. Quoc jumped at the chance, evading the French police by sneaking out of a movie theater to the Gare du Nord, taking a train to Hamburg disguised as a Chinese businessman, then sailing to Petrograd on a ship aptly named the *Karl Liebknecht*, after the founder of the German Communist Party. He arrived in the USSR on June 30, 1923. In revolutionary Russia Quoc hoped to find a new vision of colonial liberation.

Quoc spent roughly a year and a half in the Soviet Union before moving on to China at the end of 1924. After a few weeks in Petrograd he traveled to Moscow, where Comintern officials put him to work in their Far Eastern Bureau, helping to draft plans for Communist propaganda and activism in Asia. In October he represented Indochina at an International Peasant Conference held in the city, outlining the terrible oppression of the Asian peasantry under colonialism and capitalism and emphasizing their central role in revolutionary movements. The conference agreed to create an International Peasant Council, appointing Quoc to a leadership position.

In December Quoc enrolled as a student in the Communist University of the Toilers of the East. Founded in 1921 and directed by Joseph Stalin, the school had roughly one thousand students, most from Soviet Central Asia, and one hundred fifty instructors. Students learned Marxist theory, labor and revolutionary history, science, and math, as well as receiving military training and working in the kitchen. Instruction was initially in French, gradually transitioning to Russian as students' language skills improved. Although conscious of being the only Vietnamese at the school, Quoc nonetheless enjoyed his time there, spending long hours reading in the libraries and discussing matters of revolutionary theory with fellow students. During his time there he published a pamphlet, *French Colonialism on Trial*, bringing together all his critiques of imperial France.

> It is to the colonial people themselves that we appeal. The day, and that day is coming, when these masses, who have been, in effect, enslaved, regain their freedom, they will then establish a revolutionary Tribunal to try the colonial clique as it deserves.
>
> We are told—but what about civilization? It is true; French colonization brings the railroad, the electric tram, wireless telegraphy (not counting the Gospel and the Declaration of the Rights of Man); the questions are, who opens their wallets to pay for these wonders? Who sweats to build these machines? Who benefits from the welfare they bring? And who receives the dividends they yield?–Is it us, or those who exploit and oppress us? Is it the Blacks of Sudan and the yellow of Annam, or the conquistadors with pink faces, stealing our land and our herds, and taking the fruits of our labor, after killing our countrymen?
>
> France, or more precisely the French people, have repeatedly been used to undertake distant, costly, and bloody, conquests. They are prevailed upon to justify the unspeakable crimes that plague the colonies daily, but go unpunished. Do these people take the least profit from the colonial scramble, or are they exploited, like us, by the same exploiters?[10]

Quoc became well-known among Communist circles in Moscow, speaking at a variety of venues including 1924's May Day celebration and the Fifth Congress in June.

In Moscow Quoc further developed a key idea that he had begun to articulate in Paris. Traditionally Marxism had viewed socialism as a response to advanced capitalism and workers as the revolutionary class par excellence. The fact that the Communist revolution had happened in relatively backward and rural Russia, not Britain or Germany, certainly cast doubt on this perspective, but it still carried considerable weight in Marxist circles. The Bolsheviks themselves tended to consider the peasantry a problem rather than a source of support, a viewpoint that would culminate with the savage repression of Stalinist collectivization of the land in the 1930s. In contrast, Quoc argued not only that peasants in Vietnam and the colonized world were (at least potentially) a revolutionary class, but that the oppressed of colonial Africa and Asia could mount Communist revolutions without waiting for the collapse of capitalism in the West. At the Fifth Congress he addressed the issue frankly:

> I am here in order to continuously remind the International of the existence of the colonies and to point out that the revolution faces a colonial danger as well as a great future in the colonies. It seems to me that the comrades do not entirely comprehend the fact that the fate of the world proletariat, and especially the fate of the proletarian in aggressive countries that have invaded colonies, is closely tied to the fate of the oppressed peoples of the colonies ... Why do you neglect the colonies, while capitalism uses them to support itself, defend itself, and fight you?[11]

If in France Quoc had challenged and ultimately rejected French universalism as masking imperial exploitation, in Moscow he more gently but nonetheless consistently criticized Marxist universalist ideology for misinterpreting the struggles of the Vietnamese under colonial rule.

At the end of 1924 Quoc left Russia for China, settling in Canton for several years. During the rest of the interwar period, he traveled widely, returning briefly to France and for a more extended stay in the late 1930s to Russia. While Quoc lived abroad resistance in Vietnam to French rule gathered strength. During the mid-1920s Tonkinese intellectuals began staging protests against French rule, and at the end of 1927 founded the Vietnamese Nationalist Party, the first major organization advocating independence for Vietnam. The new organization soon attracted significant popular support, often in response to its brazen assassinations of French officials and Vietnamese collaborators. In February 1929 the Nationalists in Hanoi assassinated Hervé Bazin, a French labor recruiter for the rubber plantations who many considered no better than a slave trader. Exactly a year later, the Nationalists staged the biggest anti-colonial revolt in Indochina up to that time, organizing Vietnamese soldiers in the small garrison of Yen Bay to mutiny against their French officers. France suppressed the rising so brutally it effectively destroyed the Nationalist Party.

Rather than destroy Vietnamese nationalism altogether, however, the defeat of Yen Bay left the field open for other anti-colonial efforts. Communism became the most important of these. Like Quoc, many other Vietnamese drew inspiration from the Russian Revolution, especially its condemnations of Western imperialism, and in 1930 Quoc convened a meeting of Vietnamese activists in Hong Kong that founded the Vietnamese Communist Party. It soon changed its name to the Indochinese Communist Party and, although small, during the early 1930s began establishing roots in Vietnamese towns and villages. The colonial government fought back, arresting many Communist activists in the early 1930s. This changed with the advent of France's Popular Front regime in 1936, which released Communists and other political prisoners from jail. The Party was able to operate openly in Vietnam until the start of World War II, when increased the hostility from the regime forced the Vietnamese Communists to return to clandestinity.

In February 1941 Quoc returned to Vietnam for the first time in more than twenty years, adopting the new name Ho Chi Minh, or "he who has been enlightened." Much had changed in his absence. The previous July France had surrendered to Nazi Germany, and a few months later the Japanese invaded French Indochina. Upon his arrival, Minh threw himself into action against the occupiers of his country. He worked with the Communist Party and other political factions to create the "League for the Independence of Vietnam," or Viet Minh. Although dominated by the Indochinese Communist Party, the Viet Minh included people of many different political tendencies, and received foreign aid from both the United States and the Soviet Union. It launched a guerrilla campaign against the Japanese, all the while making it crystal clear that it considered both them and the French its enemies, that its goal was the independence of Vietnam. Ho Chi Minh became the clear leader of the Viet Minh and would spend the rest of his life in Vietnam, fighting for his country's liberation against first the Japanese, then the French, and finally the Americans. In many respects, however, his revolutionary path was laid during those early, seminal years in Paris and Moscow.

The experiences of Karl Marx and Ho Chi Minh in French exile have many similarities, but also some important differences. Both lived in France for only a few years, but in both cases their Parisian sojourns played a major role in their ideological and political development. Both went from their lives in Paris to become global leaders in the struggle for progressive social change. Both also had an impact on revolutionary political activism in France itself. However, whereas Marx lived and died as an expatriate political intellectual, Ho Chi Minh became the revered leader of a nation, one that fought successfully for more than thirty years for national independence. While Marx completely rejected nationalism, Ho Chi Minh integrated it and revolution in ways that dominated and typified Communist movements during the twentieth century. Moreover, the Communism of Ho Chi Minh illustrated a crucial dimension of the movement largely absent from Marx's thinking, the revolt against colonialism. Both great revolutionaries lived in France, but the differences in Parisian life during their eras illustrated and underscored important differences in their philosophies.

The story of Ho Chi Minh during the early years of the twentieth century illustrates contemporary challenges to French universalism in two different respects. The increasing presence of the empire in French life, in this case the growing Vietnamese community in Paris and the metropole, brought new visibility to the contradictions of France's universal vision when applied to the colonies. The presence of an alternate universal vision, that of Soviet Communism, also called into question republican universalism, both in the metropole and the colonies. The life of one Vietnamese activist thus illustrated the interplay of both French and global revolutionary traditions, underscoring the idea of France as a transnational nation. In developing his own vision of Vietnamese national liberation, Ho Chi Minh considered and critically evaluated both French and Marxist universalism. Ultimately the liberation of Vietnam in the years after World War II would come on the nation's own terms, but would also owe a certain debt to both traditions.

9

Foreigners for France

The Manouchian Group and the French Resistance

On the morning of Tuesday, September 28, 1943, Colonel Julius Ritter of the Nazi *Schutzstaffel* (SS) left his office in the seventh arrondissement of Paris and walked out to his waiting Mercedes sedan. Ritter was an experienced Nazi and one of the most highly placed officials in the occupied French capital. Originally trained in labor law, he had gradually risen through Nazi Party ranks to become the head of Germany's forced-labor programs (STO) in France. Reporting directly to Fritz Sauckel, the so-called slavemaster of Europe, Ritter had the responsibility of implementing the agreements between Nazi Germany and Vichy France that resulted in the deportation of hundreds of thousands of young French men across the Rhine as forced laborers during the war. Few aspects of the Occupation more dramatically underscored France's subordination that this sacrifice of its youth, and Colonel Ritter both directed and exemplified it.

Things did not go as the Colonel planned on that Tuesday morning, however. As he walked to his car four men on the sidewalk pulled out guns and staged a deadly attack on Ritter. The first assailant shot at him as he dived into the car to escape, then as he struggled to get out of the opposite side of the vehicle another emptied three bullets into him, fatally wounding him. The attackers also killed Ritter's bodyguard and driver before calmly walking away. At a time when both the Nazi regime in France and its Vichy allies were increasing their pressure on opponents of the Occupation this brazen attack, in broad daylight, on one of the leading German officials in the country represented a spectacular success for the French Resistance.[1]

Or did it? The four assailants, Marcel Rajman, Leo Kneler, Celestino Alfonso, and Spartico Fontano, were devoted to the resistance, but they were not French citizens. Rajman was a Polish Jew and Kneler was a German Jew and veteran of the International Brigades in Spain. Alfonso was a Spaniard who had also fought in the Spanish Civil War before fleeing to France, and Fontano was an Italian antifascist who had spent virtually his entire life in French exile. They were members of the Manouchian Group, which had organized the attack. One of the leading organizations of foreigners in the French Resistance, the Manouchian Group—led by Armenian Communist Missak Manouchian—exemplified the complex nature of the nation's struggle against Nazism.[2]

The history of the French Resistance during World War II is both national and transnational at the same time. The significant participation of foreigners in the struggle against the Nazi occupation testifies to the global and universal character of that struggle, while at the same time the difficulty of including that participation in the national narrative of wartime France underscores the challenge posed by a transnational perspective to traditional histories. Some of the most interesting, and poignant, examples of wartime sacrifice have to do with members of subaltern or marginal groups who commit themselves to the war effort as a way of proving their value to the nation, their worthiness of citizenship. During World War I German Jews signed up for Germany's armed forces in record numbers, to show themselves loyal members of the national community. The famous 442nd Infantry regiment of the U.S. Army, composed entirely of Japanese Americans, some of whose families were imprisoned in internment camps, became the most decorated American army unit in World War II. These and similar examples have a bittersweet flavor, showing the intense devotion of individuals and communities to nations that may very well not have deserved such self-sacrifice.

The story of the Manouchian Group belongs in this category, exemplifying the contribution of foreigners to the French Resistance. In 1943 this small group of foreigners waged war almost single-handedly against the German forces in Paris, scoring some notable triumphs before its destruction. Just as France during the interwar years was a gathering place for immigrants and refugees from throughout Europe and beyond, so did foreigners play a significant role in the struggle to liberate the nation during the dark years of the occupation. The presence of foreigners underscored the transnational character of France, its appeal as a universal nation to people from different parts of the world. Yet it also raised the question, how to consider the contributions of outsiders to what was viewed as a national resistance struggle, indeed a movement for the renewal of the nation? The story of these foreigners who fought for France casts a new light not just on the French Resistance, but on the nature of republican universalism in general.

Foreigners in the French Resistance

On the night of August 24, 1944, as Resistance fighters in Paris waged a guerrilla war of liberation against the forces of the German occupation, a small detachment of General Philippe Leclerc's Free French Armored Division entered the city, the first Allied troops to do so. The next morning the rest of the division followed them, as well as American troops. That afternoon the German head of command formally surrendered control of the capital to the Free French. That evening Charles de Gaulle gave a great speech at Paris City Hall saluting the joyous event. "Paris! Paris outraged! Paris broken! Paris martyred! But Paris liberated! Liberated by itself, liberated by its people with the help of the French armies, with the support and the help of all France, of the France that fights, of the only France, of the real France, of the eternal France!"[3] The French capital, and the nation in general, thus owed its freedom above all to the efforts of its own citizens.

But this was not the entire story. Most of the Free French troops who entered Paris on the night of August 24th were not French at all, but rather political exiles from Spain. When the forces of General Francisco Franco defeated the Republic at the end of the Spanish Civil War in March 1939, more than one hundred thousand political refugees crossed the border into France. Trapped there during the occupation, many went underground and joined the French Resistance, often forming their own organizations. Those who led the liberation of Paris in August 1944 often rode in army vehicles named after Spanish Civil War battles such as Guadalajara and Ebro. For them, the liberation of France simply constituted another phase in the antifascist armed struggle they had waged in Spain. Yet in a nation seeking to portray its liberation as the work of its own citizens, their particular story proved inconvenient and few postwar historians or commentators paid much attention to it. Not until 2004, sixty years after the fact, did the City of Paris honor these men and acknowledge their contribution to the liberation of France.[4]

If one framed the resistance, following Charles de Gaulle and many others, as the story of the French people liberating themselves, what place did that leave for those active in the movement who did not hold French citizenship? If, as in fact happened, foreigners did play a major role in the French resistance, could one still define it as the "French" resistance, a national struggle, or did it become part of the global campaign against fascism? Moreover, did resistance by immigrants and non-citizens justify the propaganda claims of Vichy that the movement as a whole was not French? Such questions go to the heart of a transnational approach to the history of France, as during the Second World War the activities of foreign resistance activists shaped the future of the French nation as a whole.[5]

By the time World War II broke out in 1939, France had some three million foreigners in its overall population of forty-one million, more than any other country in Europe. During the 1920s the growth of the French economy, and the decision of the United States in 1924 to sharply curtail immigration, made France one of the leading immigrant nations in the world. Although the Depression of the 1930s cut back labor migration into France, the political instability of the decade brought new floods of immigrants into the country from Germany, eastern Europe, and finally Spain. On the eve of the new war Paris teemed with refugees from throughout Europe, hoping against hope that France would endure the coming storm and win the new war as it had World War I.

The declaration of war in September 1939 had an immediate impact on France's foreign population. The French government interned thousands of German and Austrian refugees as enemy aliens, in some cases keeping them in custody until the German forces marched in the following June. Many other foreigners volunteered enthusiastically for the French Army, sometimes in large enough numbers so they could form their own units, and many fought with their French colleagues to resist the invasion of May 1940. Polish refugees, for example, formed their own separate army. Like their French colleagues, many sought refuge in Britain, but most were left behind in a country that now ran on German time.[6]

Foreigners in France played an active role in the French Resistance, both as members of their own national organizations and as part of the broader movement. During the interwar years millions of immigrants from Poland and Italy had settled in France, and members of both national groups organized their own resistance groups. The Poles had two organizations, one Communist and one non-Communist, with nearly twenty thousand members between them.[7] Italian resisters were most active in the south, especially near the Italian border. Spaniards were another group of foreigners who took an active role in the resistance in France. Nearly half a million had crossed the Pyrenees during the years of the Spanish Civil War, and while many returned once the war ended, more than two hundred thousand remained in France. Not only did they have firm antifascist convictions, but many of them were war veterans with very useful military experience. Other veterans of the Spanish Civil War, especially men from central and eastern Europe, fled to France in 1939 and were trapped there by the Nazi conquest.

Some of these veterans were German and Austrian exiles, and they helped form the core of German resistance movements against the Nazi occupation of France. By 1941, for example, Toulouse had an active cell of German Communists working with French Resistance organizations. As the occupation continued, from time to time German soldiers would desert and find their way into the German resistance in France, a movement that peaked in 1944 on the eve of the Liberation. As native speakers of the occupier's language, German resistance activists had special skills that they used to spread defeatist propaganda among German soldiers.[8]

In general, people from many different countries joined French Resistance movements, and in doing so underscored their own claims to be accepted as part of the nation. They represented a new version of the universalism inherited from the French Revolution, a belief that saw France as the representative par excellence of universal values of freedom, justice, and progress. Whereas some foreigner resistance activists saw themselves as fighting primarily for the liberation of their own subject lands, others saw their commitment as a way to claim membership in a liberated France after the war. The foreign resistance in France was thus both national and transnational, integrally part of the nation and at the same time connecting it to the broader world.

Not surprisingly, Jews in France played a major role in the French Resistance, in ways that both challenged and reinforced the dichotomy between citizens and foreigners. Their participation generally took two forms: activism in the mainstream resistance, and the organization of specifically Jewish groups to protect the Jewish population. Several, notably the leading postwar intellectual Raymond Aron, joined de Gaulle and the Free French in London. Others worked in the *Musée de l'Homme* group, and many contributed to the underground press, such as Jean-Pierre Lévy who founded *Franc-Tireur*, the official journal of one of the first major resistance organizations. The great historian Marc Bloch worked with the underground and paid the ultimate price for his efforts; the Germans executed him shortly before the Liberation in 1944. These resisters had a particular reason for fighting the Nazi occupation, but for the most part they did so as French citizens, not necessarily as Jews; as one commented, "If I should perish in this adventure, it is for France that I will have died; I do not wish to be considered a victim of Judaism."[9]

Many others, however, especially Jews of foreign origin and nationality, devoted themselves to working in primarily Jewish organizations, ones that often fought to protect their endangered coreligionists in particular. Zionists often played an important role in these efforts. The Amelot Committee, named after the Parisian street where it met, was organized in the summer of 1940 by Zionists and members of the Jewish *Bund* (socialists) to help Jews, especially children, escape occupied France. In 1942 Zionist activists formed the Jewish Army, which eventually had as many as two thousand members, to help Jews escape over the Pyrenees mountains into Spain. By 1944 it had evolved into a military organization fighting alongside the resistance in general.

If one group dominated the Jewish resistance in France, however, it was the Communists. Communist Jews organized their own networks under the aegis of the Party, taking incredible risks and suffering savage repression. They fought both as Communists, inspired by the struggle of the Soviet Union against Nazi Germany, and as Jews against the persecution of their people. Their story forms a key part of the history of the Manouchian group and the Communist resistance in general, to which we now turn.

The Manouchian Group

A week before World War II began, Nazi Germany and the Soviet Union astonished the world by signing a non-aggression agreement. Overnight this forced Communists in France to abandon the antifascism they had championed since the days of the Popular Front for a rather nebulous antiwar position, one that disturbed many members and challenged Party unity. The 1941 Nazi invasion of the Soviet Union completely reversed that situation, allowing Communists in France to return to a militant anti-Nazi stance and for the first time organize against the occupation. The Communists, for example, began the policy of assassinating German soldiers and officials, continuing it even when the Germans responded by executing innocent French hostages. More significantly, in 1941 the party founded the *Francs-Tireurs et Partisans*, a guerrilla army that would play a leading role in the resistance.[10]

The Manouchian group, active in Paris during 1943 before being caught and executed by the Germans, was one of the more successful partisan groups during the war. Affiliated with the Communist resistance army *Francs-tireurs et partisans* (FTP), its history begins with the efforts of the French Communist Party (PCF) to organize immigrant workers during the interwar years. The presence of a large, mostly working-class foreign population in France during the 1920s and 1930s attracted Communist organizers, with the blessings and urgings of Moscow. Inspired by proletarian internationalism, the party reached out to immigrant workers, especially those working in factories in large cities like Paris and Marseilles. Its affiliated union organization, the United General Confederation of Labor (CGTU), began creating special sections devoted to them, featuring newspapers in their own native languages. Initially named the MOE, or Foreign Labor Group, in 1932 they switched their name to MOI, Immigrant Labor Group, in response to the increasing xenophobia of the Depression years.

When the Communists organized the FTP in 1941, they included sections for foreigners that took the name FTP-MOI. Concentrated primarily in Paris, it was directed by Joseph Epstein (code name Colonel Gilles), a Polish Jewish Communist and veteran of the Spanish Civil War. The FTP-MOI was small, less than one hundred active militants at any given time organized in smaller subgroups, often but not always organized along national and religious lines. One subgroup consisted primarily of Polish Jews, for example, another of Italians. Constituted from the outset as an armed resistance unit, the real turning point for the FTP-MOI came with the Vel d'Hiver roundups of July 1942. This brought a number of young Jewish Communists, many of whom had lost their entire families, into the organization. Annie Kriegel, one member who later became a distinguished French historian, described her own reaction as a young woman:

> To understand it is necessary to start from one basic fact: the brutal collapse for them of all those systems of protection, even if sometimes oppressive, which an individual acquires from belonging to a regulated society. Homeland, name, family, house, school, neighborhood, work, everything which provides a point of fixity, and definition of self, had been swallowed up in nothingness . . . Thus the resistance provided membership of a group, a narrow group, but one which was tightly structured and hierarchical, the reconstitution of a network of interpersonal relations where the survival of each depended on the solidarity of all the others. [It] once again peopled the days with faces and gave them back a savour and a value, an existence freighted with both fear and hope.[11]

Perhaps the most famous FTP-MOI group was that directed by Missak Manouchian. Of Armenian origin, Manouchian fled his native region as a boy after the Armenian genocide left him and his brother orphans. The two escaped to Syria, under the French mandate, and were accepted into an orphanage where they learned French. In 1925, at the age of nineteen, Manouchian immigrated to Marseilles, eventually making his way to Paris and finding work in the Citroën factory. He joined the CGT and in 1934 became a member of the Communist Party, working actively with the Armenian section of the MOI. During the 1930s Manouchian also developed as a poet and intellectual, studying at the Sorbonne, founding magazines devoted to Armenian literature, and translating the works of French poets into his native language.

At the beginning of the war Manouchian left Paris for Rouen, returning to the capital after the Armistice of 1940. There he found that the PCF was now illegal and his entire political world in disarray. He was himself arrested and briefly interned in a camp in Compiègne. He went back to working in secret with the Armenian section of the MOI, before joining the FTP-MOI in early 1943. There he found others, like himself foreigners and Communists, also committed to fighting both for France and against fascism. For Manouchian and his comrades, the national and global struggles came together in the fight against the German occupation of France.

The constitution of the FTP-MOI came at a critical time for the PCF in Paris. By the end of 1942 the Germans and the French police had largely destroyed Communist organizations in the capital. The PCF leadership thus withdrew most of its operatives from the city, so that only the FTP-MOI guerrillas remained. Years later this caused a major controversy: some argued the PCF had abandoned the FTP-MOI to their fate because they were foreigners and therefore expendable, others contending the Party left them in Paris because they were so effective. Whatever the truth of the matter, during early 1943 in particular the FTP-MOI shouldered on its own Communist guerrilla activity in Paris.

Reporting to Joseph Epstein, Manouchian assumed command of a small group of guerrilla fighters, initiating a series of actions against the Germans in Paris. The Manouchian group enlisted people from a variety of backgrounds, including many foreign Jews but also Italians, Spaniards, and native French. It soon became notable for its daring. Manouchian and his followers derailed trains, ambushed and assassinated German soldiers, and published Resistance propaganda in a variety of foreign languages. On July 28 members of the group threw a bomb into the car of General von Schaumburg, the German commander of the Paris region, narrowly missing killing him. Two months later, as noted at the outset of this chapter, the group did kill SS Colonel Julius Ritter, the head of the STO in France and a personal friend of Adolf Hitler. Both men and women worked in the Manouchian group. Olga Bancic, a Jewish woman from Romania, was one of the group's most active operatives. In the space of a few months in 1943 the Manouchian group undertook some thirty attacks on German targets.

On October 5, five members of the group attacked a column of fifty German soldiers in broad daylight in the place de l'Odéon on Paris' Left Bank. They hurled two grenades at them before melting back into the crowd, successfully making their escape after killing three and wounding ten soldiers. Three days later four Manouchian commandos threw a bomb into a restaurant near the Arc de Triomphe that had been requisitioned by the Germans, again escaping without difficulty. The Manouchian group also targeted traitors. In one incident, members discovered that a Jewish man was betraying fellow Jews to the German authorities, so they tracked him down to his apartment and shot him.

In general, such small guerrilla groups did not last long in occupied France, and the end came for the Manouchian group in November 1943. After one member of the FTP-MOI cracked under torture, the French police tracked down and arrested all members of the group in mid-November. They succeeded in breaking not only the Manouchian group but the FTP-MOI in general, arresting more than sixty members. They tortured Manouchian and others, then handed them over to the Germans.

In February 1944, after several months of imprisonment and interrogation, the twenty-three core members of the Manouchian group went on trial in a German military court. To publicize the trial, and more generally underscore the foreign nature of the resistance, authorities created a lurid poster with pictures of ten of the accused and lists of their crimes. Known as the Red Poster (l'Affiche Rouge), it condemned the accused as criminals and terrorists rather than freedom fighters. As the accompanying leaflet argued: "[The Manouchian Group] is the army of crime against France. Banditry is not the expression of a wounded patriotism, it is a foreign plot against the lives of the French people and against the sovereignty of France."[12] Copies of the poster went up throughout the city, but instead of vilifying the Manouchian group as criminals it made them more famous and contributed to their image as martyrs. Anonymous individuals frequently left flowers below the posters or scrawled on them *"mort pour la France"* ("they gave their lives for France").

Missak Manouchian and most of the other members of the group were shot by firing squad at Mont Valérian outside Paris on February 21, 1944. The sole person spared, Olga Bancic, was beheaded a few months later in Stuttgart. The members of the group were allowed to write a final communication to their loved ones before they died. Manouchian's own last testament included the following words:

> I joined the Army of Liberation as a volunteer, and I die within inches of Victory and the final goal. I wish for happiness for all those who will survive and taste the sweetness of the freedom and peace of tomorrow. I'm sure that the French people, and all those who fight for freedom, will know how to honor our memory with dignity. At the moment of death, I proclaim that I have no hatred for the German people, or for anyone at all; everyone will receive what he is due, as punishment and as reward. The German people, and all other people will live in peace and brotherhood after the war, which will not last much longer. Happiness for all.[13]

Missak Manouchian died as he had lived, an internationalist until the very end.

A few members of the Manouchian group survived the war. Leo Kneler took part in the liberation of Paris in 1944 then returned to Germany after the war, spending the rest of his life in East Berlin. The group's last surviving member, Arsène Tchakarian, like Manouchian himself a survivor of the Armenian genocide, died in 2018 at the age of 105. Probably its most eminent veteran was Henri Krasucki, a Polish Jew active in the group until his arrest by the Gestapo in March 1943 and subsequent deportation to Buchenwald. Krasucki survived the concentration camp and returned to France after the war, immersing himself in Communist activism and eventually becoming the secretary general of the General Confederation of Labor (CGT), the nation's largest trade union.

How should the French, and how should we, remember the Manouchian group? In the aftermath of the Liberation the victorious Gaullists (and others) insisted that most French people had supported the Resistance, but the argument that the French were all or mostly resisters also implied that the resisters were mostly French. In such a context it was difficult to acknowledge the contributions of the FTP-MOI. Starting in the 1970s, however, French writers and artists have begun to pay serious attention to the history of the Manouchian group. Several books and films have appeared dealing with it, and the implications of its story for the broader histories of the Resistance, the PCF, and France as a whole. Missak Manouchian was posthumously awarded the Legion of Honor, and is now widely regarded as a national hero in both France and his native Armenia.

The history of the Manouchian group underscores not just the important contribution of foreigners to the French Resistance but also the thoroughly internationalist perspective of that movement. Its members saw themselves as fighting both for France and for a better world in general. Against the reactionary nationalism of Vichy, they counterposed the proudest traditions of republican and revolutionary universalism. Communist resistance fighters generally sang both *The Marseillaise* and *The Internationale* before they were executed; one, Jean-Pierre Timbaud, shouted out "Long live the German Communist Party!" as his last dying words. The members of the Manouchian group and of the FTP-MOI championed both the faith of foreigners in a just France and the French belief in universal liberty. Probably their best epitaph was provided by the great French poet Louis Aragon in 1955; the last stanza reads:

> They were twenty-three when the rifles blossomed
> Twenty-three who gave their hearts before their time
> Twenty-three foreigners but still our brothers
> Twenty-three who loved life to death
> Twenty-three who cried out "France!" as they fell.[14]

Part 4

The Rebirth of the Universal Nation

The observation that life in the contemporary era has a fundamentally trans-national and global character seems like a given, even a cliché. Historical events such as decolonization and the rise and fall of the Soviet Bloc, social movements including feminism and environmentalism, and international cultural developments in music, cinema, and television dominated the late twentieth century. The rise of the internet and other forms of instantaneous worldwide communication during the twenty-first century has only under-scored this trend, taking it to a whole new level. More than ever before, we live in a world where transnational interconnectedness is the norm.

During such an era, what remains of national independence, on a political, social, and cultural level? For France, a nation proud of its unique history and heritage, the question of how to preserve this singular culture in a global era lies at the heart of what it means to be French in the contemporary era. Ultimately this new globality would reaffirm its essential character as a universal nation, one whose culture was forged by the interchange with many other peoples and cultures throughout the world. In the contemporary era the impact of global forces on issues in French life has become more evident than ever, while at the same time France has continued to make its own distinct contributions to those global patterns.

In 1944 France emerged triumphant from the nightmare of Nazi occu-pation, and a year later stood proudly as one of the victors of World War II. Yet it did not create its liberation by itself, instead being freed by an unstable alliance of the United States and the Soviet Union, whose rivalry would go on to dominate the late twentieth century. Moreover, France's empire, which had done so much to help liberate the mother country, would increasingly demand and win recognition of its own interests. The prosperity that the nation enjoyed in the thirty years after the Liberation would further integrate France into global networks, especially those involving immigration from Europe and beyond, and the new immigrant and post-immigrant populations would spark new challenges to ideas of French identity. Finally, from battles against "Coca-Colonization" and *franglais* (French "polluted" with many English words) to Existentialism, New Wave cinema, Club Med, and French hip hop, French culture would engage with others on a global scale and continue to assert the unique character of the Hexagon. In many different spheres of life, the contemporary era has demonstrated that, perhaps more than ever before, the future of the French nation would continue to be transnational.

France Under the Fourth Republic

Charles de Gaulle's march down the Champs-Élysées with a million Frenchmen and women at the culmination of the liberation of Paris on August 25, 1944, surely constitutes one of the great moments of French history. The shame, horror, and degradation of four years of Nazi occupation had finally come to an end, to be confirmed by the utter defeat of the Axis a year later. France could at last look forward to a bright new future, a future its people could determine themselves.

Yet what form would that future take? The Nazis had left for good by the end of 1944, but they left in their wake lots of problems the new France would have to deal with. The nation was economically prostrate: if not as bad off as central and eastern Europe, France's economy generally functioned at half of prewar production levels, and the disruption of transportation and agriculture led to major food and fuel shortages for the next few years. The political future of France also remained to be determined. De Gaulle, leader of the Free French, seemed the obvious choice to head the new regime. Other forces, however, notably the internal resistance and in particular the powerful Communist party, also demanded a say in postwar political life. As the great wartime anti-fascist alliance gradually gave way to the looming

Cold War, many questioned the ability of France to remain independent of both the United States and the Soviet Union. Moreover, the war had both reaffirmed and challenged the relationship between metropolitan France and the empire. The majority of de Gaulle's Free French troops had come from the colonies, for example, so that in one sense the empire rescued the metropole. At the same time, however, the war had weakened France's links to its overseas possessions, setting the stage for the postwar traumas of decolonization. In short, France stood victorious in 1944, but it still had to find its place in a new, vastly transformed, world order.

Ironically, although the two most powerful political forces in France were de Gaulle and the Communists, in the last analysis neither ended up leading what emerged as the Fourth French Republic in 1946. After the Liberation de Gaulle established a provisional government that held its first elections in October 1945. These elections, the first in French history that allowed women to vote, created a Constituent Assembly dominated by three parties: the Communists (PCF), the Socialists (SFIO), and the new progressive Catholic party (MRP). Over the next year French politicians debated various forms for the new government. By slender majorities they rejected both a strong unicameral legislature, favored by the PCF, and a strong executive, favored by de Gaulle. In the end the constitution of the new Fourth Republic, ratified in October 1946, bore an uncanny resemblance to that of the Third, with a bicameral legislature and a weak presidency. After all the talk of political transformation and even revolution that accompanied the Liberation, France ended up with a new government strikingly similar to the old.

Charles de Gaulle haughtily refused to take part in such a regime and retreated into private life for a decade. The three main political parties struggled for the next two years to maintain a coalition government, which took the name of Tripartism, but the increasing impact of the Cold War on France soon rendered that impossible. The Americans emerged from World War II the strongest nation on earth, and of all the major powers the one least devastated by the conflict. It viewed the defeat of the Axis as a victory for democracy and capitalism, and felt the entire world should be open to American ideals and American products. In sharp contrast, the Soviet Union had been devastated by the German invasion, losing well over 10 percent of its entire population. Soviet dictator Joseph Stalin insisted above all on controlling eastern Europe politically and militarily, so that Russia would never again suffer such a catastrophe. The Soviets were perfectly happy to see France remain under American influence, but the growing conflict between the two superpowers meant that France would ultimately have to take sides, and that this choice would have both international and domestic ramifications. As a result, by the end of 1947 Tripartism collapsed with the expulsion of the PCF, paving the way for billions of dollars in foreign aid from the United States.

This foreign aid proved crucial to the Fourth Republic's greatest triumph, its restoration of the French economy. From the late 1940s to the mid-1970s France experienced a powerful economic boom, the *Trentes Glorieuses* (the thirty great years), which transformed the nation and made it more prosperous than ever. A crucial factor was the postwar baby boom, which saw French birthrates rise massively for the first time in a century and fueled demand for products ranging from milk to housing. The birth of European integration, pioneered in particular by the French statesman Robert Schuman, also facilitated economic growth by opening up continental markets to France's industries and agriculture. In 1957 France joined West Germany, Belgium, Luxembourg, the Netherlands, and Italy in signing the Treaty of Rome, which created the European Economic Community, or EEC, also known as the Common Market.

In addition, drawing inspiration from both the Resistance and Vichy, the Fourth Republic embraced centralized economic planning to rebuild the nation in the postwar years. In 1947, under the leadership of economist Jean Monnet, France launched its first five-year plan, targeting basic sectors such as coal, electricity, and transportation. In 1952 the government immediately followed this with a second five-year plan, focusing on agriculture and housing. Many had traditionally considered centralized economic planning the province of dictatorships like Nazi Germany or the Soviet Union, but the French Fourth Republic demonstrated that a democracy could use a mixture of government programs and incentives to private industry to boost a nation's economy.

As a result, during the 1950s and 1960s in particular the French economy grew at an impressive rate, increasing production, profits, and popular living standards. Working class living standards nearly doubled between 1950 and 1975, and the availability of massive amounts of subsidized public housing in the suburbs of Paris and other French cities improved the quality of life for the nation's new young families. The creation of new social benefits, above all public health care, furthered improved the living standards of the French people. Its ability to create and shape the huge postwar economic boom, and use it to transform French society for the better, was without a doubt the finest achievement of the Fourth Republic.

In contrast, its greatest weakness and ultimately fatal flaw came with its colonial policy. During World War II the empire had proved its worth to France: de Gaulle's Free French movement had been based in the colonies, which furnished the majority of his soldiers. More than ever before, the empire *was* France. In addition, in an age of superpowers many French leaders felt only the empire would enable France to remain a nation of the first rank. Yet the war also brought a new discourse of national liberation and democracy to the world, and France's colonial subjects were by no means immune. Moreover, the nation's defeat and occupation by Nazi Germany had weakened its prestige in the eyes of many in the empire, making the prospect of breaking imperial bonds and achieving national independence a more realistic one.

The Fourth Republic recognized these challenges, and the constitution that established it made some important concessions to the colonized. These were not enough, however, to prevent them from launching their own struggles for independence. Trouble first broke out in French Indochina. The colony had a long history of anticolonial resistance, and during the wartime occupation by the Japanese the Communist Viet Minh had taken the lead, demanding independence from both Paris and Tokyo. France's attempt to resume control of Indochina after 1944 soon led to a full-fledged war with the Viet Minh, a war that became entangled with Cold War politics after the 1949 Communist takeover of China. By 1954 the French had had enough; after their disastrous defeat at Dien Bien Phu in May, France withdrew its troops and recognized the independence of Vietnam, Laos, and Cambodia.

Later that same year a new revolt against the French empire broke out in Algeria. Unlike Indochina, Algeria lay at the heart of the empire, just on the other side of the Mediterranean from France, and the French were determined to maintain it as an integral part of their nation. Algeria also had a large European settler population, one fanatically committed to preserving French rule. France dispatched hundreds of thousands of troops to the rebellious colony, brutally repressing anticolonial activity. The independence movement was led by the National Liberation Front, or FLN, an organization of Algerian nationalists. It launched the initial revolt against France on November 1, 1954, and after an initial series of setbacks responded to the military's offensive with a vicious war of terror, massacring French soldiers and civilians alike. The bloody nature of the war shocked world opinion, which began increasingly to favor ending the war and granting Algerian independence. Moreover, an antiwar movement developed in France itself, horrified by reports that the French Army was torturing Algerian rebels. In May 1958 matters came to a head: the military seized power in Algeria and demanded the overthrow of the Fourth Republic, threatening to send paratroopers to invade Paris itself. With that the government collapsed, and after a complex series of negotiations Charles de Gaulle, the hero of the military rebels, agreed to return to power after twelve years in private life. He assumed power on June 1, and with that the new Fifth Republic was born.

The Fifth Republic from de Gaulle to Mitterrand

Charles de Gaulle was one of the greatest political leaders in modern France, and by most accounts the most prominent politician of the twentieth century. He returned to power in 1958 determined to rescue the nation from military disaster as he had during World War II. In order to do so he insisted on a new, more powerful form of government, departing radically from the weak parliamentarianism of the Third and Fourth republics. The constitution of the new Fifth Republic granted the president an unprecedented seven-year term, making him in effect an elected monarch. De Gaulle would use this extraordinary power to remake France, presiding over an era of strong economic growth and calm international relations. In particular, he restored the image of France as an independent nation and a leader in global affairs, a country people around the world still looked to for inspiration.

In order to accomplish these things de Gaulle first had to resolve the Algerian war, and the broader crisis of empire that it represented. De Gaulle soon realized that the situation in Algeria offered no realistic prospects for continued French rule, that no matter what the army and the settlers thought France had lost the loyalty of the majority Muslim population and thus could only hold on to the colony by force. He therefore began a series of secret negotiations to end French control and grant Algeria independence. The realization that France intended to withdraw caused a firestorm of protest among the French in Algeria, prompting a military uprising there in January 1960. The revolt failed, however, and France formally recognized Algerian independence in 1962. During the same years de Gaulle engineered the transition away from formal colonialism in other parts of the empire. In 1960, in a grand gesture France granted independence to no fewer than fourteen African colonies. This peaceful cession of formal rule enabled the French to retain important political, economic, and military links to Francophone Africa. In the end, de Gaulle wisely recognized that accepting the winds of change in the empire would ultimately enable France to maintain its position as a global power in an era of decolonization.

Given that proponents of formal empire had often emphasized its economic value to the imperial powers, it is ironic that France emerged from the era of decolonization more prosperous than ever. During the 1960s France, like much of Europe and America, enjoyed a period of unparalleled affluence, reaping the benefits of the investments made during the Fourth Republic. From 1958 to 1970 the French economy grew by nearly 6 percent a year, making it the most dynamic in Europe. Unemployment stayed low, so most people were able to take home larger and larger paychecks. This led to increasing consumer demand, fueled both by higher wages and dwindling fears of unemployment. Expenditures on the home accounted for much of this; during the 1960s the French not only spent more on their houses and apartments, but also on things to put inside them. They began indulging more in big-ticket items like refrigerators, cars, and televisions. The image of the typical Parisian inhabiting a tiny room and spending all of his or her time in cafes gave way to a new reality of families living in their own houses and driving to work.

At the heart of this transformation lay the massive postwar baby boom. France's population under de Gaulle grew from forty to fifty-two million. As the new generation grew its needs changed, from hospital care to day care, from toys to books and education, but during the decades after World War II they always played a central role not only in the French economy but increasingly in society, culture, and politics as well. By the early 1960s the children of the baby boom were maturing into adolescence, a concept that came into its own with their generation, and forcing their elders and the broader society in general to take notice of their perspectives and desires. Moreover, they increasingly identified with a global youth culture, often inspired by trends from Britain and America. French teenagers danced to rock music, both imported and home-grown, and embraced blue jeans and other youth-oriented clothing styles. As young people moved into high schools and universities, many involved themselves in politics, usually trending to the left or far left.

As in other countries, traditional institutions and society in France proved slow to adapt to this huge new generation. The resulting tensions culminated in the revolutionary year of 1968, producing a crisis that shook French society to its very foundations and almost toppled the government of Charles de Gaulle. French universities had expanded massively during the 1960s to serve the big new student population, but they often remained traditional, hidebound, and bureaucratic. The resultant student alienation combined with radical political activism to produce an explosion. In March 1968 students at the suburban Paris campus of Nanterre began a series of political actions—inspired in part by the anti-Vietnam war movement in the United States—that threw the campus into turmoil. After the administration closed the campus in early May, student radicals simply moved to Paris, invading the Sorbonne and transferring their movement from the margins to the heart of France's university system. Within a week, universities throughout the country were thrown into turmoil, while in Paris students battled police in the city's Latin Quarter. This shocked the nation, but the movement had just begun. It soon spread from the campuses to the nation's factories and offices, as workers walked out on strike in protest of the government or the capitalist system in general. By the last week of May what had begun as an isolated student movement had morphed into the largest strike wave in French history, one that seemed to threaten the survival of de Gaulle's government, if not the Fifth Republic in general.

De Gaulle ultimately won the battle, promising reforms but also mobilizing the anger and impatience of people who by the end of May had grown tired of the constant chaos in the streets. It was in effect his last major victory. After losing a national referendum on government reform in April 1969, de Gaulle abruptly resigned, returning to private life for the last time. The great leader died a year later, in November 1970, his passing symbolizing the end of France's postwar era. His successor, Georges Pompidou, certainly lacked de Gaulle's presence but did make an impact on the French landscape with a series of major projects, notably the Montparnasse Tower in Paris and the *TGV*, the new high-speed railway network.

Such projects represented all the dynamism and confidence of the *Trentes Glorieuses*, but this dynamism would soon come to an end. During the 1970s political turmoil in the Middle East triggered sharp rises in the price of oil, in many ways the key commodity to the postwar economic boom. These resulted in two major economic downturns, from 1973–1975 and from 1979–1981. France, whose economy depended heavily on imported oil, suffered greatly from the global crisis. Its economic growth rate dropped from nearly 6 percent to 2 percent by the early 1980s, and unemployment rates tripled within a decade, getting as high as 12 percent a decade later. Moreover, as often happens the crisis did not strike the French people equally. Young people suffered disproportionately, as did industrial regions of the country including the North, the East, and the Paris suburbs.

The recession of the 1970s had a major political impact. In 1981 the French Socialists led by François Mitterrand returned to power for the first time in a generation. The election of a left-wing president—at a time when conservative leaders including Ronald Reagan in American and Margaret Thatcher in Britain dominated global politics—highlighted the desire of the French to pursue a different, more populist solution to the economic downturn. The Mitterrand administration took a liberal Keynesian approach to dealing with the economy, nationalizing several key industries and raising wages. It took other progressive measures as well, such as appointing women government ministers, deregulating the radio industry and promoting new types of culture in general, and abolishing the death penalty. In the end, however, the French Socialists could not single-handedly fight the global economic conjuncture, and after a couple of years the Mitterrand government found itself forced to embrace the same deflationist policies so common elsewhere during the 1980s, cutting wages and closing unproductive state industries. By the mid-1980s, the optimism and confidence of the 1960s seemed to belong to another world, and for the rest of the century and beyond France would struggle with joblessness and anemic economic performance.

Into a New Century

In 1988 Mitterrand won a second term as president of France, serving until 1995. He died in 1996, like Charles de Gaulle leaving the earth a year after he left office. During Mitterrand's last years as president the world experienced momentous changes that in effect wrote an end to the twentieth century. In 1989 peaceful revolutions broke out in Eastern Europe against the Communist Soviet satellite system that had dominated the area since World War II. In November crowds of demonstrators tore down the infamous Berlin Wall, symbolizing a series of popular uprisings throughout the region that culminated with the collapse of the Soviet Union itself in 1991. A year later twenty-seven European nations signed the Maastricht Treaty, creating the European Union and unifying Europe economically, politically, and administratively to an unprecedented degree. In 1999 it created the Euro, the common European currency that would supersede national coinage and become a key symbol of Europe in the twenty-first century.

France under Mitterrand played a key role in bringing about this new spirit and reality of European unity, and most French people felt it would improve the quality of their own lives: even without the French franc, France would still be France. For some, the push toward European integration revived the old Gaullist dream of a united Europe led by France standing as a counterweight to the global hegemony of the United States.

A united Europe did mean a united Germany, which after 1990 resumed its traditional role as the powerhouse of the Continent. Yet in spite of Berlin's new preeminence the postwar Franco-German alliance held strong in the new era, easing Europe's transition to a post-Communist society.

In the late twentieth century France experienced greater challenges from another aspect of its relationship to the broader world: immigration. This issue went back to the years of the Fourth Republic, which to an important extent had built the postwar economic recovery on the backs of immigrant workers. By the early 1970s more than three million lived in France, and over the years the composition of this population had changed significantly. Whereas during the 1940s and 1950s, as during the interwar years, most had come from southern and eastern Europe, by the 1960s non-Europeans began arriving in larger numbers. In particular they came from France's colonies and former colonies in North Africa, sub-Saharan Africa, and the Caribbean. Many settled in the old *bidonvilles* (shanty towns) and new housing projects of the banlieue, the suburban areas around Paris and other large cities. France largely ended legal immigration in 1974 in response to the economic crisis, but many foreigners had already settled there and were raising families; few returned to their homelands.

During the 1980s and 1990s questions of immigration in French society increasingly evolved into issues of race. Many social critics discussed the so-called second-generation immigrants, young people of North African heritage who had grown up in France and spoke French fluently, yet were widely perceived as cultural and racial outsiders. Starting in the early 1980s, after the Brixton uprising in London, a series of race riots broke out in French suburbs pitting "immigrant" youth against the police. In the fall of 2005 a massive series of riots broke out in the suburbs; in spite of constant denials, France did indeed have a race problem. The spectacle of burning cars, a symbol of the frustration and lack of mobility of nonwhite youth, became a regular occurrence in the banlieue. The rise of Islamic fundamentalism played a key role in racial tensions at the end of the twentieth century in France. By the 1990s Islam had become the second largest religion in France, and in a country whose dominant political culture had long prided itself on secularism and anticlericalism, the rise of a large population seemingly devoted to integralist Islam came as a shock. The 1989 decision by a group of Muslim girls to wear the hijab to a public school, the very symbol of the secular republic, threw the nation into turmoil; in 2011 France would become the first nation in Europe to outlaw the public wearing of the niqab, or full face covering.

Questions of immigration and race reshaped French politics at the dawn of the twenty-first century. In 1972 several small neofascist parties in France joined together to found the National Front, in imitation of the analogous party created in Britain five years earlier. Its leader, Jean-Marie Le Pen, a veteran of the Algerian war, quickly brought the new party to public notice with his strong, often violent opposition to immigrants and nonwhites. At first widely dismissed as part of the lunatic fringe in French politics, the National Front began to gain strength during the 1980s and 1990s. It often filled the gap left in working class politics by the decline of the PCF. By the beginnings of the new century Le Pen's daughter, Marine Le Pen, had turned the National Front into one of the most powerful political parties in the country, and many speculated that it was only a matter of time before it captured the presidency itself.

The specter of a racist party at the center of French politics provided an ominous warning for the nation in the early twenty-first century. As in the past, France gradually integrated its new wave of immigrants into national life while at the same time being transformed by them. Food, music, and culture in general were all enriched by the presence of peoples originally from a different shore. In the 1990s a wave of so-called banlieue films such as *La Haine, Rai*, and *Bye-Bye* swept French cinema. Largely thanks to immigrants and their descendants, France now possesses a hip-hop music scene second only to that of the United States in the world. Even that holiest space of French culture, food, has been transformed by the nation's new multicultural diversity: I can recall hearing a Parisian friend say that what he wanted for dinner was a good French cous-cous. As an American journalist living in the Paris suburbs recently wrote, "My neighbors come from around the world; legal or illegal immigrants from Africa, South Asia, China and Vietnam. Most of the white faces I see are Poles, Ukrainians, Russians and Serbs . . . I don't feel despair or fear here, but something more alive than the static elegance of eternal Paris. The future of this great city is on its periphery."

Twenty-First-Century France

On Bastille Day, July 14, 1998, France experienced the greatest explosion of national joy it had seen since the Liberation. One-and-a-half million Parisians crowded onto the Champs-Élysées and spontaneous celebrations broke out throughout the country. The cause was the victory of France's national team in the World Cup. The revelers gathered to celebrate France, but also a multicultural, inclusive vision of France: the team's captain, Zinedine Zidaine, was of Algerian origin, and like him many of his teammates came from immigrant and postcolonial backgrounds. The festivities highlighted the fact that France's victory was a victory of *all* the French people, that the French had won by mobilizing the nation as a whole. As France pursues its national destiny during the twenty-first century, hopefully this vision of a global nation will guide and favor its future.

10

Universal Family
Josephine Baker and the Rainbow Tribe

Once upon a time there was a beautiful queen who lived in a magnificent castle. There she and her husband raised a wonderful family of twelve children, adopted from every corner of the realm. The children grew up with all the advantages of royalty, their own private amusement park, beautiful clothes, and lots of presents at holidays. People came from around the world to meet them and admire their lovely home. They learned to love each other and their parents, as in any good family. They never had any problems, and they all lived happily ever after. Or so the story goes . . .

Sometimes the fairy tale is the real story: it speaks to the hopes and dreams that motivated people to act, even if it doesn't necessarily represent the results of those actions. During the 1950s the performing star Josephine Baker and her husband Jo Bouillon adopted twelve young children, bringing them to live in her castle, Les Milandes. Long before the era of transnational adoptions, or celebrity adoptions like those of Angelina Jolie and Brad Pitt, or of personal fantasy parks like Michael Jackson's Neverland, Baker and Bouillon dreamed of creating a family composed of children from around the world. The children would be raised to love each other and cherish their differences, to reject racism and embrace the idea that all men and women are brothers and sisters. The Rainbow Tribe would be a shining light of universalism to all the peoples of the world.

The story of Baker's Rainbow Tribe speaks to the transnational history of France during the postwar era, much as her meteoric rise to stardom illustrated that of the 1920s. France under the Fourth Republic was a nation struggling to translate the dreams of the Resistance into postwar reality. Heroes had vanquished the dragons and trolls of the occupation, and now fought to create security and prosperity for all. The sharp increase in the national birthrate brought about the literal renewal of the nation, placing children at the epicenter of its hopes and dreams for a bright new future. Moreover, during and after the war French women and men dreamed of a future without national rivalries or hatred, of social justice for all peoples. Ideals of peace and prosperity, of children growing up in a world without intolerance or fear, these were the universal values of the Resistance that they shared with people throughout the postwar world. The story of the Rainbow Tribe thus provides one example of how France tried to realize the goals in the decades after the Liberation.

Perhaps more than anyone else in modern history, Baker brought together the worlds of African American culture and the Parisian avant-garde. Born in 1906 in St. Louis, Missouri, Baker rocketed to fame as a result of her 1925 appearance in Paris with the *Revue nègre*. Her performance took the city by storm, immediately making her, in the words of Paris correspondent Janet Flanner, ". . . the established new American star for Europe."[1] Baker settled in Paris, living a life of luxury and public acclaim during the 1920s and 1930s, opening her own nightclub and appearing on stage and in films. Whether striding down Parisian boulevards in designer gowns or singing and dancing before crowds of adoring fans, during the interwar years Baker embodied the racial tolerance and joie de vivre of the French capital.[2]

All this came to a crashing halt with the German invasion of 1940. Like millions of other Parisians Baker fled the capital in advance of the Nazi armies. She went first to the idyllic Dordogne region of central France where she rented a beautiful Renaissance chateau named Les Milandes, and there made contact with French army officers inspired by Charles de Gaulle's call for continuing the struggle against the Germans. After brief sojourns in Lisbon and Marseilles, in 1941 Baker joined the Resistance and moved to North Africa. She spent the rest of the war years there, rising to the rank of a lieutenant in the French army. Her devotion to the cause of Free France, in contrast to the attitudes of some other Parisian entertainers, won her both the Croix de Guerre and appointment as a Chevalier of the

Legion of Honor. After the Liberation Baker came back to Paris, returning in triumph in October 1944. According to one man who witnessed her return, "[There were] a million people up and down the Champs [Elysées] to see her when she came in. It was a glorious day, as big as the day they liberated Paris."[3]

The France she returned to had changed markedly from the country she first encountered in the 1920s. The lively, devil-may-care spirit of the interwar years had vanished, replaced by a much more somber tone. The German occupation had been a national embarrassment and trauma, the evil it represented symbolized above all by the deportation and murder of thousands of French Jews during the Holocaust. Just coming to terms with and rebuilding from the material damage caused by the war and occupation seemed a daunting task. France had emerged on the winning side of the Second World War, but in spite of the Resistance it had not liberated itself. Instead, the postwar era underscored its dependence on the United States, the great superpower whose tense rivalry with the other great superpower, the Soviet Union, would shape not only the future of the world in general but that of France in particular.[4]

The immediate postwar years were grim, characterized by political infighting and shortages of basic commodities like food and housing. They laid the basis, however, for one of the greatest periods of economic expansion in modern French history: the *Trentes Glorieuses*, or the thirty glorious years from the late 1940s to the mid-1970s. As in much of Europe and America, this was a time of full employment, economic modernization, and growing wealth and opportunities. For the French, one aspect in particular of these good times stood out. Since the mid-nineteenth century France had had one of the lowest birthrates in Europe. This had accelerated during the early twentieth century so that by the 1930s the nation had achieved negative population growth, an excess of deaths over births. During the occupation, however, this pattern began to reverse itself as French women began having more children. The end of the war and the gradual return of prosperity brought an explosion of the birthrate in France, part of the postwar global baby boom. Whereas during the 1930s the nation averaged six hundred thousand births per year, by the early 1950s it was producing eight hundred thousand. Comedians joked that the new national slogan should be "Liberty, Equality, Maternity."[5]

Josephine Baker's Rainbow Tribe spoke to the broader transformation of French society since the Second World War, a transformation that placed children and family at the heart of national life. It also underscored a new image of women in postwar France, and Baker's ability to embody that new image. During the 1920s she symbolized the New Woman, a feminine ideal that rejected traditional gender roles and emphasized the ability of young women to join the work force, socialize on their own terms, and in general live life free of the dictates of men.

While many women found this vision alluring, conservative forces attacked it as a perversion of traditional morality, often blaming France's low birthrate on the refusal of such women to get married, stay at home, and have babies. Monique Lerbier, the heroine and ultimate liberated women of Victor Margueritte's 1922 novel *La Garçonne* (*The Bachelor Girl*), paid the ultimate price for her dissolute lifestyle of drugs, drink, and sex by ending up sterile. Ultimately this perspective accused the liberated women of the 1920s of betraying not just traditional gender roles but the nation itself.[6]

In opting for maternity Baker in effect opted for a new vision of womanhood. After the Liberation, she transformed her image from a nightclub performer to a mother, and indeed a mother on a grand scale. Leaving behind the Parisian boulevard to raise twelve children in the French countryside, Baker embraced the child-centered society of the Fourth Republic. The Rainbow Tribe took the postwar emphasis on children and made it a key symbol of universal France.

The Rainbow Tribe spoke to another central French concern in the postwar years, the empire. Ever since the days of Napoleon the universal vision of French republicanism had often taken an imperial form, and in the late nineteenth century the Third Republic had created the largest colonial empire in the nation's history, second only to that of Great Britain. During the Second World War many French colonies had rallied to the Resistance, and a majority of its fighters came from the empire. France emerged from the war with its empire intact, yet at the same time it became increasingly evident that old forms of imperial domination could not endure in the postwar era. On a global scale, the struggle against German and Japanese imperialism had inspired colonized peoples with desires for their own independence, so that decolonization would become a central characteristic of the world in the decades after the defeat of fascism.

In the aftermath of the Liberation France generally resisted calls for colonial independence, holding tight to the idea of "a nation of one hundred million Frenchmen." The nation's economy and society had been shattered by the occupation, and many considered the resources of the empire indispensable to the work of reconstruction. Nonetheless, French policy makers recognized that the world had changed, and that this required a new vision for the empire. The 1946 constitution that established the Fourth Republic abolished the French empire, replacing it with the French Union, making all colonial residents citizens and, at least in theory, emphasizing their equality with residents of the metropole. In the best tradition of French universalism, it proclaimed, "On the morrow of the victory achieved by the free peoples over the regimes that had sought to enslave and degrade humanity, the people of France proclaim anew that each human being, without distinction of race, religion or creed, possesses sacred and inalienable rights."[7]

This was not entirely empty verbiage; for example, the new constitution converted the "old colonies" of Martinique, Guadeloupe, Guiana, and Réunion, whose inhabitants had already enjoyed French citizenship, into full-fledged departments of France. For the most part, however, France's overseas possessions had little autonomy, and all political power remained concentrated in Paris. Moreover, the paternalist vision of civilizing the natives so central to modern French imperialism remained largely intact. As the constitution stated, "Faithful to its traditional mission, France desires to guide the peoples under its responsibility towards the freedom to administer themselves and to manage their own affairs democratically."[8]

The French Union's vision of empire as a multicultural, universal brotherhood of peoples brought together under the benevolent, paternal rule of mother France had more than a little in common with Josephine Baker's Rainbow Tribe. Baker was a veteran of the French Resistance, and the Fourth Republic's embrace of its progressive ideals, especially its opposition to racism, resonated deeply with her. The family she built would symbolize the universal appeal of France, with its children carefully chosen to represent different parts of the world to be raised in a French chateau. It would represent a response and an antidote to the American racism that had shaped her own childhood, while at the same time both embracing and parodying traditions of French colonialism. Just as imperial France would train her colonial subjects to be equal members of the national community, so would Baker raise her young children to be citizens of the world.

One must therefore consider the Rainbow Tribe not simply as the peculiar fancy of a celebrity, a sort of Michael Jackson's Neverland *avant la lettre*, but equally as a phenomenon that offered important insights into French life in the decades after the Liberation. At a time when the postwar baby boom was transforming the nation, Baker created the biggest, most spectacular family of all. During an era increasingly dominated by decolonization, by the colonial subjects' rejection of France's imperial vision, the Rainbow Tribe presented a global, multiracial vision of a French family. The fact that it fell to an African American woman, also a French citizen, to create an institution that so clearly embodied the national challenges and aspirations of the postwar era underscored the idea of France as a transnational nation.

By the end of World War II Baker seemed more triumphant than ever. She was an international star of stage and screen, lionized by audiences throughout the world. In 1947 she married French bandleader Jo Bouillon, her fourth husband, and the same year bought the chateau of Les Milandes. For the next few years Baker traveled widely throughout Europe and the Americas, not only back to the United States but also to Cuba, Brazil, Mexico, and Argentina. In the U.S. she came face to face with the racism she had fled to Europe to escape, experiences that would shape her unwavering commitment to the nascent civil rights movement. In 1952 Baker visited the Argentina of strongman Juan Péron and his charismatic wife Evita, whose work on behalf of the country's poor children struck a deep chord in her.

For she was also a woman who wanted a child. She spent years undergoing medical procedures to facilitate her ability to become pregnant. At one point she exclaimed to a doctor treating her during her wartime years in North Africa that "I want a baby more than anything else in the world!"[9] It was not to be. Baker did conceive after the war, but suffered a miscarriage while on tour in Mexico. By the early 1950s it had become clear that if she was to become a mother she would have to find an alternate means of realizing that goal.

Ultimately the Rainbow Tribe became this alternative. In 1953 Baker decided that the next stage in her life would not be the stage at all, but rather motherhood. Approaching fifty and without children of her own at a time when women all over France seemed to having babies, it made sense perhaps to complement (but certainly not to replace) her dynamic public persona with a rich private life. At the same time, creating a new family, and a new type of family, appealed both to her political convictions and her essentially performative nature. Raising a group of orphans from all racial backgrounds and all parts of the world would demonstrate the essentially unity of mankind, creating a model of human harmony not through struggle but through love. As she noted: "I'm convinced that I can realize my dream because I believe in the dignity of man. Jo and I plan to adopt four little children: red, yellow, white, and black. Four little children raised in the country, in my beautiful Dordogne. They will serve as an example of true Democracy, and be living proof that if people are left in peace, nature takes care of the rest."[10] The idea of the Rainbow Tribe also illustrated Baker's dramatic, larger-than-life personality. She had to have twelve children, not one or two, and her family couldn't be just a family, it had to be a political statement and a universal vision.

Baker began assembling her family during a trip to Japan in the spring of 1954. In general, she would find her children while on tour, blending her roles as mother and performer. Visiting an orphanage, she decided to adopt two boys of mixed-race parentage, the sons of Korean mothers and American soldier fathers. Such lineage would marginalize these boys in Japanese society, but Baker happily adopted young Akio and Teruel, whom she renamed Janot. The next year she found Luis in Colombia. Later in 1955, while on tour in Scandinavia, she found Jari in a Helsinki orphanage, and then discovered Jean-Claude in an orphanage in Paris. At this point Baker's projected family had generated a lot of publicity, which led to people sending her tips about prospective children. In 1956 she brought in two young refugees from the Algerian war, Marianne and Brahim, supposedly discovered hiding under a bush. The year 1957 saw Koffi, an orphan from the Ivory Coast, join the family. In 1959 Baker adopted a native American girl named Mara in Venezuela; just before Christmas news of an infant found in a garbage dump outside Paris led to the adoption of Noel. Three years later Baker adopted Stellina, born of a poor Moroccan mother in Paris.

One of Baker's great desires was to adopt children from every race and culture. In 1955 she visited Israel on tour and approached the Israeli government about adopting an orphan there. The Israelis, trying to build up the young country's Jewish population as quickly as possible, politely refused. Baker, who had converted to Judaism after marrying her third husband, Jean Lion, was determined to have a Jewish child, and so she found a young boy, Moise, in a Paris orphanage. So eventually there were twelve children, ten boys and two girls. Many were in effect war orphans, both World War II and the Algerian war, and others had been given up for adoption for a variety of reasons. In 1957 Baker and Bouillon formally adopted the children, making them French citizens. Baker's hope was that they would be equally citizens of their nation and of the world.

In many ways the children enjoyed a fairy-tale existence. They lived in Les Milandes, where Baker had first lived in 1940. The twenty-four-room castle had been renovated in the early twentieth century, and when Baker bought it she added her own extensive renovations, including heat, running water, electricity, and six bathrooms. Gargoyles, turrets, and other decorations covered the castle, making it a fantasy vision of the Middle Ages. The chateau's extensive grounds featured not only lovely landscaping but also a miniature golf course, an outdoor theater, and a large swimming pool shaped like the letter J. The family had dogs, monkeys, and other pet animals to play with. A small army of cooks, nurses, and tutors attended to the needs of the children. Some of Baker's own family, including her mother Carrie McDonald, moved to Les Milandes to help out.

Baker wanted all of her children to grow up learning about their individual heritages, so she hired instructors to teach them their "native" languages. She loved lavishing them with presents, and at Christmas time gifts were piled up to the ceiling in the castle's main living room. Les Milandes became a regional tourist attraction, thousands coming to see both the chateau and the family that lived there. Baker and Bouillon would show guests around the castle and its grounds, often exhibiting the children dressed in their "native" costumes.

For all its idyllic setting, however, the Rainbow Tribe was a real family, and like any other had real problems. Baker was frequently absent, pursuing her career both because she loved it and because she had to pay the bills. As they grew older the children complained that they didn't see her enough, and they also at times complained about their lessons. Little Moise, for example, resolutely refused to learn Hebrew, leading his Israeli tutor to resign in frustration. He was not the only instructor to find Baker's children difficult to handle. In many ways Baker ran the Tribe like a boarding school, and her children at times resented what they saw as her master plan for their lives.

Childish rebellion against parental discipline is nothing new, of course, but there were other serpents in paradise. The pressure of raising twelve children, managing a castle, and running separate careers soon strained Baker's marriage. Jo Bouillon was a loving father who invested much of his family fortune in Les Milandes, but he often clashed with Baker over the financial management of the estate and their family. In 1957 Baker filed for divorce, and although this never became final by 1960 Bouillon had moved out of Les Milandes. His departure was a big loss for the children, as was the death of Baker's mother a year earlier. But worse would follow.

By the early 1960s Baker was clearly living beyond her means and could no longer afford the extravagant lifestyle of the Rainbow Tribe. She had never been good at financial management, never one to deny herself or her family things just because she couldn't pay for them. Bouillon had been more adept at managing their budget, and with his absence Baker's own lack of financial skills began to cause serious problems. In order to pay the bills, she performed as much as possible, but the concerts never seemed to bring in enough money, and they meant spending more time away from her children. By 1964 Baker was in way over her head; local shopkeepers and merchants were no longer willing to extend her credit, so she often had to shop for food and supplies in distant Paris. During these years the children began entering adolescence, and with an absent father and an only periodically present mother they often became uncontrollable, sneaking out at night and at times disappearing for days. More and more Les Milandes seemed to be spiraling out of control.

In February 1968 local authorities sold Les Milandes at an auction for one-tenth of its value, ordering Baker and her family to vacate the premises in May. Baker sent the children to stay with a friend in Paris but remained in the chateau, camping out there for several more months until she was forcibly evicted. Photographs of her sitting forlornly in a tattered bathrobe on the steps of Les Milandes flashed around the world. It was a sad moment, but not the end of Baker's saga. Baker had lots of powerful and wealthy friends, and they stepped in to help at this low point in her life. Princess Grace and Prince Rainier of Monaco resettled the family in a five-bedroom villa overlooking the Mediterranean in the beautiful seaside town of Roquebrune. There Baker could recover from the disastrous loss of Les Milandes. Well into her sixties she would continue to perform until her death in 1975, which came appropriately enough backstage after a triumphal comeback concert in Paris.

The loss of Les Milandes did in effect spell the end of the Rainbow Tribe, however. Most of the children moved on from Monaco to attend various boarding schools before striking out on their own as adults. Some moved in with Jo Bouillon, who had relocated to Buenos Aires. Baker had hoped that as adults they would return to their home countries as ambassadors of her universal vision, but that doesn't seem to have happened. Some continued to identify strongly with their famous mother, and with the Rainbow Tribe, whereas for others the experience became an increasingly distant part of another life. Les Milandes passed into other hands and continues to receive tourists to this day, housing a museum on the life of Josephine Baker. But the Rainbow Tribe would never live there, or anywhere, all together as a family again.

The end of the Rainbow Tribe also mirrored and spoke to changes in postwar France. By the late 1960s the infants of France's baby boom had become teenagers, and Baker's children were not the only ones to engage in adolescent rebellion. 1968, the year the Rainbow Tribe left Les Milandes, saw the highpoint of youth rebellion throughout the world, and no more so than in France itself. In May a crisis erupted at the suburban Nanterre campus of the University of Paris, quickly spread throughout the university system, and from there engulfed the nation as a whole. At one point some ten million French workers had gone on strike, and the May '68 movement nearly overthrew the government of Charles de Gaulle. At one point Baker took part in a march through Paris in support of de Gaulle and against the youthful protestors demanding a revolution. The turmoil at Les Milandes thus reflected broader challenges posed to French society by the new generation.[11]

The Rainbow Tribe's decline reflected the postwar crises of decolonization. In 1954, the year in which Baker and Bouillon's project began to take shape, also witnessed the outbreak of the Algerian war for independence. The war, which lasted until 1962, was an extremely traumatic experience for both Algeria and France, in large part due to the special role played by Algeria in French and French imperial life. Unlike France's other overseas possessions, Algeria was technically not a colony at all but rather three French departments, and French governments considered it an integral part of the nation. Yet most Algerians were not French citizens but rather subjects, dependents of the imperial state charged with the task of civilizing them. An anti-colonial revolt broke out in November which soon engulfed the territory in a bloody cycle of terror attacks and brutal military repression.[12]

In 1958 the seemingly insoluble crisis caused the collapse of the Fourth Republic and the return of Charles de Gaulle to power in Paris. In establishing the new Fifth Republic de Gaulle took the opportunity to replace the French Union with the new French Community, which in theory granted equality to all its citizens but in practice reserved key aspects of governance, such as economic policy and defense, to the metropole. As a result, after initially accepting membership most French colonies in 1960 opted for full independence, effectively destroying the French Community. The teenagers had revolted and demanded the full rights of adulthood. Although France retained important economic and military links to its former colonies, especially in Africa, the ideal of the French empire as a universal family basically died after 1960.

In one final irony, the Rainbow Tribe effectively ceased to exist right as the global demographic diversity it represented was becoming more the norm in French society as a whole. As historians such as Gerard Noiriel have shown, France has been a country of immigrants for most of its modern history, in particular during the twentieth century.[13] Before the *Trentes Glorieuses*, however, most of the newcomers had come from elsewhere in Europe, especially Italy, Spain, Portugal, and Ireland. After World War II, in increasing contrast, many colonial and former colonial subjects chose to seek opportunity in France, so that more and more French immigrants came from North Africa, West Africa, Southeast Asia, and elsewhere in the postcolonial world. The African street sweeper and the Arab corner grocer became fixtures of the French urban landscape in the 1950s and beyond. In adopting members from Asia, North Africa, and beyond, Josephine Baker's Rainbow Tribe anticipated the demographic diversity of France as a whole in the years and decades beyond the Second World War.[14]

The Rainbow Tribe thus belonged very much to its time and place. In a nation that emphasized children and large families, it was the largest, most grandiose family of them all. Baker's attempt to mold her children along the lines of her own universalist vision, and the failure of that attempt, in some ways echoed the failure of France's colonial project during the era of decolonization. Much of the inspiration for the Rainbow Tribe, such as the very idea of a casual extended family, came out of the African American tradition. In some ways, it embodied in living form the post-racial society the civil rights movement hoped to achieve. At the same time, the very idea of a cosmopolitan group of children living in a chateau, a part of France's national heritage, resonated with the egalitarian vision of the Resistance, one in which princes and paupers should be able to live side by side. It thus represented a blend of French and American influences in a France increasingly shaped by its great transatlantic ally. In a country— one of whose key cultural and political values was *fraternité*—the Rainbow Village offered a new take on the ideal of universal brotherhood, and of France as a global nation.

11

Transnational France on Vacation
A History of Club Med

A major part of consumer society during the postwar years, both in France and throughout the developed world, has been vacation. The rise of mass travel for the purpose of leisure had a double impact on France during the *Trentes Glorieuses*: the nation became one of the world's leading destinations for tourists, especially Americans, while at the same time more and more French began holidays beyond their national borders. The ability to go on vacation became a main goal for, and symbol of, the growing middle class during the late twentieth century. In the years after World War II tourism became a powerful symbol and key component of the good life, playing a key role in shaping the economy and culture of the French people and the broader world in which they lived.[1]

During these years the French created one of the greatest and most innovative vacation companies in the world, *Club Méditerranée*, universally known as Club Med. The study of Club Med provides a fascinating view of postwar French consumer culture, and how it played out on a global stage. The creators of Club Med sought to create a fantasy world, one where the individual or family on vacation could escape all the pressures of modern life, at least for a time. In doing so, however, it also illustrated the challenges of affluence, and in particular the interactions between France and the wider world in the construction of modern consumer culture. By the 1970s Club Med had created a worldwide network of vacation "villages," where one could enjoy both the local scenery and French cuisine: croissants under the coconut palms. It represented a new vision of transnational France, based both in traditions of French universalism and in global consumer culture.[2]

In spite of the fact that one can find references to the idea of vacation as early as the fourteenth century, in Chaucer's *Canterbury Tales* for example, for the most part the idea of taking time off work is a modern practice. It first began to emerge in the late nineteenth century, often associated with health: the practice of going to a spa or "taking the waters" at places like Bath England or Vichy France had existed since ancient times. The rise of organized tourism, such as that pioneered by Thomas Cook & Sons, both benefitted from and contributed to the idea of vacation. By the early twentieth century social and political groups throughout Europe and America organized vacation activities, especially for children and young people. Historian Laura Lee Downs has shown, for example, how Catholic, Socialist, and Communist organizations created summer camps for the children of the working-class Paris suburbs during the interwar years.[3]

When the leftwing Popular Front coalition won control of the French government in 1936, it granted all French workers two weeks paid vacation, creating the tradition of the *congé annuel* (yearly vacation) that has endured down to the present. That summer reporters marveled at the spectacle of working-class families from the slums of French cities and suburbs seeking out relaxation in the sun for the first time in their lives. Those whose lives were defined by work had the right to play as well. The idea of vacation for the people became a part of the broader emphasis on the good life for all championed by the Popular Front. Club Med's vision of organized holidays for all thus fit into the idea that leisure was not a privilege but a right for the citizens of a democratic nation.

At the same time, Club Med reflected the rise of a new middle class and the unprecedented prosperity of France in the decades after the Liberation. The era of the *trentes glorieuses*, the thirty glorious years of economic good times from the mid-1940s to the early 1970s, brought a new desire for consumer goods, and more importantly a new ability to satisfy that desire. During the 1950s and 1960s French people poured money into acquiring refrigerators, televisions, cars, and other symbols of the good life. As noted in the last chapter, much of this prosperity went to nurturing the huge new baby boom generation, so that family expenses assumed pride of place in the budgets of the new middle class.[4]

They also made spending money on vacation a priority. By 1968 French citizens could take up to four weeks of paid time off a year, and more and more used this time to get away on vacation. Nothing says one has to spend time off work traveling to vacation areas far away from home; many French people in the postwar era spent their time at home, or in vacation homes in the countryside increasingly popular among Parisians in particular as the nation became more urban. Yet more and more during the decades after World War II the idea of traveling to some place new, scenic, and exotic captivated the imaginations, and wallets, of French families. In a nation increasingly focused on children, moreover, vacation time was family time, a chance to enjoy (or sometimes maybe not) quality time with one's offspring. From 1950 to 1970 French spending on leisure activities more than doubled, and most families spent 6 to 8 percent of their budgets on vacation. By the 1960s the month of August had emerged as the prime vacation time, with Paris and other cities given over to foreign tourists while the French headed for vacation spots.

Moreover, the rise of consumer spending, especially on transportation, interacted with the new vacation culture. When French workers got their first paid vacations in 1936 photographs and newsreels showed smiling families waving from packed trains as they headed out to the countryside. By the 1960s, in contrast, most French drove to vacation spots in their own cars. The private automobile, a key symbol of postwar consumerism and prosperity, also became a centerpiece of vacation culture. In the late 1960s and 1970s the rise of mass aviation further broadened ideas about tourism and travel. Not only the affluent but now many members of the middle classes could fly to destinations beyond France and even Europe. As much as anything, vacation symbolized the good life in postwar France; as French scholar Claude Goguel noted, the year was now divided between two periods, vacation and waiting for vacation.[5]

This broader context produced the business and cultural phenomenon that became Club Med. It was founded in the spring of 1950 by Gérard Blitz, an amateur water polo player from a family of Jewish diamond cutters in Antwerp. His socialist father had also played water polo and was one of several Jewish athletes to win a medal at the 1936 Olympic Games in Nazi Germany. Blitz had served in the Belgian resistance during the war, and after 1945 had worked in a hotel in the French Alps run by the Belgian government to help recuperate concentration camp survivors. Discovering the importance of fresh air, natural beauty, and exercise to people who had literally been through hell convinced Blitz of the benefits of such leisure, and how they could help all people live better lives.

Blitz was also strongly influenced by his wife, Claudine Coindeau, who had lived in Tahiti during the war and become enamored with the primitivist ideal of Tahitian culture as a life without artifice, spontaneous, carefree, and sensuous. She brought to Club Med the idea of the colony as escape from daily life in the metropole. The fledgling organization thus drew inspiration both from the empire and the Holocaust. After the war Blitz also met Gilbert Trigano, whose family owned the camping store which would supply the new Club Med with tents. Trigano was born in Paris, of Algerian Jewish origin, and had fought as a Communist in the Resistance during the war. Their work together would eventually make Club Med a global phenomenon, a leader of the vacation industry of the late twentieth century.

The fact that Blitz and Trigano were both Jews, and veterans of the Resistance, deserves mention. In contrast to much of the rest of Europe, most French Jews had survived the war and Nazi occupation, but the community had nonetheless been devastated by the experience, and in particular those who returned to France after the liberation of the concentration camps and who struggled to put the traumas of the past behind them and resume a normal life. When the two first met Blitz impressed Trigano with his desire to help Holocaust survivors, to help them heal from the horrors they had suffered in a place of beauty and spiritual peace. The Club Med village would be the exact opposite of, and antidote to, the concentration camp, a community based in pleasure and love rather than terror, slave labor, and murder. It represented a way of fighting against Nazism very different from, but in some senses as important, as their work during the Resistance. Moreover, both Trigano and Blitz strongly supported Zionism, and the communalism of Club Med significantly resembled that of the Zionist movement and of Israeli culture during the early years of the Jewish state; the Club Med village as kibbutz. Although Club Med focused on play and the kibbutzim on work, both emphasized personal empowerment, the healing of traumas, and the importance of community. Trigano and Blitz founded a Club Med in Israel in 1961, and one of the first vacationers there was the Baron Edmond de Rothschild, who would go on to buy the company after enjoying his stay there. Jews accounted for many of the vacationers and employees at Club Med during its first decades, and in general Club Med, like the Alliance Israélite Universelle before it, spoke to a blending of French and Jewish universalism.

The first Club Med opened in the summer of 1950 at a beach on the Spanish island of Majorca. Over the course of the summer 2,500 people came for two-week stays. Most of the vacationers were young and middle class, and most came from France, Belgium, or elsewhere in Europe. Blitz provided an orchestra and sports equipment, and his guests played sports, swam, and ate at communal tables. Conditions were rudimentary: there were no hotels or even cabins, and no running water, so guests slept in U.S. Army surplus tents; moreover, the threat of a hurricane led many guests to threaten to leave, until Blitz promised them complete satisfaction or their money back. Eventually most stayed, and after their return Blitz used photos and a newsletter to keep in touch with the *gentils membres* (nice guests, or GMs).

Over the next few years, Blitz and Trigano developed Club Med from a rather quirky vacation concept into a major transnational corporation devoted to leisure. Originally started as a non-profit agency, Trigano in particular transformed it into a modern business. The first resorts were all located on the Mediterranean, but in 1956 Club Med opened a ski village for winter holidays in Switzerland. In 1955 it branched beyond Europe, opening a club in Tahiti, followed by a resort in Morocco in 1965. When the Baron de Rothschild bought Club Med he used his resources and vision to expand its operations significantly. In 1968 Club Med expanded into the Americas, opening its first village there in the French Caribbean island of Guadeloupe. It also opened a business office in New York as well as signing an agreement with American Express, giving itself new visibility in the North American market. By the early 1970s Club Med had twenty-eight villages spread around the world. Also in the late 1960s Club Med began experimenting with its own cruise ships, making the experience of total relaxation and indulgence a sea-going one as well. In 1989 this new practice culminated with the launching of *Club Med 1*, an ocean-going Club Med village and the world's biggest cruise ship.

Several aspects of Club Med made it unique at its time, and laid the bases for its success. Club Med presented itself to its guests, the G Ms, as not just a vacation but an alternate utopian world. Upon arrival the G Ms were expected to divest themselves of their regular clothing and spend their time at the resort in beachwear. The resort was supposed to be an isolated, closed world, cut off from everyday life. To facilitate this the resort pioneered the all-inclusive concept, where everything was paid for in advance and the G Ms had no need of cash during their vacation. G Ms were expected simply to enjoy themselves, to play and relax. There was no pedagogical agenda, no duty beyond the escape from civilization.

Part of this emphasis on nature was a focus on sex and the body. Club Med ads touted the native sensuality of the tropics, part of the escape from civilization. G Ms were encouraged to exercise and cultivate a better physique, although the emphasis was always on physical conditioning rather than dieting. Each resort had a number of employees, or *gentils organisateurs* ("G Os") who worked as swimming instructors, physical trainers, and sports coaches. Club Med also quickly acquired a reputation as places where sexual encounters were normal, and even expected, where a summertime romance was both a reward for improving one's physique and part of relaxing one's traditional, everyday inhibitions.

More generally, Club Med emphasized the idea of total vacation, where the G Ms would spend their time without plans or cares, in a culture that emphasized pure simple enjoyment. Sports loomed large in Club Med villages as a way of relaxing and enjoying the body rather than as a rigid regimen of physical improvement. Unlike traditional health clubs and vacations, Club Med did not promote a strict dietary regimen, rather lavishing a wide range of (all you can eat) delicious food and drink on its guests. The company carefully kept its villages isolated from their surroundings, although it would at times arrange excursions to see exotic local cultures. It strove to welcome the GM to an Eden-like paradise, far removed from all cares and from time itself.

The popularity of this vision, of a desire to escape all the problems of contemporary bourgeois society, ironically made Club Med a pillar of the very world it at least implicitly criticized. By the late 1960s Club Med was a big capitalist company, with more than thirty vacation villages in Europe alone and some twenty million dollars in business annually. Although it started as a non-profit organization in 1950, the Baron de Rothschild's investments in the early 1960s made it more and more like any other capitalist concern. Increasingly it worked closely with other companies involved in the vacation business, such as Air France and American Express. The dream of an egalitarian tropical paradise thus rested upon and grew out of modern corporate culture.

The company's clientele also reflected this paradox. Club Med definitely catered to the cadres, the new middle classes that became so prominent during the boom years of the Fifth Republic. The majority of GMs were teachers, lawyers, doctors, secretaries, managers, and other members of the prosperous wage-earning sector of French society. Although more and more French people started to go on vacation during the 1960s, very few workers could afford to do so. Moreover, the majority of those who took holidays did so within France, often going camping. This was not tourism for the elite, however; it did not aspire to the world of grand hotels and luxury restaurants. Rather, it catered to people who could afford to set a little money aside to enjoy themselves, every once in a while, in a different kind of setting, to experience life in a tropical fantasy paradise.

At the same time, Club Med tried to create a fantasy world beyond social classes and distinctions. Both Blitz and Trigano came from leftwing backgrounds, and the alternate vision of society that Club Med represented included aspects of socialist utopia. It replicated the social egalitarianism of many in the French Resistance, their conviction that they fought for a future France free not only from German rule but from capitalism in general. The emphasis on wearing vacation clothes, for example, served to mask social distinctions. GMs were encouraged to wear bathing suits and sarongs, to appear as natural as possible. Such minimal clothing both highlighted the sensuality of the vacation experience and also tended to suppress class distinctions; as Club Med claimed, "there are no social differences when everyone is in a bathing suit." In this way Club Med heralded the 1960s triumph of the ultimate symbol of egalitarian clothing, blue jeans. Another aspect of this egalitarianism was the suppression of cash. Since the resort was all-inclusive, GMs paid for their meals and sporting activities in advance. To purchase drinks and other extra items, they bought colored beads that they wore around their necks, a bodily decoration as much as a type of money. In general, Club Med tried to mask the fact that it was a business for profit, that the GMs paid for their experience. To an important extent, a cashless society thus seemed a classless society. Club Med represented the idea that growing prosperity would tend to erase social distinctions, a core belief of many who served in the Resistance, at a time when in reality the opposite was happening.

Club Med also represented a new vision of France's colonial encounter. It began during the era of decolonization, creating a new global empire of commercial vacations right as the old republican empire was falling apart. In many ways, the idea of Club Med as an antidote to civilization rested upon earlier primitivist ideas of the colonies. Claudine Coindeau translated her experiences in Tahiti during the war into a fascination with Polynesian culture as naïve and sensual, and it became a key theme of Club Med life even before the creation of a resort in Tahiti itself. GMs often lived in Tahitian-style grass huts that replaced the army tents of the early years. Welcoming ceremonies to the resorts often mimicked those of Polynesian villages—both GMs and GOs usually wore sarongs and pareos—and Club Med would routinely bring Tahitians to their resorts to teach the GMs native customs. During the 1960s the company helped pioneer the idea of the lush tropical island as the ultimate vacation destination, at a time when the rise of mass market jet travel was causing an explosion in tourism to Hawaii and the Caribbean. At the same time, the focus on islands replicated changes in the French empire itself. By the early 1960s islands in the Caribbean and Pacific were essentially what remained of overseas France, the so-called confetti of empire. To romanticize them was to idealize France's continued presence beyond the borders of the metropole.[6]

The image of colonial life presented by Club Med was of course far removed from the reality. The image of the natives as happy-go-lucky, lazy, and sensual had been used to justify French rule, and forced labor in particular. In Club Med, by contrast, it became a positive value, the antithesis of a civilized lifestyle seen as oppressive. Or at least, oppressive for the overwhelmingly European and white GMs. Club Med resorts could not exist without labor, of course: someone had to cook and serve the food and clean the rooms. Even the ultimate image of tropical leisure, the white sand beach, had to be raked and cleaned regularly to maintain its idyllic, pristine appearance. But such labor was supposed to be as unobtrusive as possible, and it was done mostly by the local residents, the real-life version of the colonial natives. For them, of course, laziness was not a virtue. Ultimately what Club Med offered was the chance to experience the lifestyle of a colonial settler for a short time, to be a "Sahib for a week."

Moreover, such considerations raise the question of how Club Med acquired its properties, and what existed there before it built its primitive wonderlands for western tourists. Did it simply purchase unused land and develop it both for the benefit of the tourists and the locals who found jobs there, or did it use its resources to displace existing communities? One poignant example is the village Club Med established in Israel, like so many places in the country built on the ruins of a Palestinian Arab village. As historian Peter Lagerquist has noted:

> When Club Med arrived in Israel in 1961, it found on the country's northern coast a golden beach with picturesque ruins and no people— the kind of place where a weary European could "feel so far away, yet be so near." Palestinians who once lived in the coastal village of al-Zib feel the same way. Driven from their homes in 1948, some returned to the vicinity of their destroyed village after the war, to resettle on the margins of Israel's conscience and the globalized fantasies of leisure that have since been enacted on the ruins of their homes.[7]

Club Med certainly bore no responsibility for the destruction of al-Zib, but it benefitted from it. In this instance at least, and quite possibly others, a tourist paradise for affluent Westerners rested upon the disappearance of those traditional communities it often encouraged its guests to celebrate. Recently a satirical version of the classic fairy tale "The Three Little Pigs" described the destruction of the house of sticks in terms uncomfortably close to the Club Med experience: "The wolf huffed and puffed and blew down the house of sticks. The pigs ran to the house of bricks, with the wolf close at their heels. Where the house of sticks had stood, other wolves built a time-share condo resort complex for vacationing wolves, with each unit a fiberglass reconstruction of the house of sticks, as well as native curio shops, snorkeling and dolphin shows."[8]

Finally, Club Med in its early years represented an interesting mix of French and global cultures. Until the company began creating resorts specifically designed for Americans, the lingua franca was French and the GOs usually came from France. As the organization became more international, however, more and more people spoke English. The focus on French cuisine also characterized Club Med villages and became a selling point for non-French visitors. What could be more wonderful, after all, than eating fresh croissants on a beautiful tropical beach? At the same time, especially once the company started catering to families, it began providing standard international fare such as pizza and hamburgers. Club Med thus came to represent both the global reach of French culture and the transnational reconfiguration of that culture.

By the 1980s Club Med had gone far beyond its French and Mediterranean roots to become a global vacation industry. During that decade it opened several new villages around the world, including ones in Japan in 1984 and in the United States. As the times changed, Club Med changed with them. The impact of AIDS in the 1980s led it to deemphasize its sex-in-the-sun appeal, and as more young vacationers returned as middle-aged parents it developed extensive child-care programs to give them a break and keep everyone happy. By the turn of the century some Club Med villages were discretely catering to a gay clientele. Ideas of vacation might change, but Club Med remained committed to giving its clients a taste of paradise for a week.

The final years of the twentieth century brought new challenges to Club Med. In the 1990s new vacation companies like EuroDisney successfully copied Club Med's appeal and began eating into its profits. In response to what it perceived as a new era of mass low-budget travel, Club Med launched several new inexpensive resort villages, but the large expenses this strategy entailed did not result in the desired profits. As a result, the company began losing hundreds of millions of euros annually, leading some to wonder whether the legendary company's time had come. This troubled era culminated with the September 11, 2001, terrorist attacks on the World Trade Center, which for a brief period brought global tourism to a screeching halt.

At that point Club Med faced a fundamental choice, evolve or die, and evolve it did. Henri Giscard d'Estaing, the son of the former French president, bought the troubled company and began shifting its image from middle class tourist paradise to luxury resorts. Giscard spent a billion euros upgrading Club Med villages to attract a more upscale clientele. Many traditional Club Med families, those who vacationed there every year, sharply attacked this new orientation, feeling it betrayed the essence of what Club Med was supposed to be. Yet Giscard d'Estaing's new direction proved successful, both because he implemented it in a way that preserved many Club Med traditions, and because it corresponded to broader changes in global society and economy. The early years of the twenty-first century were not the 1960s: instead of a growing middle class, the world economy now emphasized the rise of the super-wealthy, an escalating gap between rich and poor, and the decline of the middle class. Its retail landscape centered increasingly around stores like Gucci, not Sears or JCPenney. In 2015 a Chinese conglomerate took control of Club Med, keeping Giscard d'Estaing in his role as president of the company. Today Club Med is more successful than ever, with eighty vacation villages that have preserved the tradition of cocktails and croissants on the beach.[9]

Over the years Club Med has thus represented both the consumer culture of the postwar years in France, and various challenges and alternatives to that culture. As a symbol of consumerism, it came under attack from the rebellious students of May 1968. One example of a hostile slogan was, "See Nanterre and live. Go to Naples with Club Med and die." At one point students assaulted the Club Med headquarters, whereupon the company responded by offering some of them free Club Med vacations and hiring Paul Thorez, the son of P C F leader Maurice Thorez. For the students of May 1968, Club Med symbolized much they despised about bourgeois society and consumer culture. At the same time, however, one of the most popular chants during the near-revolution was "*Sous les pavés la plage*" ("Underneath the cobblestones [used to build barricades] the beach," an expression that connotes transcending the rigid social barriers of France). The young *enrages* (activists) of the French New Left represented the avant-garde of the baby boom generation that had so profoundly transformed postwar France. They both rejected consumer society and were very much a central part of it. In very different ways, both Club Med and May 1968 represented alternate visions of modern French life, and both exemplified the continuing global reach of French culture in the late twentieth century.

12

Postcolonial Soundtrack
Hip-Hop Music and Culture in Contemporary France

In 2003 interior minister Nicholas Sarkozy threatened to sue the hip-hop group Sniper for songs that recommended young people burn cars in protest against the inequities of French society and contained lines such as "France is a bitch." Calling the group racist, anti-Semitic, and a disgrace to France, Sarkozy pushed through a law making "offending the dignity of the republic" a punishable offense. Two years later another French rapper, Monsieur R, released an inflammatory video titled *FranSSe*, implicitly comparing the Fifth Republic to Nazi Germany and featuring nude white women gyrating and fondling a French flag. Outraged legislators pushed to have the song banned, only to see the case thrown out of court. In both instances, the rappers protested, emphasizing the politics of their attacks on French racism and neocolonialism.[1]

Welcome to the world of French hip-hop. Few aspects of life in the modern era have been more global than popular music, and this has been true for centuries. The *Marseillaise* carried the message of the French Revolution around the world, and during the twentieth century France integrated different types of music from abroad into its artistic and cultural life. The invention of vinyl records, cassettes and CDs, and the birth and dissemination of radio and television all contributed to the formation of a global music sphere. More recently the rise of the internet in the 1980s and the invention of YouTube in 2005 have enabled listeners to access an enormous variety of musical forms instantaneously and repeatedly. There has always been a tension in music between the lyrics—understanding of which is limited to speakers of the same language—and the melodies and harmonies themselves, accessible to all those who can hear. The global dissemination of music has both highlighted and complicated this tension. It has created a world marketplace in music, while at the same time musicians continue to express ideas drawn from national and often intensely local experiences. In many ways, therefore, music is the ultimate transnational language.[2]

With the sole exception of the United States, contemporary France has the largest hip-hop music industry in the world today. All of its major cities, and many rural areas, have active hip-hop music cultures, with frequent concerts and festivals. While a variety of musicians perform it, and a huge range of French young people listen to it, French hip-hop has become tightly associated with the postcolonial experience in modern France, the world of jobless Black and Brown young people, suburban housing projects, crime, discrimination, and despair. Hip-hop originated in America, specifically in the Black and Latino communities of New York City; by the end of the twentieth century, it had not only largely displaced rock music as the chosen sound of young people but had also gone global in a serious way. This is not just musical imitation or faddism: the worldwide popularity of hip-hop expresses the social and political conflicts that constitute the underside of neoliberal globalization in the contemporary era.

Like jazz before it, hip-hop first came to France as an African American import, but also like jazz it was rapidly integrated into the nation's musical traditions. Musicians and cultural commentators debate to this day whether hip-hop in France is authentically French or rather a reflection of America's global dominance of popular music. I reject the idea of this as an either-or dilemma, suggesting instead that both arguments have some truth to them, that while French hip-hop is inseparable from its American big brother, at the same time it has been so successful precisely because it maps onto important aspects of contemporary French culture and society. In terms of society, the gritty urban realities of the nation's postcolonial banlieues were perfectly suited to a musical form that emerged from America's minority ghettos. Moreover, in areas without their own cultural traditions, only a few decades old and largely composed of immigrants from elsewhere, hip-hop corresponded to and helped shape their new realities. One can be authentically and transnationally French at the same time.

From New York to the World: The Origins of Hip-Hop

Barely fifty years old, the hip-hop genre, including rap music, is one of the great cultural achievements of the contemporary world. It is both very much a part of the long tradition of African American music, a successor to jazz and rhythm and blues, and a premier example of global cultural fusion. The origins of hip-hop music and culture go back to New York City, in particular the Bronx, during the 1970s. Interactions between African Americans and immigrants from the Caribbean gradually brought a new form of musical culture into being, one that drew upon the heritages of both groups. Although most noteworthy as a musical style, hip-hop also embraced other cultural patterns, notably break dancing, disc jockeying, and graffiti art. In 1973 DJ Kool Herc, a Jamaican immigrant in New York, began the practice of simultaneously using two record players to produce a new sound, "scratching." This style was soon picked up by other disc jockeys, notably Grand Master Flash and Afrika Bambaataa, starting in house parties and gradually moving to larger outdoor venues. A crucial aspect of hip-hop music and culture was rapping, a performative combination of singing and speaking with deep roots in African American and ultimately African music.[3]

By the late 1970s hip-hop was emerging out of its birthplace in the Bronx to become a national phenomenon. In 1979 the Sugarhill Gang recorded "Rapper's Delight," widely regarded as the first rap song to reach a mainstream audience. By the mid 1980s hip-hop music had become big business, and more diverse than ever. Critics often referred to this era as the golden age of hip-hop, a period in which it became more and more central to American popular music while at the same time retaining a strong innovative streak. Hip-hop had also branched well beyond its New York roots to establish centers in many other cities, notably Los Angeles where gangsta rap developed in the mid to late 1980s. The 1988 album *Straight Outta Compton* by N.W.A highlighted the emergence of this new genre, illustrating not only the diversity but also the exceptional popularity of the new musical and cultural style. In 1990 albums by rappers such as Public Enemy and MC Hammer climbed to the top of the pop charts in America, making hip-hop more than ever the sound of the age.[4]

The spread of hip-hop across the United States went together with an even more impressive dissemination around the world. Like jazz and rock and roll earlier in the twentieth century, hip-hop both shaped and was shaped by the increasingly globalized character of world life in the contemporary era. Given the Latinx roots of many of the first rappers in New York, hip-hop soon spread throughout Latin America and the Caribbean. By the late 1980s most European nations, notably the United Kingdom and Germany as well as France, had vibrant rap subcultures. Hip-hop music scenes also popped up throughout Africa, Asia, and the Middle East. Their existence testified both to the importance of America's worldwide cultural influence, but also to the universality of the social and political concerns that drove hip-hop culture. Today there is probably not a place in the world that does not have its own hip-hop music scene.[5]

Hip-hop's global reach underscored its diversity as a musical and cultural phenomenon, but at the same time highlighted key themes that inspired many of its practitioners. At its heart hip-hop was the music of the excluded and the oppressed, those who suffered discrimination, marginalization, and despair. It first arose in the South Bronx, one of America's most impoverished and crime-ridden neighborhoods during the 1970s, a phenomenon replicated by the gangsta rap of South Central Los Angeles in the 1980s. It also illustrated and frequently protested against the impact of racial discrimination, and not just in the United States. Many rappers in Europe and Latin America came from minority and immigrant backgrounds, and used their music as a weapon against racism. At the end of the twentieth century, hip-hop achieved success around the world largely by voicing the cultural anguish of those who felt success had passed them by in real life.

B-Boyz in the Banlieue

The rise of hip-hop in France took place in the context of the nation's version of economic decline and racial trauma.[6] Hip-hop first arrived in France in 1982, when a French journalist persuaded the radio station Europe

1 to organize a tour of American hip-hop musicians and dancers in France. Leading performers such as Afrika Bambaataa, the Rock Steady Crew, and Fab 5 Freddy played concerts at ten cities in the country, including a major show in Paris. The "New York City Rap Tour" marked the beginnings of hip-hop culture in France. Of particular importance was Afrika Bambaataa, a Black hip-hop disc jockey from the South Bronx, and his Universal Zulu Nation, which in 1984 established a branch in the Paris suburbs, complete with its own king and queen, its own fanzine, and regular dance parties. It had a major influence on many of the earliest French hip-hop performers. At the same time French youth began listening to American hip-hop on the radio, and watching American movies featuring breakdancing like *Flashdance* and *Footloose*. In 1984 Sydney Duteil, a young man from Guadeloupe, began hosting his own dance show on French television. Entitled *Hip-Hop*, it was the first French television program hosted by a Black person and became a force in the dissemination of the new music. By this time hip-hop had become popular in France, especially in the nation's multicultural suburbs.[7]

In terms of culture, the intense lyricism of hip-hop, its strong focus on words rather than melodies and harmonies, not only constituted a sharp departure from traditions of American popular music but also meshed well with French musical traditions, notably the *chanson*, or song. The oldest surviving work of French literature, *The Song of Roland* from the eighth century, is a chanson, and contemporary French hip-hop has more in common than one might think with the chansons sung by working class Parisian women like Edith Piaf in the early twentieth century. The heroic posing, verbal jousting, and bitter sociological analysis of rap spoke to many young people experienced in French music who lived in conditions all too reminiscent of the South Bronx or Chicago. For working class French youth, rap expressed the global dimensions of their lives both politically and aesthetically.

At the heart of French hip-hop lay the experience of life in the banlieue, the massive suburban rings outside Paris and other French cities that in the late twentieth century became the center and symbol of postcolonial France. For more than a century the suburbs of the capital have symbolized social, cultural, and political marginality in French life. In contrast to America, where "the suburbs" usually stand for middle class comfort and affluence, in France the suburbs are generally home to the working-class poor, people without the resources to succeed in Paris itself. In the late nineteenth century heavy industry developed there first rather than in the city, ringing Paris with a zone of factory towns and cheap housing. The working class that settled there during the interwar years became the natural constituency for the young French Communist Party (PCF), so that by the 1930s social commentators had christened the area the Paris Red Belt. In the decades after World War II the PCF increased its power in Paris suburbs that grew by leaps and bounds due to the nation's population growth and the desire of many young families for better housing. Under the Fourth Republic the French state invested massively in public housing in the area, building huge complexes known as *habitation à loyer modéré* (HLM). Many immigrants, drawn to the booming industrial economy of the Paris area, settled in the suburbs during the postwar era. As a result, by the end of the twentieth century the suburban communities were home to nearly ten million people, many more than lived in Paris itself and well more than 10 percent of the nation's population as a whole.

During the last quarter of the century the Paris suburbs increasingly began to represent marginality grounded not just in class but also in race. In response to the economic downturn of the early 1970s France terminated most overseas immigration, but did enable the (largely male) foreign residents to bring in their families as a way to promote social stability. "Family reunification" resulted in the creation of new immigrant communities, composed especially of people from North and sub-Saharan Africa, throughout the Paris suburbs. By the early 1980s suburban nonwhite youth, often born in France and speaking native French, had begun to make a mark on the society and culture of the banlieue. Their emergence into adolescence and adulthood coincided with the deindustrialization and stagnation of the French economy (in particular the decline of the industries which had built the suburbs) and the physical decay of the HLMs in which they lived all added up to a sense of crisis, for them and for French society as a whole.[8]

The difficulties of the "second generation immigrants," a term that underscored their difficult integration into the society in which they were born and raised, made issues of race and racism a key social issue in France at the end of the twentieth century. Many French had traditionally viewed racism as an American problem: after all, France had gladly welcomed illustrious African Americans such as Josephine Baker and Richard Wright, refugees from bigotry in the United States. Yet the country now had its own suburban ghettos populated by disaffected brown and Black people in many ways alienated from the mainstream of French society, which generally regarded them with suspicion. In the early 1980s riots broke out in the Paris suburbs, often featuring minority youth blowing up automobiles and fighting with the police. The kinds of social and racial problems French intellectuals had so often decried in the United States had clearly crossed the Atlantic.[9]

The election of the Mitterrand administration also played an important role in the rise of French hip-hop. The victory of the Socialists in the presidential and legislative elections of 1981 brought a powerful wind of change to French society and culture. Culture Minister Jack Lang used the power of the French state to embrace nontraditional forms of artistic expression and appeal to a broader, more youthful audience. In 1982 Lang established the *Fête de la Musique*, a national celebration when the French government encouraged everyone to be musical for a day. Lang also decentralized the nation's broadcast system, encouraging the rise of the so-called *radios libres*, or free radio stations, which brought music of all different kinds into French households. By the end of the decade Lang had recruited the famed Florida A & M University marching band to take part in the bicentennial celebration of the French Revolution, treating Parisians to the sight of African American musicians and performers break dancing down the Champs-Élysées.

In 1984 French rapper Dee Nasty released the first major hip-hop album in France, *Paname City Rappin'*. Dee Nasty, a white Frenchman (born Daniel Bigault) from the Paris suburbs, first encountered hip-hop music in 1979. At the end of 1981 he began working in a free radio station in Paris, Carbone 14, that broadcast hip-hop and other types of popular music twenty-four hours a day. Hostility and skepticism from the French commercial music establishment forced Nasty to produce and sell his album independently. Sales of the album were slow at first, but the new style quickly caught on.

By 1990 Virgin Records would sponsor an anthology album of French rappers named *Rapattitude*, and in the new decade hip-hop would become one of the most popular genres of music in the country.

Paname City Rappin' illustrated the centrality of the Paris region to French hip-hop. *Paname* (Panama) is an old slang term for Paris, in particular for the city's popular culture and style. It comes both from the ruinous Panama Canal financial scandal of the late nineteenth century, and from the fashion for Panama hats, originally worn by the workers who dug the canal and fashionable among Parisian men in the early twentieth century. In using this term Dee Nasty underscored the idea that Parisian rappers represented a new version of popular Parisian style, linking the cultures of the *faubourg* and the banlieue. As the song's refrain went:

> Panama, Panama, oh city of dreams;
> But life in Paris is not what it seems;
> You will lose your head, find yourself on the street;
> If you can't keep up with the city's beat;
> It's too much, there are too many people;
> It's too much, it's too much;
> There are too many people;
> It's too much.[10]

This pessimistic view of Paris replicated the perspective from the city's suburbs, home to few of the city's attractions and many of its problems.

Paris did not hold a monopoly on hip-hop in France, however. Marseilles, the nation's second city, also hosted a vibrant rap music scene. In many ways Marseilles fit the image of a hip-hop center: familiar to Americans as a result of the film *The French Connection*, Marseilles was a big working-class port city with many immigrants and strong ties to North Africa as well as other Mediterranean ports such as Barcelona and Naples. Unlike Paris, Marseilles had never developed a major suburban belt, so the poor still had a visible place in the city center, a downtown full of gangsters and illicit drugs. In the late 1980s six young men from Marseilles formed what would become one of France's most successful hip-hop groups, I A M. The musicians were both Black and white, and all foreign-born. I A M underscored the cosmopolitan, interracial nature of French hip-hop. It also highlighted the local culture of Marseilles, which it portrayed as linked to the colonial world and Africa in particular. IAM often adopted an Afrocentric perspective, frequently referring to the civilization of ancient Egypt. For IAM, the hip-hop world of Marseilles had both global and local dimensions.

One of the first major French rappers, and to this day probably the best known, was MC Solaar. Born in Senegal in 1969, Solaar came to France with his family as an infant, settling in the Parisian suburb of Villeneuve-St-Georges where he grew up. He discovered the Universal Zulu Nation in Cairo, where he lived with his uncle for a year when he was twelve. Upon returning to France he began playing rap music while pursuing his education, earning a degree in philosophy from the University of Paris at Jussieu. Early on he teamed up with American hip-hop artists, notably music producer Jimmy Jay, and in 1990 released his first single, *Bouge de là* ("Get out of there"), which rose to number five on the national charts. Solaar followed this a year later with his first album, *Qui Sème le Vent Récolte le Tempo* ("He who sows the wind harvests the beat"), which sold four hundred thousand copies.[11]

By the early 1990s hip-hop had become all the rage in France, and numerous groups were performing it. Some of the most notable early groups included IAM, Assassin, Suprême NTM, and New Generation MC. French hip-hop emphasized very fast and complex lyrics, often sung in *Verlan*, a type of linguistic inversion pioneered in the suburbs, or other forms of slang. Although audiences and listeners were very diverse, most performers were second generation immigrants, young people from the suburbs who embraced the music as speaking to their own experience. At the same time, many in France assumed that rap music had to be created and performed by suburban Black and Brown youth to be authentic. In 1995 film director Matthieu Kassovitz released *La haine* (*Hate*), a study of banlieue life modeled on American ghetto-centric films like *Boyz in the Hood*. In sharp contrast to the United States, where the political establishment harshly condemned hip-hop culture, the political and aesthetic establishment in France often embraced it. François Mitterrand allowed himself to be photographed with a group of young French rappers wearing a baseball cap backward, and his culture minister Jack Lang promoted the teaching of hip-hop music and dance in schools throughout the country.

French hip-hop embraced a variety of themes, some similar to those of American rap music, some less so. Just as Americans focused on life in the inner-city ghetto, so did their French peers address the experience of the banlieue, and its implications for French identity in general. For French rappers the suburbs were not only home, but a symbol of the racism and oppression inherent in French society as a whole. In particular, French hip-hop musicians focused on the hypocrisy of republican universalism which didn't seem to have a place for them. As Yazid, a rapper of North African origin, sang:

> I'm the Arab, stopping oppression is my mission.
> The country of secularism doesn't tolerate Islam.
> Unemployment ravages, they talk of immigration.
> And when the *banlieue* burns, they talk of integration.[12]

One should note that, as in America, hip-hop in France was not limited to music and music performance. Dance played a major role in the emergence of a French hip-hop culture. In fact, because unlike vocal music it did not have to contend with the difficulties of translating the idiom from English into French, dance became a primary venue for the introduction of rap culture into France. Its predominant form, break-dancing, borrowed from the martial arts and other combat dance styles like Brazilian *capoeira* which also became popular in France during the 1980s and 1990s. Graffiti art, or tagging, also became very widespread in the Paris suburbs in particular, if not as much as in New York. It became the hip-hop generation's way of inscribing its name in public space. By the end of the twentieth century, hip-hop culture thus posed a multifaceted challenge to French traditional life.

The Politics of French Hip-Hop

Much of French hip-hop took an overtly political stance, voicing the rage of the banlieue. As in the United States it frequently targeted the police, the state forces of order widely seen as the oppressors of Black and Brown youth. In 1993 the popular rap group Suprême NTM recorded the song

"Police" (on the album *I Pull the Trigger*) which harshly attacked the police as racist. Two years later, during a Bastille Day concert called to protest the right-wing National Front, the group not only sang the song but also encouraged concertgoers to attack the security guards. This led a French court to sentence the band members to six months in jail and a fifty thousand euro fine, prompting protests and demonstrations in what soon became known as the NTM Affair. Eventually the band got off with a suspended sentence, but the incident sharply increased its popularity as rebels against the system. French hip-hop thus came to symbolize protests against racial injustice in France. At times it ventured into the frankly revolutionary, such as the photo of the group Assassin holding a copy of Karl Marx's *Civil War in France*.

It was only a step from symbolic protest to political and revolutionary action. For years since the 1980s observers of the French suburbs had viewed them as an area waiting to explode, and in October 2005 explode they did. Only a few months after French authorities tried to ban *FranSSe*, on October 27 two young men fleeing the police were electrocuted while hiding in a power substation in the Paris suburb of Clichy-sous-Bois. Outraged by what many saw as yet another instance of police harassment, young people across the Paris suburbs took to the streets in protest. By the second week of November the movement had spread throughout the nation, with protesters firebombing cars and battling the police. The French government eventually declared a state of emergency, arresting nearly three thousand rioters. By the time the movement came to an end in late November protestors had burned thousands of cars and caused hundreds of millions of dollars of property damage.[13]

After the 2005 uprising many rightist French politicians sought to censor rap music, arguing that it called for and contributed directly to violence and social upheaval. Many French rappers had in fact trumpeted the revolutionary and insurrectional nature of life in the banlieue, and the 2005 riots struck many across the political spectrum as a verification of their perspective: Suprême NTM at one point called hip-hop "the loudspeaker of the ghetto." In response, more than two hundred French Members of Parliament signed a petition in late November calling for legal action against several rappers, claiming they had incited racism and violence. As François Grosdidier, a member of the conservative U M P party, put it, "When people hear this all day long and when these words swirl round in their heads, it is no surprise that they then see red as soon as they walk past policemen or simply people who are different from them."[14] Such attempts to make French hip-hop legally culpable for the 2005 riots failed in the end, but the association between rap music and violent protests against racism and the establishment endured for many on both sides of the barricades.

Another major theme in French hip-hop was historical connections to Africa and slavery. By no means were all French rappers Black or of African ancestry, but many of those who were sought to link their current oppressed situation in France to the ravages of the slave trade. The Universal Zulu Nation had had a strongly Afrocentric philosophy, and some of the bands it influenced adopted this perspective. IAM's song *The Tom-Toms from Africa* portrayed a lost African paradise destroyed by Western oppression, to a sampled version of Stevie Wonder's *Past Time Paradise*. More than American rappers, many French hip-hop musicians and artists had direct family ties to the African continent, a place they considered victimized by the legacy of slavery and colonialism.

In addition, French rap at times embraced the gangsta culture of American hip-hop, complete with some of its misogynistic overtones. Most French rappers have been young (and gradually not so young) men, with some notable exceptions like Diam and Ladéa. The sole female performer on the *Rapattitude* album, Saliha, went on to a successful career, but few women followed in her trail. France did not produce an equivalent of the American singer Queen Latifah, who started as a rapper before going on to a mainstream career in music and movies. Hip-hop in France thus illustrated and exemplified the sexism of both hip-hop and mainstream French culture.[15]

The hypermasculine gangsta pose of some French rap finds expression in hostile attitudes toward France as a woman, for example, or patriarchal views of young women as sexual pawns. At the same time, it expresses a desire to shock established society, and to play into existing stereotypes of banlieue culture as intrinsically sexist. Sexism often thus mirrors the hostility directed toward the police, or society as a whole. The rap group

Suprême NTM claimed that the acronym part of its name stood for "*le nord transmet le message*," or "message from the north," referring to its origins in the north Paris suburbs. However many argued the word stood for *Nique ta mère*, "F--k your mother," a common insult in the banlieue.

Finally, a major theme of French hip-hop, one that differs from its American equivalent, has been interracial unity. In contrast to American rap music, strongly identified with African American musical traditions and politics, hip-hop in France involves performers from different immigrant backgrounds as well as white French musicians. Dee Nasty and several members of Suprême NTM are white, for example, MC Solaar came from Senegal, and Saliha's parents were Arab and Italian. One major group, Alliance Ethnik, pointed with pride to the diverse ethnic and racial origins of its members. The banlieue is portrayed as a place where people with origins in Africa and the Caribbean, and white French society will hopefully come together to fight the racist and class oppression of the national establishment. As Suprême NTM sang in its album *Authentik*, "Our society is multiracial/ So let's work together and create unity."[16] In contrast to the United States, therefore, often viewed as a nation of racial separation, the world of the French suburbs involves many different types of French people united in a desire to create a truly universal nation, one that will acknowledge the crimes of its past and move beyond them to embrace a future of respect and justice for all.

French hip-hop, disparaged by many in and outside France as the symbol of the nation's ghetto pathology, also thus speaks to the hope for a new form of republican universalism. This is perhaps one reason why it has had much more of an impact on mainstream politics in France than in the U.S. or other nations. In his presidential campaign of 2012 François Hollande released a campaign video titled "48 Hours with FH" complete with a soundtrack of *Niggas in Paris* by American rappers Kanye West and Jay-Z. The video, which made quite the splash on YouTube before suddenly being yanked from the public domain, showed Hollande riding the RER train through the Paris suburbs then speaking to a crowd of Brown and Black people showing their identity cards and declaring their intention to vote for him. The video cleverly weaves its way through banlieue and African

American hip-hop culture to portray Hollande as hip and sympathetic to all the people of France, unlike his opponent Nicholas Sarkozy. More importantly, it portrays the world of French hip-hop as the true face, and future, of France.

The view of hip-hop as symbolizing modernity and the new face of the nation, one that is global and multicultural rather than traditional, resonates with the image of the banlieue as the ungainly yet potent representative of France in the twenty-first century. The suburbs represent the national experience lived by ordinary French women and men, not the tourist France of the Eiffel Tower and the Champs-Élysées. In 2013 an American reporter living in the Paris suburbs described this perspective on the region and its place in contemporary France:

> My neighborhood is in Pantin, where the infamous northeastern suburbs—the banlieues—begin. When I told one Parisian where I lived during casual chatter at a dinner party in the chic Marais quarter, he actually stepped away from me and blurted: "*Quelle horreur!*" But it isn't a horrible place. And it's where, for better or worse, a new France is being forged . . . I don't feel despair or fear here, but something more alive than the static elegance of eternal Paris. The future of this great city is on its periphery.[17]

French hip-hop has succeeded both as a transnational and French cultural amalgam, a product of transnational France. It both expresses the agonies of life in the banlieue, and at times offers ideas about how to move beyond them. At its best, it suggests a new type of universalism, postcolonial and inclusive, to replace the paradoxes and inadequacies of the old. In short, it is a vision of the France of the future, one that can be terrifying and hopeful at the same time.

Conclusion

A Nation of Stories Large and Small

As a French historian, I have devoted my professional life to the proposition that France is a great and endlessly fascinating nation, full of people and peoples who have made important contributions to their own history and that of the world. Students of other national histories will no doubt say and believe the same. But as tempted as we are to take refuge in ironclad certainty about the essential value of this one country, we must nonetheless be prepared to answer the question, what makes France great? Or, as skeptics might wonder, what's so great about France? Why in particular should those of us who were born and have lived our lives elsewhere devote so much time and attention to studying the history of a nation in the last analysis not our own?

One can come up with many responses to these questions, responses no doubt familiar to many readers of this book. Answers that point to France's great national traditions, its formative role in the rise of modern ideas, intellectual schools, and ideologies, its role in shaping European and world histories, its pioneering role in developing the modern nation-state; all these rationales frequently appear in books and articles about French history. For me, this book underscores another reason for studying French history, one that makes this topic so attractive. France in the modern era has often brought together intensely localized community lives with an expansive, universalist political culture, facilitating their interactions in the context of a powerfully articulated nation-state. I do not argue that France is the only nation to do so, but I do nonetheless believe that its history gives us a powerful and exceptional example of the complex interrelationships between local, national, and global. Approaching French history from a transnational perspective not only explores these intersections, but also invites historians from both near and far to deploy that history in an exploration of their own pasts. National origins and differences certainly count for a lot, but to consider them from both global and local perspectives turns them from a barrier into a resource for a greater appreciation of the human condition in general. The study of transnational French history therefore gives me, as an American historian, important insights into how my own life, community, and traditions have shaped the past of my nation and the world.

One of the best examples of the history of local life in modern France, and its relationship to the national context, is Emile Guillaumin's great novel, *The Life of a Simple Man*. The novel relates the life story of a share-cropper in nineteenth century France, drawn to a significant degree from Guillaumin's own peasant background. In it the hero, Tiennon, gives a rich description of life in provincial France and the ways in which it interacted with the world outside. Near the end, the elderly Tiennon describes his conversations with his young grandson Francis, interchanges that illustrate changing ideas of memory and history:

> Francis would very often beg me to tell him stories; he remembered having heard me tell them to his sister and his cousin, and he wanted to learn them. I knew some of the old stories which we hand down on the farms from generation to generation. I knew "The Green Mountain," "The White Dog," "Tom Thumb," "The Devil's Bag of Gold," and "The Beast with Seven Heads."
>
> But it was not long before Francis knew my collection of stories and riddles and funny tales as well as I did, and I was no longer able to amuse him. He then began to tell me the things he was learning at school. He talked of kings and queens, of Joan of Arc, of Bayard, and Richelieu, of crusades and wars and massacres. He had the air of knowing all that had happened during those dead centuries.[1]

One can easily read this intergenerational exchange as a contrast between tradition and modernity, as an example of the displacement of folk tales so dear to Tiennon by the standardized curriculum Francis learned in his public school. But it also illustrates the relationship between local and national life in France at a time when the French state, as scholars such as Eugene Weber have demonstrated so convincingly, was increasing shaping the contours of village society and culture.[2] One must note that the interplay between local and national shaped the lives of *both* Tiennon and his grandson; Tiennon worked in an agrarian economy that formed part of a national and in fact global market economy, and tales he told his grandson originated far from his native soil. "Tom Thumb," for example, comes from seventeenth-century England. Other aspects of the novel also betray this important international dimension of French local life: the Franco-Prussian War of 1871 and the Prussian invasion of France occupy an important role in the text, and one of Tiennon's sons serves with the French army in Algeria. *The Life of a Simple Man* portrays traditional French village life in a glocalized way, one that shows its involvement with national and global factors.

I chose to comment on this particular section of the novel because it emphasizes and illustrates the importance of stories and their relationship to the telling and writing of history. History is in many ways a story writ large, of course; it represents the attempt of historians to bring together many different stories into an organized and coherent narrative. The act of doing so represents an important achievement, but it also involves sacrificing many peculiar details and experiences that don't necessarily fit into the broader tale. One cannot by any means prevent this from happening, or fully restore all the individual details and life experiences of people whose history we set out to write; no one ever knows *everything* about any other person, even those that one loves best. Nonetheless, a historical study based on case studies, on individuals, specific organizations, and events hopefully helps give us a better idea of that which is lost in crafting the broad sweep of history.

In conclusion, therefore, what does a book like *From Near and Far* reveal about the modern history of France, and of the world as a whole? To what extent does this transnational and glocal approach bring us new insights about French history? In answering these questions, I focus on a few essential observations about my study and this perspective more generally. First, I would simply argue that the stories in this book show how many people and events seen as integral parts of French history have an important international dimension. The fact that Paul Gauguin, for example, was partly Peruvian in origin and had a Danish wife and family exemplifies this, as does the complex influence of African American culture on French hip-hop music. The global dimensions of haute couture, in many ways the Parisian industry par excellence, also underscores this pattern.

Second, I believe the reverse is also true, that individual French people and the French nation as a whole have had an important impact on global cultures. The rise of Paris, especially after its redesign by Baron Haussmann under the Second Empire, as one of the world's great examples of modern urbanity is a classic example, but there are many others. The fact that the term and concept "Latin America" originated in France constitutes one example of this, as does the influence of Karl Marx's life in Paris on the subsequent development of Marxism as a global ideology and political movement. The study of the Alliance Israélite Universelle demonstrates the important French influence on Jewish politics and ideas of Jewish universalism in the modern era. So, in general, this book underscores the fact that France is a part of the world, and the world is a part of France, using a variety of individual stories to hammer home that point.

More specifically, I have tried to integrate the history of the French empire and French colonialism into the national and transnational narrative. Empire in France took different forms historically, and colonialism had an impact on French life in both the colonies and the metropole. As the story of Tiennon and his son who served in Algeria demonstrates, even French men and women who never left their native regions often had connections to the colonies. Josephine Baker's vision of a universal family drew heavily upon the colonial experience, many of her children having their origins in the colonies, and in a larger sense replicating the nation's familial narrative of empire. France's character as an imperial nation thus forms a key part of its transnational history, one that exemplifies the many ways in which local, national and global life have interacted across its modern history.

In the last analysis, therefore, France is a nation whose history can be read across all these levels, and that doing so will add to our understanding of what it means to be French in the modern world. I hope this book will contribute to that endeavor, at least modestly. In particular, I hope it shows that an attention to local and to global historical perspectives strengthens rather than weakens each, that one cannot fully understand local events without attention to their transnational context, and vice versa. People build nations by attending to and negotiating between both levels of human existence, and attempts to write the historical record must take this into account. Transnational and local are thus different faces of a diverse, unified history, and studying the history of a nation like France richly demonstrates this. In this way, like many others, France forms a vital part of the heritage of humanity.

Permit me to end this book at the beginning, with a story that brings us back there in more than one sense. Roughly a century and a half after the French settled in Gallipolis, a young African American couple traveled there from their home across the river in Lakin, West Virginia. Their destination was the town's Holzer Hospital, where the woman planned to give birth to their first child. Since Holzer had the closest maternity facility to their home it made sense to go there, but other factors entered into their decision. The expectant father, in particular, wanted his first child to be born on "free soil," in the North. So, like Eliza Harris in *Uncle Tom's Cabin*, the couple crossed the Ohio River with their child in search of a future grounded in freedom.

The town that received them not only had a historical legacy of French settlement but also a significant African American presence. In 1818 Blacks in Gallipolis founded Bethel Church, which endured for over a century. During the early nineteenth century its congregation and other groups in town made Gallipolis an important stop on the Underground Railroad, one of many in Ohio helping refugee slaves escape to liberty in Canada. On September 22, 1863, townspeople held a formal celebration of Abraham Lincoln's signature of the Emancipation Proclamation exactly a year earlier. Gallipolis has continued to celebrate that anniversary every year from then to the present day without fail, the only town in America to do so.

That is where my parents brought me into the world, a few months after the *Brown vs. Board of Education* Supreme Court decision that marked the beginning of the civil rights movement. They doubtless had high hopes for me at my birth, but probably would never have predicted that I would become a historian of France, still less one that would put into dialogue French, American, and African American history with a transnational vision of the subject. A coincidence, certainly, seeing that I haven't been back to Gallipolis since my earliest days, but one that nonetheless highlights some of the broader themes of this book. In my case a very small story links together the different levels of French history, in one sense bringing it full circle. France's national past, like that of any country, consists of such stories, and I feel privileged to tell the tale of a nation whose history has been as grand as the French Revolution and at the same time as intimate as the place where I first saw the light of day. As this book has endeavored to demonstrate, stories like this constitute the heart of French history, a history both local and transnational at the same time.

CONCLUSION

NOTES

INTRODUCTION

1. Stovall, *Transnational France*.
2. The classic theoretician of narrative and history is Hayden White. See his *Metahistory*. See also Louch, "History as Narrative."
3. Ben-Rafael and Sternberg, *Transnationalism*.
4. On transnational history, see Iriye, *Global and Transnational History*; Tyrell, *Transnational Nation*; and Bayly et al., "AHR Conversation."
5. Ginzburg, *The Cheese and the Worms*; Levi, "On Micro-History"; Crew, "Alltagsgeschichte?"; Lüdtke, *The History of Everyday Life*.
6. Vincent and Lingo, *The Human Tradition in Modern France*.
7. Sahlins, *Boundaries*.
8. Robertson, "Glocalization," 26.
9. Schor, "The Crisis of French Universalism"; Samuels, *The Right to Difference*.

1. STRANGERS IN A STRANGE LAND

1. *Prospectus*, cited in Fouré-Selter, *Gallipolis*, 152.
2. Works Progress Administration, *Gallipolis*, 11.
3. Cited in Desan, "Transatlantic Spaces of Revolutions," 468.
4. Cited in Moreau-Zanelli, *Gallipolis*, 142.
5. Fouré-Selter, *Gallipolis*, 34.
6. Cartier, *The Voyages of Jacques Cartier*; Douglas, *Old France in the New World*; Vidal, *Caribbean New Orleans*.
7. Podruchny, *Making the Voyageur World*; Skinner, *The Upper Country*.
8. Cited in Belote, "The Scioto Speculation," 35.
9. Cited in Belote, "The Scioto Speculation," 73–74.

10. Sleeper-Smith, *Indigenous Prosperity and American Conquest*; O'Donnell, *Ohio's First Peoples*; Hurt, *The Ohio Frontier*.

11. Work Projects Administration, *Gallipolis*, 16.

2. WORLD REVOLUTIONARY

1. Cited in Raddatz, *Karl Marx*, 58.

2. Toth, *An Exiled Generation*; Garrison, *German Americans on the Middle Border*.

3. Grandjonc, *Marx et les communistes allemands à Paris*, 11–12.

4. Harvey, *Consciousness and the Urban Experience*; Chevalier, *Laboring Classes and Dangerous Classes*.

5. Cited in Kramer, *Threshold of a New World*, 18.

6. Cited in Kramer, *Threshold of a New World*, 144–45.

7. Cited in Raddatz, *Threshold of a New World*, 85.

3. THE OTHER SECOND EMPIRE

1. Shawcross, *France, Mexico and Informal Empire in Latin America*; Williams, *Latin Blackness in Parisian Visual Culture*.

2. Hazareesingh, *From Subject to Citizen*; Plessis, *The Rise and Fall of the Second Empire*; Price, *The French Second Empire*.

3. Ridley, *Maximilian and Juárez*, 148.

4. Cited in Ridley, *Maximilian and Juárez*, 74.

5. Cited in McAllen, *Maximilian and Carlota*, 7–8.

6. Cited in McAllen, *Maximilian and Carlota*, 182.

7. Cited in McAllen, *Maximilian and Carlota*, 209.

PART 2. THE RISE OF THE IMPERIAL REPUBLIC

1. Merriman, *A History of Modern Europe*, 866.

4. CAPITAL OF FASHION

1. Boussahba-Bravard and Rogers, *Women in International and Universal Exhibitions*; Prochasson, *Paris 1900*; Mandell, *Paris 1900*.

2. Currie, *A Cultural History of Dress and Fashion in the Renaissance*.

3. Brachmann, *Arrayed in Splendor*.

4. Cited in Steele, *Paris Fashion*, 20.

5. Mansel, *King of the World*.

6. Cited in Steele, *Paris Fashion*, 24.

7. Cited in Troy, *Couture Culture*, 342.

8. Cited in Hegermann-Lindencrone, *In the Courts of Memory*, entry of May 7, 1863.
9. Cited in Steele, *Paris Fashion*, 3.
10. De Marly, *Worth*, 23.
11. Bouvier, *Mes Memoires*, cited in Traugott, *The French Worker*, 372–73.

5. UNIVERSALISM FROM THE MARGINS

1. Samuels, *The Right to Difference*.
2. Benbassa, *The Jews of France*.
3. Cited in Graetz, *The Jews in Nineteenth-Century France*, 26–27.
4. Jaher, *The Jews and the Nation*.
5. Abitbol, "The Encounter," 32.
6. Benbassa, *The Jews of France*, xv.
7. *L'Appel de L'Alliance*, May 17, 1860, cited in the AIU website: https://www.aiu .org/fr/notre-histoire-0#lct-2.
8. Cited in Rodrigue, *French Jews, Turkish Jews*, 55–56.
9. Cited in Abitbol, "The Encounter," 53.
10. Cited in Rodrigue, *French Jews, Turkish Jews*, 51.
11. Cited in Graetz, *The Jews in Nineteenth-Century France*, 252.

6. PAINTER OF EMPIRE

1. Sweetman, *Paul Gauguin*; Hoog, *Paul Gauguin, Life and Work*; Hudson, *Gauguin*.
2. Clark, *The Painting of Modern Life*; King, *The Judgment of Paris*.
3. Clark and Fowle, *Globalizing Impressionism*.
4. Rewald, *Post-Impressionism*.
5. Cited in Sweetman, *Paul Gauguin*, 171.
6. Salmond, *Aphrodite's Island*; Sheriff, *Enchanted Islands*; Howarth, *Tahiti, A Paradise Lost*.
7. Letter of July, 1891, cited in Gauguin, *Paul Gauguin: Letters*, 163.
8. Gauguin, *Noa Noa*.
9. Broude, *Gauguin's Challenge*, 3.

7. LAFAYETTE, WE ARE HERE!

1. On the historical relationship of France and the United States see Kuisel, *Seducing the French*; Mathy, *French Resistance*.
2. On the history of World War I, see Hart, *The Great War*; Ferro, *The Great War*; Eksteins, *Rites of Spring*.
3. Flood, *First to Fly*.

4. Englund, *March 1917*; Cronin and Sirianni, *Work, Community, and Power*.

5. Kaspi, *Le temps des américains*.

6. These included Private Otha Fuller of West Virginia, my grandfather. On African American soldiers in World War I see Lentz-Smith, *Freedom Struggles*; Williams, *Torchbearers of Democracy*.

7. Cited in Stovall, *Paris Noir*, 18.

8. Stovall, *Paris Noir*, 18.

9. Stovall, *Paris Noir*, 18.

10. Lunn, *Memoirs of the Maelstrom*.

11. Cited in Freidel, *Over There*, 97.

12. Cited in Freidel, *Over There*, 246–47.

8. COLONIAL AND GLOBAL REVOLUTIONARY

1. Duiker, *Ho Chi Minh*, 48.

2. On the history of French Indochina see Norindr, *Phantasmatic Indochina*; Jennings, *Imperial Heights*; Vann, "White City on the Red River."

3. Cited in Duiker, *Ho Chi Minh*, 32. On the life of Ho Chi Minh see also Lacouture, *Ho Chi Minh*; Brocheux, *Ho Chi Minh*.

4. Cited in Duiker, *Ho Chi Minh*, 50.

5. Crowe, *Hemingway and Ho Chi Minh in Paris*.

6. Macmillan, *Paris 1919*; Stovall, *Paris and the Spirit of 1919*.

7. Michael Goebel, *Anti-Imperial Metropolis*.

8. Goebel, *Anti-Imperial Metropolis*, 64.

9. Duiker, *Ho Chi Minh*, 85.

10. Ho Chi Minh/Nguyen Ai Quoc, *French Colonialism on Trial*.

11. Duiker, *Ho Chi Minh*, 99–100.

9. FOREIGNERS FOR FRANCE

1. Zucotti, *The Holocaust, the French, and the Jews*.

2. On the Manouchian group see Tchakarian, *Les commandos de l'Affiche rouge*; Robrieux, *L'Affaire Manouchian*.

3. Cited in Neiberg, *The Blood of Free Men*, 237.

4. Stein, *Beyond Death and Exile*.

5. On the history of the French Resistance see Wieviorka, *The French Resistance*; Gildea, *Fighters in the Shadows*.

6. On France during World War II see Jackson, *France, the Dark Years*; Paxton, *Vichy France*; Drake, *Paris at War*.

7. Jackson, *France, the Dark Years*, 494.

8. Brès, *Un maquis d'antifascistes allemands en France*.

9. Cited in Jackson, *France, the Dark Years*, 364. On the Jewish resistance in France see Latour, *The Jewish Resistance in France*; Lazare, *Rescue as Resistance*.

10. McPhillips, *From Vacillation to Resolve*; Courtois, *Le PCF dans la guerre*.

11. Cited in Jackson, *France, the Dark Years*, 369.

12. Musée national de l'histoire de l'immigration, "L'affiche rouge," https://www
.histoire-immigration.fr/dossiers-thematiques/les-etrangers-dans-les-guerres
-en-france/l-affiche-rouge.

13. Cited in Duclos, *Lettres des fusillés*.

14. Aragon, "Strophes pour se souvenir."

10. UNIVERSAL FAMILY

1. Flanner, *Paris Was Yesterday*, xxi.

2. On the life of Josephine Baker see Baker and Bouillon, *Josephine*; Jules-
Rosette, *Josephine Baker in Art and Life*; Rose, *Jazz Cleopatra*.

3. Cited in Stovall, *Paris Noir*, 150.

4. Bourg, *After the Deluge*; Pulju, *Women and Mass Consumer Society in Postwar France*; Nord, *After the Deportation*.

5. Fishman, *From Vichy to the Sexual Revolution*; Sirinelli, *Les baby-boomers*.

6. Roberts, *Civilization without Sexes*; Maza, *Violette Nozière*.

7. UNHCR, "France: Preamble to the Constitution of 27 October 1946,"
https://www.refworld.org/docid/3ae6b56910.html; Joseph-Gabriel,
Reimagining Liberation; Cooper, *Citizenship between Empire and Nation*.

8. Cooper, *Citizenship between Empire and Nation*.

9. Cited in Guterl, *Josephine Baker and the Rainbow Tribe*, 15.

10. Guterl, *Josephine Baker and the Rainbow Tribe*, 85.

11. Wolin, *The Wind from the East*; Ross, *May '68 and Its Afterlives*; Singer,
Prelude to Revolution.

12. Vince, *The Algerian War, the Algerian Revolution*; Horne, *A Savage War of
Peace*; Shepard, *The Invention of Decolonization*.

13. Noiriel, *The French Melting Pot*.

14. Nasiali, *Native to the Republic*; Germain, *Decolonizing the Republic*.

11. FRANCE ON VACATION

1. On the history of tourism to modern France see Gordon, *War Tourism*;
Endy, *Cold War Holidays*; Levenstein, *Seductive Journey*.

2. On the history of Club Med see Blednick, *Another Day in Paradise?*; Furlough, "Making Mass Vacations" and "Packaging Pleasures."

3. Downs, *Childhood in the Promised Land*.

4. On the *Trentes Glorieuses* see Hanley, *Contemporary France*; Fourastié, *D'une France à une autre*.

5. Furlough, "Making Mass Vacations," 264.

6. Aldrich and Connell, *France's Overseas Frontier*; Marsh, *Narratives of the French Empire*.

7. Lagerquist, "Vacation from History," 45.

8. Garner, *Politically Correct Bedtime Stories*, 17.

9. *France Today* eds., "Club Med," August 21, 2014.

12. POSTCOLONIAL SOUNDTRACK

1. Monsieur R, *FranSSe*, https://www.youtube.com/watch?v=GiPm-m6hvui.

2. Wade and Campbell, *Global Music Cultures*; Miller and Shahriari, *World Music*.

3. On the origins and history of hip-hop in America, see Rose, *Black Noise*; Chang and Kool Herc, *Can't Stop Won't Stop*; George, *Hip Hop America*.

4. On gangsta rap see Westhoff, *Original Gangstas*.

5. Mitchell, *Global Noise*; Fernandes, *Close to the Edge*; Nitzsche and Grünzweig, *Hip-Hop in Europe*.

6. Brooks, "Gangsta in French," *New York Times*, November 10, 2005. See also Rosen, "David Brooks, Playa Hater," *Slate*, November 10, 2005.

7. On the history of hip-hop in France, see Durand, *Hip Hop en Français* and *Black, Blanc, Beur*; McCarren, *French Moves*; Hélénon, "Africa on Their Mind."

8. On the Paris suburbs see Stovall, *The Rise of the Paris Red Belt*; Selby, *Questioning French Secularism*; Slooter, *The Making of the Banlieue*.

9. Schneider, *Police Power and Race Riots*.

10. Dee Nasty, *Paname*, https://www.youtube.com/watch?v=6b4NEQiAFJc.

11. Baker, "Preachers, Gangsters, Pranksters."

12. Cited in Drissel, "Hip-Hop Hybridity."

13. Schneider, *Police Power and Race Riots*; Moran, *The Republic and the Riots*.

14. Cited in "French MP blames riots on rappers," *BBC News*, November 24, 2005.

15. Iandoli, *God Save the Queens*.

16. Cited in Loupias, "Les raps pour le dire."

17. Kamdar, "The Other Paris, Beyond the Boulevards."

CONCLUSION

1. Emile Guillamin, *The Life of a Simple Man*, translated by Margaret Holden, 239, 244.

2. Eugene Weber, *Peasants into Frenchmen*.

BIBLIOGRAPHY

Abitbol, Michel. "The Encounter between French Jewry and the Jews of North Africa: Analysis of a Discourse (1830–1914)." In *The Jews of Modern France*, edited by Frances Malino and Bernard Wasserstein. Hanover NH: University Press of New England, 1985.

Aldrich, Robert, and John Connell. *France's Overseas Frontier: départements et térritoires d'outre-mer.* Cambridge: Cambridge University Press, 2006.

Aragon, Louis. "Strophes pour se souvenir." Paris: Walusinski, 2005.

Baker, Geoffrey. "Preachers, Gangsters, Pranksters: MC Solaar and Hip-Hop as Overt and Covert Revolt." *Journal of Popular Culture* 44, no. 2 (April 2011): 233–55.

Baker, Josephine, and Jo Bouillon. *Josephine.* New York: Harper & Row, 1977.

Bayly, Christopher A., et al. "AHR Conversation: On Transnational History." *American Historical Review* 111 (2006).

Belote, Theodore Thomans. "The Scioto Speculation and the French Settlement at Gallipolis: A Study in Ohio Valley History." *University Studies* 3, no. 3 (September–October 1907).

Ben-Rafael, Eliezer, and Yitzhak Sternberg. *Transnationalism: Diasporas and the Advent of a New Disorder.* Leiden: Brill, 2009.

Benbassa, Esther. *The Jews of France: A History from Antiquity to the Present.* Princeton NJ: Princeton University Press, 1999.

Blednick, Patrick. *Another Day in Paradise? The Real Club Med Story.* Toronto: Macmillan of Canada, 1988.

Bourg, Julian, ed. *After the Deluge: New Perspectives on the Intellectual and Cultural History of Postwar France.* Lanham MD: Lexington, 2004.

Boussahba-Bravard, Myriam, and Rebecca Rogers. *Women in International and Universal Exhibitions, 1876–1937*. New York: Routledge, 2018.

Bouvier, Jeanne. *Mes Memoires*, cited in *The French Worker: Autobiographies from the Early Industrial Age, edited by* Mark Traugott. Berkeley: University of California Press, 1993.

Brachmann, Christoph. *Arrayed in Splendor: Art, Fashion, and Textiles in Medieval and Early Modern Europe*. Turnhout: Brepols, 2019.

Braskén, Kaspar. et. al. *Anti-Fascism in a Global Perspective: Transnational Networks, Exile Communities, and Radical Internationalism*. New York: Routledge, 2021.

Brès, Eveline. *Un maquis d'antifascistes allemands en France, 1942–1944*. Montpellier: Presses du Languedoc, 1987.

Brocheux, Pierre. *Ho Chi Minh: A Biography*. Translated by Claire Duiker. New York: Cambridge University Press, 2007.

Brooks, David. "Gangsta in French." *New York Times*, November 10, 2005.

Broude, Norma. *Gauguin's Challenge: New Perspectives After Postmodernism*. London: Bloomsbury Visual Arts, 2018.

Chang, Jeff, and DJ Kool Herc. *Can't Stop Won't Stop: A History of the Hip-Hop Generation*. New York: St. Martin's, 2007.

Chevalier, Louis. *Laboring Classes and Dangerous Classes in Paris during the First Half of the Nineteenth Century*. Translated by Frank Jellinek. Princeton NJ: Princeton University Press, 1973.

Clark, Alexis, and Francis Fowle, eds. *Globalizing Impressionism: Reception, Translation, and Transnationalism*. New Haven: Yale University Press, 2020.

Clark, T. J. *The Painting of Modern Life: Paris in the Art of Manet and His Followers*. Princeton NJ: Princeton University Press, 1999.

Connor, Hillary. *I Hope This Reaches You: An American Soldier's Account of World War I*. Detroit: Wayne State University Press, 2020.

Cooper, Frederick. *Citizenship between Empire and Nation: Remaking France and French Africa, 1945–1960*. Princeton NJ: Princeton University Press, 2014.

Courtois, Stéphane. *Le PCF dans la guerre: De Gaulle, la Résistance, Staline*. Paris: Ramsay, 1980.

Courtois, Stéphane, et al. *Le sang de l'étranger: les immigrés de la MOI dans la résistance*. Paris: Fayard, 1989.

Cowley, Malcolm. *Exile's Return: A Literary Odyssey of the 1920s*. New York: Penguin Classics, 1994.

Crew, David F. "Alltagsgeschichte: A New Social History 'From Below?.'" *Central European History* 22, no. 3–4 (September–December 1989).

Crowe, David. *Hemingway and Ho Chi Minh in Paris: The Art of Resistance.* Baltimore: Fortress, 2020.

Cunningham, Michele. *Mexico and the Foreign Policy of Napoleon III.* New York: Palgrave, 2001.

Currie, Elizabeth, ed. *A Cultural History of Dress and Fashion in the Renaissance.* London: Bloomsbury, 2017.

de la Haye, Amy, and Valerie D. Mendes. *The House of Worth, 1858–1914: Portrait of an Archive.* London: V & A, 2014.

de Hegermann-Lindencrone, Lillie. *In the Courts of Memory.* New York: Da Capo, 1980.

De Marly, Diana. *Worth: Father of Haute Couture.* Singapore: Elm Tree, 1980.

Desan, Suzanne. "Transatlantic Spaces of Revolution: The French Revolution, *Sciotomanie*, and American Lands." *Journal of Early Modern History* 12 (2008).

Downs, Laura Lee. *Childhood in the Promised Land: Working-Class Movements and the Colonies de Vacances in France, 1880–1960.* Durham NC: Duke University Press, 2002.

Drake, David. *Paris at War, 1939–1945.* Cambridge MA: Harvard University Press, 2015.

Drissel, David. "Hip-Hop Hybridity for a Glocalized World: African and Muslim Diasporic Discourses in French Rap Music." *Global Studies Journal* 3, no. 2 (2009).

Duclos, Jacques, ed. *Lettres des fusillés.* Paris: Éditions sociales, 1970.

Duiker, William J. *The Comintern and Vietnamese Communism.* Athens OH: Ohio University Center for International Studies, 1975.

———. *Ho Chi Minh: A Life.* Paris: Hachette, 2000.

Durand, Alain-Philippe. *Black, Blanc, Beur: Rap Music and Hip-Hop Culture in the Francophone World.* Lanham MD: Scarecrow, 2002.

———. *Hip Hop en Français: An Exploration of Hip-Hop Culture in the Francophone World.* Lanham MD: Rowman & Littlefield, 2020.

Eisenhower, John S. D. *Yanks: The Epic Story of the American Army in World War I.* New York: Free Press, 2002.

Eisenman, Stephen F. *Gauguin's Skirt.* New York: Thames & Hudson, 1997.

Eksteins, Modris. *Rites of Spring: The Great War and the Birth of the Modern Age.* Boston: Houghton Mifflin, 1989.

Endy, Christopher. *Cold War Holidays: American Tourism in France.* Chapel Hill: University of North Carolina Press, 2004.

Englund, Will. *March 1917: On the Brink of War and Revolution.* New York: W. W. Norton, 2017.

Faulkner, Richard S. *Pershing's Crusaders: The American Soldier in World War I.* Lawrence: University Press of Kansas, 2017.

Fernandes, Sujatha. *Close to the Edge: In Search of the Global Hip Hop Generation.* London: Verso, 2011.

Ferro, Marc. *The Great War, 1914–1918.* New York: Routledge, 2001.

Fishman, Sarah. *From Vichy to the Sexual Revolution: Gender and Family Life in Postwar France.* New York: Oxford University Press, 2017.

Flanner, Janet. *Paris Was Yesterday, 1925–1939.* New York: Viking, 1972.

Fourastié, Jean. *D'une France à une autre: avant et après les Trentes Glorieuses.* Paris: Fayard, 1987.

Fouré-Selter, Hélène. *Gallipolis: Histoire de l'établissement de cinq cents Français dans la vallée de l'Ohio à la fin du XVIIIe siècle.* Paris: Jouve & Cie, 1939.

France Today Editors. "Club Med: The Story Behind the Iconic French Brand." *France Today*, August 21, 2014.

Freidel, Frank. *Over There: The Story of America's First Great Overseas Crusade.* Boston: Little, Brown, 1964.

Furlough, Ellen. "Making Mass Vacations: Tourism and Consumer Culture in France, 1930s to 1970s." *Comparative Studies in Society and History* 40, no. 2 (April 1998).

———. "Packaging Pleasures: Club Méditerranée and French Consumer Culture, 1950–1968." *French Historical Studies* 18, no. 1 (April 1993).

Garner, James Finn. *Politically Correct Bedtime Stories.* New York: John Wiley & Sons, 1994.

Garrison, Zachary Stuart. *German Americans on the Middle Border: From Antislavery to Reconciliation.* Carbondale: Southern Illinois University Press, 2019.

Gaspard, Thu Trang. *Ho Chi Minh à Paris, 1917–1923.* Paris: L'Harmattan, 1992.

Gauguin, Paul. *Noa Noa. The Tahiti Journal of Paul Gauguin.* Edited by John Miller. San Francisco: Chronicle, 1994.

———. *Paul Gauguin: Letters to His Wife and Friends.* Edited by Maurice Malingue. Translated by Henry J. Stenning. Cleveland: Cleveland World, 1949.

George, Nelson. *Hip Hop America.* New York: Penguin, 2005.

Germain, Felix F. *Decolonizing the Republic: African and Caribbean Migrants in Postwar Paris, 1946–1974.* East Lansing: Michigan State University Press, 2016.

Gildea, Robert. *Fighters in the Shadows: A New History of the French Resistance.* Cambridge MA: Harvard University Press, 2016.

Ginzburg, Carlo. *The Cheese and the Worms: The Cosmos of a Sixteenth-Century Miller*. Translated by John Tedeschi and Anne Tedeschi. Baltimore: Johns Hopkins University Press, 1980.

Goebel, Michael. *Anti-Imperial Metropolis: Interwar Paris and the Seeds of Third World Nationalism*. Cambridge: Cambridge University Press, 2017.

Gordon, Bertram. *War Tourism: Second World War France from Defeat and Occupation to the Creation of Heritage*. Ithaca NY: Cornell University Press, 2018.

Gottreich, Emily Benichou, and Daniel J. Schroeter, eds. *Jewish Culture and Society in North Africa*. Bloomington: Indiana University Press, 2011.

Graetz, Michael. *The Jews in Nineteenth-Century France: From the French Revolution to the Alliance Israélite Universelle*. Translated by Jane Marie Todd. Stanford CA: Stanford University Press, 1996.

Grandjonc, Jean. *Marx et les communistes allemands à Paris, 1844*. Paris: Maspero, 1974.

Guillamin, Emile. *The Life of a Simple Man*. Translated by Margaret Holden. London: Selwyn and L. Blount, 1919.

Guterl, Matthew. *Josephine Baker and the Rainbow Tribe*. Cambridge MA: Belknap, 2014.

Hanley, D. L. *Contemporary France: Politics and Society Since 1945*. New York: Routledge, 1984.

Hargreaves, Alec. *Multi-Ethnic France: Immigration, Politics Culture and Society*. London: Routledge, 2007.

Hart, Peter. *The Great War: A Combat History of the First World War*. Oxford: Oxford University Press, 2015.

Harvey, David. *Consciousness and the Urban Experience: Studies in the History and Theory of Capitalist Urbanization*. Baltimore: Johns Hopkins University Press, 1989.

Hazareesingh, Sudhir. *From Subject to Citizen: The Second Empire and the Emergence of Modern French Democracy*. Princeton NJ: Princeton University Press, 2016.

Hélénon, Veronique. "Africa on Their Mind: Rap, Blackness, and Citizenship in France." In *The Vinyl Ain't Final: Hip-Hop and the Globalisation of Black Popular Culture*, edited by Dipannita Basu and Sidney J. Lemelle, 151–66. Ann Arbor MI: Pluto, 2006.

Ho Chi Minh/Nguyen Ai Quoc. *French Colonialism on Trial*. Translated by Joshua Leinsdorf. Paris: Workers' Library, 2017.

Hoog, Michel. *Paul Gauguin, Life and Work*. New York: Rizzoli, 1987.

Horne, Alastair. *A Savage War of Peace: Algeria, 1954–1962*. New York: NYRB Classics, 2006.

Howarth, David. *Tahiti, A Paradise Lost*. New York: Penguin, 1983.

Hudson, Belinda. *Gauguin*. New York: Thames and Hudson, 1987.

Hurt, R. Douglas. *The Ohio Frontier: Crucible of the Old Northwest, 1720–1830*. Bloomington: Indiana University Press, 1998.

Iandoli, Kathy. *God Save the Queens: The Essential History of Women in Hip-Hop*. New York: Dey Street, 2019.

Ibsen, Kristine. *Maximilian, Mexico, and the Invention of Empire*. Nashville TN: Vanderbilt University Press, 2010.

Iriye, Akira. *Global and Transnational History: The Past, Present, and Future*. New York: Palgrave, 2012.

Jackson, Julian. *France, the Dark Years: 1940–1944*. Oxford: Oxford University Press, 2001.

Jaher, Frederic Cople. *The Jews and the Nation: Revolution, Emancipation, State Formation, and the Liberal Paradigm in America and France*. Princeton NJ: Princeton University Press, 2002.

Jennings, Eric T. *Imperial Heights: Dalat and the Making and Undoing of French Indochina*. Berkeley: University of California Press, 2011.

Joseph-Gabriel, Annette K. *Reimagining Liberation: How Black Women Transformed Citizenship in the French Empire*. Urbana: University of Illinois Press, 2020.

Jules-Rosette, Bennetta. *Josephine Baker in Art and Life: The Icon and the Image*. Urbana: University of Illinois Press, 2007.

Kahler, Miles. *Decolonization in Britain and France: The Domestic Consequences of International Relations*. Princeton NJ: Princeton University Press, 1984.

Kamdar, Mira. "The Other Paris, Beyond the Boulevards." *New York Times*, November 9, 2013.

Kaspi, Andre. *Le temps des américains: le concours américain à la France en 1917–1918*. Paris: Publications de la Sorbonne, 1976.

Keene, Jennifer D. *Doughboys, the Great War, and the Remaking of America*. Baltimore: Johns Hopkins University Press, 2003.

King, Ross. *The Judgment of Paris: The Revolutionary Decade that Gave the World Impressionism*. New York: Bloomsbury, 2007.

Kramer, Lloyd S. *Threshold of a New World: Intellectuals and the Exile Experience in Paris, 1830–1848*. Ithaca NY: Cornell University Press, 1988.

Kuisel, Richard F. *Seducing the French: the Dilemma of Americanization*. Berkeley: University of California Press, 1997.

Lacouture, Jean. *Ho Chi Minh: A Political Biography*. Translated by Peter Wiles. New York: Random House, 1968.

Lagerquist, Peter. "Vacation from History: Ethnic Cleansing as the Club Med Experience." *Journal of Palestine Studies* 36, no. 1 (Autumn 2006).

Laskier, Michael M. *The Alliance Israélite Universelle and the Jewish Communities of Morocco, 1862–1962*. Albany: State University of New York Press, 1983.

Latour, Anny. *The Jewish Resistance in France, 1940–1944*. New York: Schocken, 1981.

Lazare, Lucien. *Rescue as Resistance: How Jewish Organizations Fought the Holocaust in France*. New York: Columbia University Press, 1996.

Lentz-Smith, Adriane. *Freedom Struggles: African Americans and World War I*. Cambridge MA: Harvard University Press, 2011.

Levenstein, Harvey. *Seductive Journey: American Tourists in France from Jefferson to the Jazz Age*. Chicago: University of Chicago Press, 1998.

Levi, Giovanni. "On Micro-History." In *New Perspectives on Historical Writing*, edited by Peter Burke. University Park: University of Pennsylvania Press, 1992.

Louch, A. R. "History as Narrative." *History and Theory* 8, no. 1 (1969).

Loupias, Bernard. "Les raps pour le dire." *Le nouvel observateur*, June 20–26, 1991.

Lüdtke, Alf. *The History of Everyday Life: Reconstructing Historical Experiences and Ways of Life*. Translated by William Templor. Princeton NJ: Princeton University Press, 2018.

Lunn, Joe H. *Memoirs of the Maelstrom: A Senegalese Oral History of the First World War*. Portsmouth NH: Heinemann, 1999.

Macmillan, Margaret. *Paris 1919: Six Months that Changed the World*. London: John Murray, 2001.

Mandell, Richard. *Paris 1900: the Great World's Fair*. Toronto: University of Toronto Press, 1967.

Mansel, Philip. *King of the World: The Life of Louis XIV*. Chicago: University of Chicago Press, 2020.

Marsh, Kate. *Narratives of the French Empire: Fiction, Nostalgia, and Imperial Rivalries, 1784-Present*. Lanham MD: Lexington, 2013.

Mathy, Jean-Philippe. *French Resistance: The French-American Culture Wars*. Minneapolis: University of Minnesota Press, 2000.

Mathews, Nancy Mowll. *Paul Gauguin: An Erotic Life*. New Haven: Yale University Press, 2001.

Maza, Sarah C. *Violette Nozière: A Story of Murder in 1930s Paris*. Berkeley: University of California Press, 2011.

McAllen, M. M. *Maximilian and Carlota: Europe's Last Empire in Mexico*. San Antonio TX: Trinity University Press, 2014.

McCarren, Felicia. *French Moves: The Cultural Politics of le hip hop*. Oxford: Oxford University Press, 2013.

McLellan, David. *Karl Marx: A Biography*. New York: Palgrave Macmillan, 2006.

McPhillips, Julian Lenwood, Jr. *From Vacillation to Resolve: The French Communist Party in the Resistance*. Montgomery AL: NewSouth, 2018.

Merriman, John. *A History of Modern Europe: From the Renaissance to the Present*. 4th ed. New York: W. W. Norton, 2019.

Miller, Terry E., and Andrew Shahriari. *World Music: A Global Journey*. New York: Routledge, 2020.

Mitchell, Tony. *Global Noise: Rap and Hip Hop Outside the USA*. Middletown CT: Wesleyan University Press, 2002.

Moran, Matthew. *The Republic and the Riots: Exploring Urban Violence in French Suburbs, 2005–2007*. Bern: Peter Lang, 2012.

Moreau-Zanelli, Jocelyne. *Gallipolis: Histoire d'un mirage américain au XVIIIe siècle*. Paris: Harmattan, 2000.

Nasiali, Minayo. *Native to the Republic: Empire, Social Citizenship, and Everyday Life in Marseille since 1945*. Ithaca NY: Cornell University Press, 2016.

Neiberg, Michael. *The Blood of Free Men: The Liberation of Paris, 1944*. New York: Basic, 2012.

Nitzsche, Sina A,. and Walter Grünzweig, eds. *Hip-Hop in Europe: Cultural Identities and Transnational Flows*. Zurich: LIT, 2013.

Noiriel, Gérard. *The French Melting Pot: Immigration, Citizenship, and National Identity*. Translated by Geoffroy de Laforcade. Minneapolis: University of Minnesota Press, 1996.

Nord, Philip G. *After the Deportation: Memory Battles in Postwar France*. Cambridge: Cambridge University Press, 2020.

Norindr, Panivong. *Phantasmatic Indochina: French Colonial Ideology in Architecture, Film, and Literature*. Durham NC: Duke University Press, 1997.

O'Donnell, James H., III. *Ohio's First Peoples*. Athens: Ohio University Press, 2004.

Paxton, Robert O. *Vichy France: Old Guard and New Order, 1940–1944*. New York: Knopf, 1972.

Plessis, Alain. *The Rise and Fall of the Second Empire*. Translated by Jonathan Mandelbaum. Cambridge: Cambridge University Press, 1988.

Podruchny, Carolyn. *Making the Voyageur World: Travelers and Traders in the North American Fur Trade*. Lincoln: University of Nebraska Press, 2006.

Pollock, Griselda. *Mary Cassatt: Painter of Modern Woman*. New York: Thames & Hudson, 1998.

Prashad, Vijay. *Red Star over the Third World*. London: Pluto, 2019.

Price, Roger. *The French Second Empire: An Anatomy of Political Power*. Cambridge: Cambridge University Press, 2001.

Prochasson, Christophe. *Paris 1900: Essai d'Histoire Culturelle*. Paris: Calmann-Lévy, 1999.

Pulju, Rebecca, *Women and Mass Consumer Society in Postwar France*. Cambridge: Cambridge University Press, 2011.

Quinn-Judge, Sophie. *Ho Chi Minh: The Missing Years, 1919–1941*. Berkeley: University of California Press, 2002.

Raddatz, Fritz J. *Karl Marx: A Political Biography*. London: Weidenfeld and Nicolson, 1978.

Rewald, John. *Post-Impressionism: From Van Gogh to Gauguin*. New York: Museum of Modern Art, 1978.

Ridley, Jasper. *Maximilian and Juárez*. New York: Ticknor and Fields, 1992.

Roberts, Mary Louise. *Civilization without Sexes: Reconstructing Gender in Postwar France, 1917–1927*. Chicago: University of Chicago Press, 1994.

Robertson, Roland. "Glocalization: Time-Space and Homogeneity-Heterogeneity." In *Global Modernities*, edited by Mike Featherstone, Scott Lash, and Roland Robertson. London: Sage, 1996.

Robrieux, Philippe. *L'Affaire Manouchian*. Paris: Fayard, 1986.

Rodrigue, Aron. *French Jews, Turkish Jews: The Alliance Israélite Universelle and the Politics of Jewish Schooling in Turkey, 1860–1925*. Bloomington: Indiana University Press, 1990.

———. *Images of Sephardi and Eastern Jewries in Transition: the Teachers of the Alliance Israélite Universelle, 1860–1939*. Seattle: University of Washington Press, 1993.

Rose, Phyllis. *Jazz Cleopatra: Josephine Baker in Her Time*. New York: Doubleday, 1989.

Rose, Tricia. *Black Noise: Rap Music and Black Culture in Contemporary America*. Middletown CT: Wesleyan University Press, 1994.

Rosen, Jody. "David Brooks, Playa Hater." *Slate*, November 10, 2005.

Ross, Kristin. *May '68 and Its Afterlives*. Chicago: University of Chicago Press, 2002.

Sahlins, Peter. *Boundaries: The Making of France and Spain in the Pyrenees*. Berkeley: University of California Press, 1991.

Salmond, Anne. *Aphrodite's Island: The European Discovery of Tahiti*. Berkeley: University of California Press, 2011.

Samuels, Maurice. *The Right to Difference: French Universalism and the Jews.* Chicago: University of Chicago Press, 2019.

Saunders, Edith. *The Age of Worth: Couturier to the Empress Eugenie.* Bloomington: Indiana University Press, 1955.

Schor, Naomi. "The Crisis of French Universalism." *Yale French Studies* 100 (2001).

Schneider, Cathy Lisa. *Police Power and Race Riots: Urban Unrest in Paris and New York.* Philadelphia: University of Pennsylvania Press, 2014.

Selby, Jennifer. *Questioning French Secularism: Gender Politics and Islam in a Parisian Suburb.* New York: Palgrave Macmillan, 2012.

Sewell, William H., Jr. *Work and Revolution in France: The Language of Labor from the Old Regime to 1848.* Cambridge: Cambridge University Press, 1980.

Shawcross, Edward. *The Last Emperor of Mexico: The Dramatic Story of the Habsburg Archduke Who Created a Kingdom in the New World.* New York: Basic, 2021.

———. *France, Mexico and Informal Empire in Latin America, 1820–1867.* Cham, Switzerland: Palgrave Macmillan, 2018.

Shepard, Todd. *The Invention of Decolonization: the Algerian War and the Remaking of France.* Ithaca NY: Cornell University Press, 2006.

Sheriff, Mary D. *Enchanted Islands: Picturing the Allure of Conquest in Eighteenth-Century France.* Chicago: University of Chicago Press, 2018.

Silverstein, Paul. *Postcolonial France: The Question of Race and the Future of the Republic.* London: Pluto, 2018.

Singer, Daniel. *Prelude to Revolution: France in May 1968.* New York: Hill and Wang, 1970.

Sirinelli, Jean-François. *Les baby-boomers: une génération, 1945–1969.* Paris: Fayard, 2003.

Skinner, Claiborne A. *The Upper Country: French Enterprise in the Colonial Great Lakes.* Baltimore: Johns Hopkins University Press, 2008.

Sleeper-Smith, Susan. *Indigenous Prosperity and American Conquest: Indian Women of the Ohio River Valley, 1690–1792.* Chapel Hill: University of North Carolina Press, 2018.

Slooter, Luuk. *The Making of the Banlieue: An Ethnography of Space, Identity and Violence.* Cham, Switzerland: Springer International, 2019.

Solomon-Godeau, Abigail. "Going Native: Paul Gauguin and the Invention of Primitivist Modernism." In *The Expanding Discourse: Feminism and Art History,* edited by Norma Broude and Mary D. Garrard. London: Routledge, 2019.

Sperber, Jonathan. *Karl Marx: A Nineteenth-Century Life*. New York: W. W. Norton, 2013.

Steele, Valerie. *Paris Fashion: A Cultural History*. New York: Bloomsbury, 2017.

Stein, Louis. *Beyond Death and Exile: The Spanish Republicans in France, 1939–1955*. Cambridge MA: Harvard University Press, 1979.

Stovall, Tyler. *Paris Noir: African Americans in the City of Light*. Boston: Houghton-Mifflin, 1996.

———. *Transnational France: The Modern History of a Universal Nation*. New York: Routledge, 2015.

———. *The Rise of the Paris Red Belt*. Berkeley: University of California Press, 1990.

Sweetman, David. *Paul Gauguin: A Life*. New York: Simon and Schuster, 1996.

Tchakarian, Arsène. *Les commandos de l'affiche rouge: la verité historique sur la première section de l'Armée secrete*. Monaco: Rocher, 2012.

Teilhat-Fisk, Jehanne. *Paradise Reviewed: An Interpretation of Gauguin's Polynesian Symbolism*. Ann Arbor: University of Michigan Research Press, 1983.

Toth, Helena. *An Exiled Generation: German and Hungarian Refugees of Revolution, 1848–1871*. Cambridge: Cambridge University Press, 2020.

Traugott, Mark, ed. *The French Worker: Autobiographies from the Early Industrial Era*. Berkeley: University of California Press, 1993.

Troy, Nancy J. *Couture Culture: A Study in Modern Art and Fashion*. Cambridge MA: MIT Press, 2004.

Tyrell, Ian. *Transnational Nation. United States History in Global Perspective Since 1789*. Basingstoke: Palgrave Macmillan, 2007.

Vann, Michael G. "White City on the Red River: Race, Power, and Culture in French Colonial Hanoi, 1872–1954." PhD diss., University of California, Santa Cruz, 1999.

Vince, Natalya. *The Algerian War, the Algerian Revolution*. New York: Palgrave Macmillan, 2020.

Vincent, K. Steven, and Alison Klairmont Lingo. *The Human Tradition in Modern France*. Lanham MD: Rowman and Littlefield, 2000.

Wade, Bonnie C., and Patricia Shehan Campbell, eds. *Global Music Cultures: An Introduction to World Music*. Oxford: Oxford University Press, 2020.

Weber, Eugene. *Peasants into Frenchmen: The Modernization of Rural France, 1870–1914*. Stanford CA: Stanford University Press, 1976.

Westhoff, Ben. *Original Gangstas: The Untold Story of Dr. Dre, Eazy-E, Ice Cube, Tupac Shakur, and the Birth of West Coast Rap*. New York: Hachette, 2016.

White, Hayden. *Metahistory: The Historical Imagination in Nineteenth-Century Europe*. Baltimore: Johns Hopkins University Press, 1973.

Wieviorka, Olivier. *The French Resistance*. Translated by Jane Marie Todd. Cambridge MA: Harvard University Press, 2016.

Williams, Chad L. *Torchbearers of Democracy: African American Soldiers in the World War I Era*. Chapel Hill: University of North Carolina Press, 2013.

Williams, Lyneise E. *Latin Blackness in Parisian Visual Culture, 1852–1932*. New York: Bloomsbury Visual Arts, 2019.

Wolin, Richard. *The Wind from the East: French Intellectuals, the Cultural Revolution, and the Legacy of the 1960s*. Princeton NJ: Princeton University Press, 2010.

Works Progress Administration. *Gallipolis: Being an Account of the French Five Hundred and of the Town They Established on La Belle Riviere*. Columbus: Ohio State Historical Society, 1940.

Zucotti, Susan. *The Holocaust, the French, and the Jews*. Lincoln: University of Nebraska Press, 1999.

INDEX

Illustrations are indicated by F with a numeral

International Peasant Council, 153
Iroquois Indians, 33
Islam, 183–84
Israel, 89, 194, 203, 207–8
Italy, 62, 78

Jacobins, 17, 18–19
Janot (Teruel, Baker adoptee), 193
Jari (Baker adoptee), 193
Jay, Jimmy, 219
Jay-Z: "Niggas in Paris," 223
jazz, 139, 143–44
Jean-Claude (Baker adoptee), 193
Jewish Army, 164
Jewish Enlightenment, 91–92
The Jewish State (Herzl), 99
Jews: and Baker family, 194; in Club
    Med heritage, 201–3; history of,
    in France, 89–93; treatment of, by
    France, 15, 21; and universalism,
    89–90, 94, 95–96, 100–101, 228;
    during World War II, 129–30, 164–
    65. *See also* AIU *(Alliance Israélite
    Universelle)*; Manouchian, Missak,
    and Manouchian Group
Johnson-Reed Act, 124
Juárez, Benito, 55, 56, 57–58, 61–62
July Monarchy, 23–24, 42, 45–46, 81

Karl, Archduke, 57
Karl Liebknecht (ship), 153
Kassovitz, Matthieu, 219
Klimt, Gustav, 113
Kneler, Leo, 160, 169
Koffi (Baker adoptee), 194
Krasucki, Henri, 169
Kriegel, Annie, 166
Kroc, Ray, 134

labor issues, 120, 129, 207
Lacascade, Théodore, 112
Ladéa (rapper), 222
Lafayette, Marquis de, F2, 137
Lafayette Escadrille, 134–35
La Garçonne (Margueritte), 190
Lagerquist, Peter, 207
La Haine (film), 184, 219
Lang, Jack, 217, 220
Laos, 74, 146, 177
Latin America, 53, 228
the League of the Just, 45, 47
Leclerc, Philippe, 161
Le Figaro (Moréas), 113
Left Bank, 124, 143, 151, 168
Legion of Honor, 170, 188–89
Lenin, Vladimir, 136, 151–52
Le Paria, 152
Le Pen, Jean-Marie, 184
Le Pen, Marine, 184
Les Milandes (Baker home), 188, 192,
    194–97
Levi, Giovanni, 2
Lévy, Jean-Pierre, 164
Lezay-Marnésia, Count de, 32, 35, 36
liberalism, 16, 26, 45, 54–55, 60, 67–69,
    94
Liberals, Mexican, 55, 57, 60, 61
Liberation (1944), 131, 160–61, 173–74
The Life of a Simple Man (Guillaumin),
    226–27
Lingo, Alison Klairmont: *The Human
    Tradition in Modern France*, 3
Lion, Jean, 194
London Missionary Society, 110–11
Lorraine, 70, 137. *See also*
    Alsace-Lorraine
Loti, Pierre: *The Marriage of Loti*, 109

Wilson, Woodrow, 135, 142, 143, 149

The Woman in the Green Dress (Monet), 87

Woman with a Flower (Gauguin), 113

women's rights, 16, 68, 84, 124

The Workers' Union (Tristán), 103

working class: and communism, 165; European, 120; Germans in France in, 43, 45; global economy affecting, 66, 67; increased power of, 65, 67–68, 72; in interwar era, 123–24; living standards of, 177; music of, 215; and National Front, 184; Parisian artisans in, 44; revolutionary spirit of, 69–70; and socialism, 24, 42, 47–49, 50–51, 142–43; as suburban residents, 216; and vacations, 200

World Cup, 185

World Trade Center attacks (2001), 209

World War I, F8; American civilian participation in, 134–35; American diplomatic participation in, 122, 142; American military participation in, 7, 121–22, 133–34, 136–41; France changed by, 119–20; Germany in, 135; global nature of, 121–22; legacy of, 142–44

World War II: approach of, 125–26; beginning of, 127; Communist resistance in France during, 165–70; foreign resistance in France during, 130–31, 160–62, 163–65; French government during, 177; Germany in, 127, 128–31; Jewish resistance in France during, 164–65; legacy of, 173, 175–76, 189

Worth, Charles Frederick, F5, 82–84, 85–88

Worth, Jean-Philippe, 88

Yazid (rapper), 220

Young Hegelians, 46, 48

youth rebellion (1968), 180–81, 196–97

Zhou en Lai, 150

Zidaine, Zinedine, 185

Zimmerman telegraph, 135

Zionism, 99–100, 164, 202–3

Zuloaga, Felix, 55

Franco America in the Making:
The Creole Nation Within
Jonathan K. Gosnell

Endgame 1758: The Promise,
the Glory, and the Despair of
Louisbourg's Last Decade
A. J. B. Johnston

The Albert Memmi Reader
Edited by Jonathan Judaken
and Michael Lejman

Colonial Suspects: Suspicion,
Imperial Rule, and Colonial Society
in Interwar French West Africa
Kathleen Keller

The New White Race: Settler
Colonialism and the Press in
French Algeria, 1860–1914
Charlotte Ann Legg

A Frail Liberty: Probationary Citizens
in the French and Haitian Revolutions
Tessie P. Liu

French Mediterraneans: Transnational
and Imperial Histories
Edited and with an introduction
by Patricia M. E. Lorcin
and Todd Shepard

Apostle of Empire: The
Jesuits and New France
Bronwen McShea

The Cult of the Modern: Trans-
Mediterranean France and the
Construction of French Modernity
Gavin Murray-Miller

Cinema in an Age of Terror:
North Africa, Victimization,
and Colonial History
Michael F. O'Riley

Medical Imperialism in French North
Africa: Regenerating the Jewish
Community of Colonial Tunis
Richard C. Parks

Making the Voyageur World:
Travelers and Traders in the
North American Fur Trade
Carolyn Podruchny

A Workman Is Worthy of His Meat:
Food and Colonialism in Gabon
Jeremy Rich

Empire and Catastrophe:
Decolonization and Environmental
Disaster in North Africa and
Mediterranean France since 1954
Spencer D. Segalla

The Moroccan Soul: French
Education, Colonial Ethnology, and
Muslim Resistance, 1912–1956
Spencer D. Segalla

From Near and Far: A
Transnational History of France
Tyler Stovall

Silence Is Death: The Life and
Work of Tahar Djaout
Julija Šukys

The French Colonial Mind,
Volume 1: Mental Maps of Empire
and Colonial Encounters
Edited and with an introduction
by Martin Thomas

The French Colonial Mind,
Volume 2: Violence, Military
Encounters, and Colonialism
Edited and with an introduction
by Martin Thomas

Beyond Papillon: The French
Overseas Penal Colonies, 1854–1952
Stephen A. Toth

Madah-Sartre: The Kidnapping,
Trial, and Conver(sat/s)ion of Jean-
Paul Sartre and Simone de Beauvoir
Written and translated by
Alek Baylee Toumi
With an introduction by
James D. Le Sueur

To order or obtain more information on these or other University
of Nebraska Press titles, visit nebraskapress.unl.edu.

CPSIA information can be obtained
at www.ICGtesting.com
Printed in the USA
LVHW101645171122
733396LV00003B/303